THE STRANGER'S RELIGION

BOSTON UNIVERSITY STUDIES IN PHILOSOPHY AND RELIGION
General Editor: M. David Eckel

Other Titles in this Series:

Myth, Symbol, and Reality
Transcendence and the Sacred
Meaning, Truth, and God
Foundations of Ethics
Religious Pluralism
On Nature
Knowing Religiously
Civil Religion and Political Theology
Human Rights and the World's Religions
On Freedom
Celebrating Peace
On Community
Selves, People, and Persons
Can Virtue Be Taught?
The Changing Face of Friendship
In Pursuit of Happiness
The Longing for Home
Is There a Human Nature?
Loneliness
Religion, Politics, and Peace
Civility
If I Should Die
Courage
Promise and Peril

The Stranger's Religion

Fascination and Fear

Edited by
Anna Lännström

UNIVERSITY OF NOTRE DAME PRESS
Notre Dame, Indiana

Copyright © 2004 by University of Notre Dame
Notre Dame, Indiana 46556
www.undpress.nd.edu
All Rights Reserved

Published in the United States of America

Library of Congress Cataloging-in-Publication Data

The stranger's religion / edited by Anna Lännström.
   p. cm. — (Boston University studies in philosophy and religion)
   Includes bibliographical references and index.
   ISBN 0-268-03366-8 (alk. paper)
   ISBN 0-268-03367-6 (pbk. : alk. paper)
   1. Religions—Relations. 2. Religion, Psychology of.
3. Strangers—Religious aspects. I. Lännström, Anna.
II. Series.
BL410 .S77   2004
201'.5—dc22   2003025375

To Leroy S. Rouner
Believer, Teacher, and Philosopher

His work on this series and elsewhere crosses the boundaries of academic disciplines in its continuing struggle to diminish our fear of the stranger and his religion through knowledge, dialogue, and increased mutual understanding.

Contents

Preface	ix
Acknowledgments	xi
Contributors	xiii
Introduction • *Anna Lännström*	1

PART I: TALKING WITH STRANGERS

Hinduphobia and Hinduphilia in U.S. Culture • *Stephen Prothero*	13
Christianity, Judaism, and Islam and the Restoration of Justice in South Africa • *John W. de Gruchy*	38
Mahatma Gandhi and Osama bin Laden: An Imaginary Dialogue • *Bhikhu Parekh*	54

PART II: UNDERSTANDING DIFFERENCE

Other Peoples' Religions, Other Peoples' *Kama* and *Karma* • *Wendy Doniger*	79
Holy Otherness: Religious Differences Revisited • *Eliot Deutsch*	99
Toward a Theology of World Religions: The Existential Threats • *Robert Cummings Neville*	113

PART III: CROSSING BORDERS

When Hindus Become Christian: Religious Conversion
and Spiritual Ambiguity • *John B. Carman* — 133

Christian-ish and Jew-ish: Childhood on a Religious Shuttle
• *Werner Gundersheimer* — 154

The Convert—Stranger in Our Midst: Crossing Borders
in Two Worlds • *Pravrajika Vrajaprana* — 169

Author Index — 187

Subject Index — 189

Preface

Boston University Studies in Philosophy and Religion is a joint project of the Boston University Institute for Philosophy and Religion and the University of Notre Dame Press. The essays in each annual volume are edited from the previous year's lecture program and invited papers of the Boston University Institute. The director of the Institute, who is also the general editor of these Studies, chooses a theme and invites participants to lecture at Boston University in the course of the academic year. The editor of each volume selects and edits the essays to be included in the volume. In preparation is volume 26, *Responsibility*.

    The Boston University Institute for Philosophy and Religion was begun informally in 1970 under the leadership of Professor Peter Bertocci of the Department of Philosophy, with the cooperation of Dean Walter Muelder of the School of Theology, Professor James Purvis, chair of the Department of Religion, and Professor Marx Wartofsky, chair of the Department of Philosophy. Professor Bertocci was concerned to institutionalize one of the most creative features of Boston personalism, its interdisciplinary approach to fundamental issues of human life. When Professor Leroy S. Rouner became director in 1975, and the Institute became a formal part of the Boston University Graduate School, every effort was made to continue that vision of an ecumenical and interdisciplinary forum.

    Within the university the Institute is committed to open interchange on fundamental issues in philosophy and religious study which transcend the narrow specializations of academic curricula. We seek to counter those trends in higher education which emphasize technical expertise in a "multi-versity" and gradually transform undergraduate liberal arts education into preprofessional training.

Our programs are open to the general public and are often broadcast on WBUR-FM, Boston University's National Public Radio station. Outside the university we seek to recover the public tradition of philosophical discourse which was a lively part of U.S. intellectual life in the early years of this century before the professionalization of both philosophy and religious reflection made these two disciplines virtually unavailable even to an educated public. We note, for example, that much of William James's work was presented originally as public lectures, and we are grateful to James's present-day successors for the significant public papers which we have been honored to publish. This commitment to a public tradition in U.S. intellectual life has important stylistic implications. At a time when too much academic writing is incomprehensible or irrelevant or both, our goal is to present readable essays by acknowledged authorities on critical human issues.

After twenty-eight years as Director of the Institute, which presents the lecture series and produces these volumes, Leroy S. Rouner is retiring from Boston University in September 2003. The Institute's interdisciplinary investigation of fundamental human issues will continue under the leadership of new director M. David Eckel, Associate Professor of Religion at Boston University.

Acknowledgments

First and foremost, this series would not be possible without the authors. They have provided us with thoughtful and interesting essays, for which they have received only modest compensation. In addition, their cheerful acceptance of editorial changes and strict deadlines as well as their willingness to do requested revisions has made the editing process easy and enjoyable.

Lee Rouner has generously provided invaluable assistance whenever a second set of eyes was needed, and I am eternally grateful to Barbara Darling-Smith for her attention to detail and her meticulous copy editing. Most of all, however, I am grateful to both of them for being such delightful colleagues and friends. I also owe many thanks to Jessica Habalou, Timothy Rodriguez, and Celia Tam for their help in running the lecture series that formed the basis for this volume and to Celia Tam for her assistance in preparing the manuscript. Adam Wright of Wheaton College—by now a valued member of our team—has constructed the author index for the third year in a row.

As usual, Barbara Hanrahan, Jeffrey Gainey, Rebecca DeBoer, Wendy McMillen, and the rest of the staff at the University of Notre Dame Press have been a joy to work with. We continue to be grateful for their confidence in the Institute's work and their professional expertise in publishing this series.

Finally, we are grateful to the PEW Charitable Trust, the Institute for Religion and World Affairs, the Stratford Foundation, and the Boston University Graduate School of Arts and Sciences for their financial support of our lecture series on the Stranger's Religion from which these essays came.

Contributors

JOHN BRAISTED CARMAN was born in India of missionary parents, and lived there until entering Haverford College, where he graduated in 1950 with highest honors in philosophy. He also holds a B.D. *summa cum laude* from Yale Divinity School, and Master's and Ph.D. degrees from Yale. From 1957 to 1962 he was Research Fellow at the Christian Institute for the Study of Religion and Society in Bangalore, India. He is currently Parkman Professor of Divinity and Professor of Comparative Religion Emeritus at Harvard Divinity School, where he has also served as acting dean and, from 1973 until 1989, as director of the Center for the Study of World Religions. Perhaps best known for his book *The Theology of Ramanuja: An Essay in Interreligious Understanding*, he is the author of numerous articles in comparative religion, and several books, including *Village Christians and Hindu Culture: Study of a Rural Church in Andhra Pradesh, South India* (with P. Y. Luke) and, most recently, *Majesty and Meekness: A Comparative Study of Contrast and Harmony in the Concept of God*.

JOHN W. DE GRUCHY is Robert Selby Taylor Professor of Christian Studies and Director of the Graduate School in Humanities at the University of Cape Town, South Africa. He holds degrees from Rhodes University, Chicago Theological Seminary, the University of South Africa, and the University of Cape Town. Since 1972, when he published *The Dynamic Structure of the Church: A Comparative Analysis of the Ecclesiologies of Karl Barth and Dietrich Bonhoeffer*, he has been known as a major interpreter of Karl Barth's theology, and in 2000 he was awarded the Karl Barth Prize by the Evangelische Kirche der Union in Germany. He has lectured widely, including named lectureships at Cambridge University, Oxford University, Princeton Theological Seminary, the University of Edinburgh, the University of Durham, and Union Theological Seminary in Richmond, Virginia. Among his many books are several dealing with religion and politics in South Africa, and his recent *Christianity, Art, and Transformation: A Study in Theological Aesthetics.*

ELIOT DEUTSCH is Professor of Philosophy and Chair of the Philosophy Department at the University of Hawaii. For many years he was editor of the journal *Philosophy East and West.* He has been Visiting Fellow at Clare Hall, University of Cambridge, England, where he was elected a Life Member in 1999, and at St. Edmund's College, Cambridge. He has also been Visiting Professor at Harvard University and at the University of Chicago. He served on the steering committee for the Fifth East-West Philosophers' Conference in 1969 and was the director of the Sixth East-West Philosophers' Conference from 1987 to 1989. The author of more than a dozen books and numerous articles, he is known both for early books in Indian philosophy—*The Bhagavad Gita; Advaita Vedanta: A Philosophical Reconstruction;* and *A Source Book of Advaita Vedanta*—and original statements of his own philosophy which draw on both Eastern and Western resources, including *On Truth: An Ontological Theory; Creative Being: The Crafting of Person and World;* and *Religion and Spirituality.*

WENDY DONIGER studied dance as a teenager under George Balanchine and Martha Graham, but later turned to Sanskrit and Indian Studies at Radcliffe College, where she graduated *summa cum laude* in 1962. She then earned two doctoral degrees, a Ph.D. from Harvard in Sanskrit and Indian Studies in 1968 and a D.Phil in Oriental Studies from Oxford in 1973. She held lectureships at the University of London and the University of California, Berkeley, and an associate professorship at the Graduate Theological Union in Berkeley before going to the University of Chicago, where she is now Mircea Eliade Professor of the History of Religion and Distinguished Service Professor. A prolific writer, she is author, translator, or editor of almost thirty books, and has published well over two hundred articles and many reviews. Her current best-seller is *The Kamasutra of Vatsyayana,* and she is at work on *The Mythology of Horses in India,* and a novel, *Horses for Lovers, Dogs for Husbands.*

WERNER GUNDERSHEIMER is Director Emeritus of the Folger Shakespeare Library in Washington, D.C., and has most recently been a Fellow of the Sterling and Francine Clark Art Institute and a Visiting Professor of History at Williams College. He was a Junior Fellow at Harvard before moving eventually to the University of Pennsylvania, where he served as chair of the History Department and director of the Center for Italian Studies. He has written on the Italian and French Renaissance, including, among others, *Life and Works of Louis LeRoy, The Italian Renaissance,* and *Ferrara: The Style of a Renaissance Despotism.* He has been active in civic and community service, including numerous trusteeships, and has chaired the Visiting Scholar Committee for Phi Beta Kappa, the Overseers' Visiting Committee to the Harvard University Libraries, and the Board of Advisors, Dumbarton Oaks. His fellowships include a John Simon Guggenheim Memorial Fellowship and a Rotary Fellowship at the University of Paris, and he was invited to the Woodrow Wilson Center for Scholars of the Smithsonian Institution.

ANNA LÄNNSTRÖM is Assistant Professor at Stonehill College. Her B.A. is from the State University of New York at Potsdam (*summa cum laude*). She has held a Presidential Fellowship at Boston University and received her M.A. in 1999 with a thesis in Indian philosophy on the role of myth and metaphor in Advaita Vedanta. Her Ph.D. thesis (Boston University, 2002) argues that Aristotle's ethics is a viable option for contemporary ethical theory. Her work in progress is tentatively titled *Loving the Fine: Virtue and Happiness in Aristotle's Ethics.*

ROBERT CUMMINGS NEVILLE is the newly appointed Dean of Marsh Chapel at Boston University, having previously served for two years as chair of the Department of Religion and director of the Graduate Division of Religious and Theological Studies, and for fourteen years as Dean of the School of Theology. Before moving to Boston University as Professor of Philosophy, Religion, and Theology, he taught philosophy at Yale, Wesleyan, Fordham, and the State University of New York at Stony Brook, where he was also Dean of Humanities and Fine Arts, 1982–85. He has been on the board of numerous trusts and professional organizations, serving as president of the Metaphysical Society of America and the International Society for Chinese Philosophy, and as co-director of the Twentieth World Congress of Philosophy. He has edited ten books and authored eighteen others, including his major study, *God the Creator: On the Transcendence and Presence of God; The Cosmology of Freedom; Creativity and God: A Challenge to Process Theology; The Tao and the Daimon: Segments of a Religious Enquiry; The Truth of Broken Symbols;* and *Religion in Late Modernity.*

BHIKHU PAREKH graduated from the University of Bombay and received his Ph.D. from the London School of Economics. He taught briefly at the London School of Economics and the University of Glasgow, and then for many years was Professor of Political Theory at the University of Hull. He is currently Centennial Professor at the London School of Economics. He is the author of a number of books, including *Hannah Arendt and the Search for a New Political Philosophy; Marx's Theory of Ideology; Contemporary Political Thinkers; Colonialism, Tradition, and Reform; Gandhi;* and *Rethinking Multiculturalism.* He has lectured widely in the United States, Europe, and India, and has been an active participant in public debate through newspaper and magazine articles, and radio and television broadcasts. In 1992 he was elected British Asian of the Year, and in 1999 was given the BBC's Special Lifetime Achievement Award. He has served the British government as co-chair of the Commission on Racial Equality, and was appointed to the House of Lords in 2000.

STEPHEN RICHARD PROTHERO was elected to Phi Beta Kappa as a junior at Yale, where he received his B.A. *summa cum laude* in 1982. He went on to Harvard for his M.A. and Ph.D. He has received a number of honors and awards, including Best First Book in the History of Religions (for *The White Buddhist*) from the American Academy of Religion, and the Best of Reference

1996 (for *The Encyclopedia of American Religious History*) from the New York Public Library. He taught at Harvard, Yale, and Georgia State University before going to Boston University, where he is now Associate Professor of Religion and chair of the Religion Department. His research interests focus on American religious history with a specialty in the growing role of Asian religions in America. His published books include *Purified by Fire: A History of Cremation in America; Asian Religions in America: A Documentary History;* and *The White Buddhist: The Asian Odyssey of Henry Steel Olcott*. His next book will be *American Jesus: How the Son of God Became a National Icon*.

PRAVRAJIKA VRAJAPRANA was born in California in 1952 and did her undergraduate and graduate work at the University of California at Santa Cruz, where she also served briefly as Associate Professor of Literature. In 1977 she moved to Santa Barbara where she joined the Sarada Convent of the Vedanta Society, the Western branch of the Ramakrishna Order of India. She took the vows of *brahmacharya* in 1983 and final vows of *sannyasa* in 1988. Her responsibilities at the Vedanta Society in Santa Barbara include book manager at Sarada Convent Books, the Vedanta Society's bookstore, and management of the Vedanta Society's website. Apart from her vocation as a Hindu nun, she has an avocation as a choral singer and is an active member of the Santa Barbara Choral Society. She has published five books, and is currently completing a study tentatively titled *Kali's Child Revisited: Language, Culture, and Documentation*, coauthored with Swami Tyagananda. Her other books are *Vedanta: A Simple Introduction; Seeing God Everywhere; A Portrait of Sister Christine; Living Wisdom: Vedanta in the West;* and *My Faithful Goodwin*.

Introduction
ANNA LÄNNSTRÖM

Ours is a world of many religions. At times, human beings have lived among people of their own faith in relative isolation from other religions. Ours is not such a time. On the contrary, we are exposed to a bewildering array of religious views and practices, some of which are completely foreign, and we are forced to come to terms with them. It is a difficult task because our natural reaction to "the stranger" and her religion seems fundamentally ambiguous, involving both fascination and fear. We are often afraid of what we do not understand. Our fear is compounded when religious and political divisions coincide, as they do in places like Palestine/Israel, Northern Ireland, and Sri Lanka. Because the stranger's strange beliefs are coupled with political goals that we suspect can be promoted only at the expense of our own, she becomes even more frightening.

But our fear of the stranger's religion is often mixed with fascination, especially if the stranger lives so far away that his political aims do not threaten us. We devour every detail in travel reports of bizarre practices and rites from remote cultures. We might even resist attempts to find commonalities between us and the stranger, preferring to cast him as the exotic stranger—essentially different and eternally other. The essays in this volume argue that we must not give in to that temptation but must try to understand the stranger as he is—different in some ways and similar in others. They maintain that we can overcome our fear of the stranger only by understanding him better, and they show ways in which we can do that, suggesting that if we understand the other better, we thereby acquire a richer understanding of ourselves and of the world we share.

The first section of this book—"Talking with Strangers"—discusses what happens when religious strangers meet, asking how we can find common ground and how we can understand each other better. In "Hinduphobia and Hinduphilia in U.S. Culture," Stephen Prothero considers the ambivalent reception of Hinduism in the United States, ranging from newspaper reporters denouncing fat swamis seducing and robbing innocent U.S. women to Thoreau's celebrations of the Bhagavad Gita, from interventions to save youngsters from suspected Hindu cults to yoga fads in health clubs. Prothero stresses that the negative reaction to Hindu immigrants in this country was primarily a matter of religion (not race), and he notes that it has strong similarities to classic Protestant prejudices against Catholicism. Both Catholicism and Hinduism were regarded as involving authoritarian priests, superstition and idolatry, mistreatment of women, illicit sex, and ill-gotten financial gain.

Prothero notes that both Hinduphobes and Hinduphiles tend to misunderstand Hinduism because they focus on part of it and ignore the rest. They separate literary from lived Hinduism, its ancient scriptures from its contemporary practices. Hinduphobes focus upon the rites and uneducated Hinduism, upon sati, untouchability, and child marriages; and they recoil in disgust and fear. Hinduphiles argue that lived Hinduism is not really Hinduism. Real Hinduism, they say, is found within its noble scriptures and sages, and it is an inexhaustible source of deep insights about the nature of reality and the divine. Prothero argues that this tendency to either aggrandize or vilify Hinduism (or any other religion) and then define "real Hinduism" still persists, and that it must be resisted. Scholars of religion must recognize and describe both the good and the bad aspects and, more generally, must recognize that all religions justifiably evoke fascination and fear.

In "Christianity, Judaism, and Islam and the Restoration of Justice in South Africa," John de Gruchy discusses the relationships among the three Abrahamic faiths. Referring to the conflict in the Middle East, he wonders if it is possible for two of the three to overcome their estrangement without also including the other, and he suggests that a threefold conversation seems to be required. He notes that given the problematic history of the relations among the three, it is essential that we learn how to see through the stereotypes and overcome our mutual alienation. But he cautions that religious dialogue is not enough; we must also address the connected political and social issues.

De Gruchy focuses upon the recent South African experience, apartheid and its aftermath. Might the South African experience, he asks, provide a model for similar conversations elsewhere? The work of the Truth and Reconciliation Commission has been viewed as a model for dealing with the past and achieving reconciliation between estranged groups. De Gruchy urges some caution. He notes that the divisions concerning apartheid did not coincide with religious borders; there were Jews, Christians, and Muslims on both sides. Furthermore, he stresses, the situation in South Africa is far from perfect. While there are many agreements between the three traditions, important divisions remain, both between members of the three faiths and between members of the same faith in different cultures. Perhaps the most important division is between traditional and progressive believers. Setting aside divisive theological issues, conservative members of the three faiths have formed coalitions which argue against a wide range of human rights–related issues—gender equality, gay rights, and abolition of the death penalty—on the grounds that the liberal South African constitution mandating these policies violates God's justice. De Gruchy responds that the concept of human rights originates within the Abrahamic tradition and thus should not be understood as alien to that tradition. He ends his essay with a call for continued dialogue and mutual engagement in seeking justice.

Bhikhu Parekh explores the nature and limits of dialogue by engaging two strangers in imaginary conversation in "Mahatma Gandhi and Osama bin Laden: An Imaginary Dialogue." Parekh observes that Gandhi and bin Laden have some common concerns: They are critical of the West and argue for an alternative vision of the good life; they are anti-imperialist and are struggling against the greatest world power in their time; they are deeply religious and believe that religion has an important place in public life. But they are of course also very different. Most importantly, Gandhi rejected violence and focused upon nonviolent resistance, whereas bin Laden argues that violence is necessary and trains his followers in terrorism. In addition, bin Laden views human beings as either completely good or completely evil, arguing that those who are good have the right to punish their evil oppressors; Gandhi argued that all humans (and societies) are mixtures of good and evil and that our anger should be directed at the system and not at those who benefit from it.

In Parekh's imaginary dialogue, Gandhi and bin Laden listen carefully to each other and respond to what the other says. Parekh suggests that if each would listen with an open mind, their differences would narrow. They would gain a better understanding of the view of the other and then use that view to reconsider their own. However, he notes, deep differences would remain. One difference is decisive: Whereas Gandhi always opposed violence in principle, arguing that when one is wronged, one should act as the higher self of the other, bin Laden thinks that violence justifies a violent response. Parekh does not believe that either would change his view on this point. However, he suggests that we might be able to circumvent this disagreement because Gandhi also presented pragmatic arguments against terrorism, indicating that terrorism simply does not work, and that bin Laden cannot create a stable Muslim world through terrorism.

Parekh concludes that even though bin Laden and Gandhi would continue to disagree, dialogues like theirs are important because they help the speakers to understand the view of the other, the nature of their disagreements, and the limitations of their own view. Furthermore, dialogue shows each participant a different way of looking at the world, thus enriching their perspective. Finally, Parekh notes, the effects the dialogue has on listeners—Muslims and Westerners—might be more important than its effect on the speakers. If the bulk of the listeners were sympathetic to Gandhi's argument, bin Laden would lose public support and would be forced to change.

The essays in the second section of the book—"Understanding Difference"—continue the focus on dialogue and stress its potential for teaching us to see the world through more than one perspective. They provide scholarly discussions of our attempts to understand the other and present methodological approaches within the philosophy of religion. In the first essay, "Other Peoples' Religions, Other Peoples' *Kama* and *Karma*," Wendy Doniger argues for an approach to cross-cultural studies that recognizes both the similarities and the differences between us and the other and that encourages us to try to think and feel with the alien tradition. When done well, she argues, comparative studies force us to come to terms with the other. This means that we must see in what ways the other is like us. However, we must not end there. Rather, we must also come to see that we are like the other, no longer taking ourselves as the norm but rather trying to see through the lens of the other. We might have to end with a recognition of difference, allowing that there are ways in which we simply are different.

Doniger illustrates her thesis by considering the *Kamasutra* and the theory of *karma*. She argues that much of the *Kamasutra*, its magical formulas, harems, and courtesans, is and remains foreign to us. Other parts of the text, like the importance of betel as an aphrodisiac, start to become accessible if we compare them to something analogous in the West. And yet other parts about courtship and flirtation or about cooking for one's partner seem perfectly familiar. We can learn much about human nature, she argues, by considering this alternation of similarity and difference.

In the final part of her essay, Doniger asks to what extent a Westerner can come to terms with the *karma* theory, noting that her own understanding of it has changed radically over the years. While she used to dismiss it, she now takes it very seriously. According to the *karma* theory, what happens to us now and what makes us who we are are in large measure the result of forces from the past, including forces generated by our actions in our past lives. In addition, we acquire guilt and credit for the deeds of other people because they are somehow us. By noting how interconnected we are to others, especially our parents, and how we benefit or are punished by their deeds (smoking in pregnancy, childhood neglect, and so on), Doniger develops an argument which suggests that the *karma* theory is much less strange than it initially appears, that even Westerners might be able to view themselves as karmically linked to others and perhaps even to strangers. Differences will remain but we will also discover important similarities. If we have the patience to learn to use the stranger's lens, we might discover that her view of the world is not so strange after all.

Eliot Deutsch continues the theme of similarity and difference in "Holy Otherness: Religious Differences Revisited." He argues for a pluralistic approach to religion, which recognizes that different religious paths may lead to different spiritual ends and which encourages cross-religious dialogue. According to his pluralism, we can make sound critical judgments about the beliefs of the other, but there is no single true system of religious beliefs that provides a standard by which to judge others. Thus, his pluralistic perspective enables us to both appreciate and appraise a variety of religions.

Deutsch begins with an epistemological discussion, considering how we go about criticizing beliefs. He argues that it is a two-step affair. We begin by examining the beliefs involved to see if they might be true. Most importantly, we ask whether they are internally consistent. If the beliefs pass this test, we then examine whether the beliefs fulfill the conditions that the appropriate community considers to be necessary for them to be considered true. He cautions that we must not take ourselves to be mere judges of the values and convictions of the other. While we indeed are trying to see whether the reasoning underlying her beliefs is adequate, we should also remain open to the possibility that her views include new and important insights which should inspire us to reevaluate our own attitudes and question our own deep presuppositions.

In the remainder of his essay, Deutsch shows how this methodology can be applied to a consideration of religious differences. He argues that we must allow that, in some respects, the religion of the other will remain foreign to us. There are indeed irreducible differences. For example, some aim at an impersonal contemplative life, others at an emotional engagement with a personal God. So what philosophical basis do we have for a critical evaluation of religious traditions? Deutsch suggests that we must answer these questions within the domain of religious belief and also within the realm of faith. Within the domain of belief, we answer by following the procedure outlined above, asking whether the beliefs are internally consistent and the reasoning sound and whether they adhere to criteria agreed upon in that particular belief community. Within the domain of faith, in our attempts to judge whether a particular faith is effective, we focus on its results. There is no reason to assume that criteria for evaluating results are universal, however. At least some of them may be internal to the tradition.

Finally, Deutsch stresses that the focus on judging is misleading. The pluralist should not be an objective judge evaluating the religious traditions, but rather somebody who is engaged with these traditions and who expects that examining them will change his own beliefs and make new ways of seeing available to him.

Robert Neville continues the conversation about whether we can evaluate religions in "Toward a Theology of World Religions: The Existential Threats." His essay argues against reductionism in theology. It challenges our tendency to view other religions through the lens shaped by our own faith tradition and thus to use categories derived from our own religion, setting it up as a model.

In considering religious practitioners' attitude to other religions, we often divide them into exclusivists, inclusivists, and pluralists. Neville argues that this division is inherently problematic because it treats religions as homogeneous and unchanging entities. He suggests that in order to better understand the differences between the world religions, we must abandon these categories and take a new approach to a theology of religions. An essential part of that new approach is to develop fair and stable categories of the religious concepts that we want to compare cross-culturally—for instance, the concept of the ultimate. We should begin with a dialogue between members of different religions in order to ensure that our categories do not privilege one religion over another (for example, by suggesting that the ultimate is best understood as personal). Then, we instantiate these categories (Chinese sky god, Dao, Brahman, Christian God, and so on). Finally, once we have specified the category in a multitude of ways, we should be able to say how these ways disagree, agree, overlap, or talk past each other.

But that is not enough. We also need a procedure for determining whether a particular religious interpretation is true. Is the Christian conception of God *true,* for instance? Neville argues that the only appropriate criteria in evaluating the truth of religious interpretations are pragmatic and contextual: Interpretations are true when they both genuinely engage their object and also transmit what is important in the object to the interpreter. This means that the truth of a religious interpretation always will be contextual rather than universal; a symbol might work in one context but not in another, and it might work for one person but not for another. Assessing the truth of a religious interpretation, then, becomes an empirical inquiry, and it involves figuring out whether or not the symbol transmits what is important and valuable in the religious object to the particular interpreter. We are profoundly mistaken, Neville argues, if we believe that we can justifiably claim that a particular religion is wholly and universally true.

"Crossing Borders"—the final section of the book—discusses religious conversions and converts, people who have crossed religious borders and who thereby have become the ultimate strangers—"traitors" to their own faith and "impostors" in the new one. John Carman considers conversions from Hinduism to Christianity in "When Hindus Become Christian: Religious Conversion and Spiritual Ambiguity." He argues that too much of the discussion of Hindu conversions to Christianity has focused upon the conversions of upper-class, well-educated Hindus in the cities, neglecting the sometimes very different experiences of poor and often illiterate village converts. Carman's discussion focuses on conversion experiences among untouchable and often illiterate villagers in rural India. The conversion stories reveal a variety of attitudes toward conversion as well as diverse views about how much of one's religious heritage can be retained after the conversion.

Carman notes that Protestant missionaries saw an outward and inward conversion as ideal: outwardly, the convert should reject Hindu idolatry and notions about caste; inwardly, the convert should recognize that Christ delivers us from our sinful state. The decision to convert should also be individual. While some villagers attained this individualistic inward and outward conversion and subsequently refused to participate in village festivals to local deities, many others continued to participate. They also often viewed the decision to convert as a communal one. Sometimes, their decision to convert was also influenced by the hope that conversion would bring material benefits, that it would alleviate injustice and bring the chance to reach a higher social status. Carman notes that such hopes often have remained unfulfilled.

Roman Catholic missionaries found it easier than did Protestants to accept conversions that seemed less than ideal. Because they were less focused on the initial decision for baptism than on the ongoing process of being a Christian, Carman argues, they found it easier to adopt and adapt Hindu forms of worship, creating a synthesis of Catholic and popular Hindu rituals. Carman illustrates this point by discussing festivals which evolved as such a synthesis and which attract both Hindu and Christian worshippers, including the festival of Velankanni, worshipped both as the Virgin Mary and as a powerful Hindu goddess. Velankanni thus expresses the ambiguity of the converts. Carman finds the same sort of ambiguity in the writings of some high-caste Hindus concerning their conversions to Christianity. They too deny that they had to abandon their religious heritage in becoming Christian. However, Carman finds no agreement among them concerning what elements to keep or about how their new and old faiths differ. He stresses that we can learn much by considering the different ways in which the converts have synthesized their new and old traditions.

Werner Gundersheimer discusses his two crossings of the border between Christianity and Judaism in "Christian-ish and Jew-ish: Childhood on a Religious Shuttle." Gundersheimer comes from a family of German Jews. After encountering great difficulties in trying to leave Germany, he and his parents finally came to the United States when he was two years old (1940), sponsored by a small congregation of the Church of England. His father was an art historian and had great difficulty finding an academic position in the United States. The only position available at a college turned out to be a housekeeper position for Mrs. Gundersheimer, with Dr. Gundersheimer tagging along to offer an occasional unpaid lecture. But the college was not willing to accept a child in the servants' quarters. His parents struggled with the decision but finally decided to accept the offer. Gundersheimer became a foster child for a year in New England in a Congregationalist minister's family, the Tuckers.

Gundersheimer recounts his encounter with rural New England Protestantism. He quickly became accustomed to many of the rituals—holding hands during grace before dinner, singing hymns at the piano, going to church, trimming the tree, dyeing the eggs—and they began to feel like his own. The Tuckers reminded him that he was Jewish but since he did not know what that meant, it left little impression on him. When his father finally found an academic position in Philadelphia, Gundersheimer was no longer a stranger to Congregationalism or to the Tuckers—he had become one of them. He came back to his parents as a foreigner both to them and to their religion. What should have been a happy reunion did not feel like one at first. He missed all the Tuckers and felt desperately lonely. The Jewish rituals in the Sephardic synagogue that his parents had joined struck him as alien, but they were neither fascinating nor frightening—just boring. The prayers were spoken in a foreign language; there were strange rules for what to eat; and he didn't like any of the melodies. That gradually changed, however, and for a short period, Gundersheimer immersed himself in Judaism. But it didn't last. Gundersheimer reports that while he still identifies himself as Jewish, his spiritual seeking soon became nondenominational. He remains fascinated by religion, but he confesses that he is a bit frightened by institutionalized religion. Ultimately Gundersheimer considers himself a hybrid of many different faiths—Anglicanism, Quakerism, Congregationalism, Sephardic and Askenazic Judaism, and, last but not least, agnosticism.

Unlike Gundersheimer, Pravrajika Vrajaprana *stayed* on the other side of the border; she is a Caucasian American who has become a Vedanta (Hindu) nun. In "The Convert—Stranger in Our Midst: Crossing Borders in Two Worlds," Vrajaprana uses her own conversion as an illustration in discussing the reception of Hinduism in America as well as the difficulties converts encounter, especially when they convert to a religion considered foreign and inferior. Vrajaprana argues that other people's misperceptions of Hinduism and of what Hindus should look like have been especially difficult. An Indian Hindu priest refused to admit her to the Viswanath temple because she clearly could not be a "real" Hindu. She has found some Westerners even less accepting, and discusses some of their negative misconceptions of Hinduism as well as their refusal to believe that a white woman could be a "real" Hindu. Converts, she argues, often become strangers within both their new and their inherited religious communities. Vrajaprana notes that it is difficult for predominantly Protestant secular America to understand conversion to Hinduism for at least two reasons: It involves taking religion so seriously that one converts, and it involves converting to a strange religion which is thought to be only for Indians. So should this particular border be crossed? Can non-Indians become "real" Hindus? Vrajaprana argues that they can and points out that Vivekananda, who spread Hinduism to the West via the Vedanta Societies he founded, has made great strides in making Hinduism a global religion, disassociating it from problematic aspects of Indian culture like the caste system.

Vrajaprana argues that Hinduism often is portrayed as irrational, mystical, and primitive. It becomes the Oriental Other, irrational in contrast to our rationality, primitive in contrast to our sophisticated modernity. She notes that media reports on Hindu religion often emphasize strange and bizarre behaviors and practices. In responding to Hinduism, Americans often express Protestant horror over its graven images and accuse it of idolatry, unaware that the images are symbols of the divine; they are not themselves thought to be divine. Vrajaprana argues that we must be careful to avoid misunderstanding Hinduism and to remember that we are often looking at it through a Western, Protestant lens. She recommends more border crossings, temporary or permanent, as broadening experiences which enable us to see both sides of any border more clearly.

The focus upon learning about the other is perhaps the most important of the themes that emerge from the essays in this volume. Learning about, listening to, and empathizing with the stranger can lead to understanding. And as we begin to understand the stranger, we can come to see that he is not as frightening as we imagine. We recognize that he is indeed different from us, but we might learn to appreciate him for those very differences. We must hope and trust that the stranger will become familiar and hence our fear will evaporate, even while our fascination with the other's religion remains.

PART I

Talking with Strangers

Hinduphobia and Hinduphilia in U.S. Culture
STEPHEN PROTHERO

In 1911, Hinduism went on trial in the United States. At issue was the last will and testament of Mrs. Sara Bull. The widow of Ole Bull (a celebrated violinist from Norway), Mrs. Bull was one of the principals at Green Acre, a spiritual retreat center in Eliot, Maine, devoted to interreligious dialogue. She was also a convert to Hinduism.

At her "Studio House" at 168 Brattle Street in Cambridge, Massachusetts, Mrs. Bull presided over a fashionable salon. There East Coast intellectuals met Indian teachers such as Swami Vivekananda, the founder of the Vedanta Society and the most popular speaker at the World's Parliament of Religions, held in Chicago in 1893. Among the intellectuals who conversed with Mrs. Bull's swamis at the Studio House was a heady crowd of Harvard professors, including the Sanskrit scholar Charles Lanman, the philosopher Josiah Royce, and the psychologist William James.

After Mrs. Bull died in 1911, it was discovered that she had left almost all of her half-million-dollar estate to Vedanta Society members. Her daughter, Olea Bull Vaughan, challenged the will on the theory that her mother was mentally incompetent when she signed it. The trial that ensued in the small town of Alfred, Maine—"one of the strangest cases in the history of will contests in this country," according to the *New York Times*—was covered closely by U.S. newspapers and produced a "stream of scandal" in Norway. The key issue before the judge was Mrs. Bull's state of mind. Yet Hinduism was on trial too, since the main argument of Sherman Whipple, the daughter's attorney, was that Hindus had driven Mrs. Bull insane.[1]

Over the course of the five-week affair, Whipple called a variety of colorful witnesses, including a cook, a maid, and a "psychic barber," in an effort to build a case for Mrs. Bull's religiously induced insanity. One witness said her "excitable" employer "frequently lost control of herself, upsetting furniture and screeching loudly for help from imaginary dangers." Others said Mrs. Bull communed regularly with spirits of the dead, dabbled in astrology, and talked to pumpkins as if they were people. Still others testified to her odd eating habits and unorthodox nutritional theories, for example, her belief that a truly spiritual person could subsist on grain alone (or, in another version, a bit of milk and six almonds a day). Reportedly, Mrs. Bull employed a "professional masseur and magnetic healer" who "used to put [her] to sleep by passing his hands in wavy motion" over her breasts and face. She also befriended a woman who claimed to be able to heal the sick by lying in bed with them (a rite she allegedly performed with some regularity with Mrs. Bull herself). As Mrs. Bull grew older, witnesses testified, she came to believe that her enemies exerted "malignant psychic powers" over her, and "could propel those killing thoughts over the telephone." In an effort to chase away that "hypnotic power," she had her furniture rubbed regularly with a special mixture of ammonia and olive oil. On one occasion, she locked herself in a room when her daughter came to visit, fearing that Olea Vaughan was unwittingly carrying this malicious magnetism.[2]

Together these arguments were quite damning to Mrs. Bull's case. But they were peripheral to the main argument of the daughter's lawyers, who asserted that Hindus had driven Mrs. Bull mad—or, as her petition put it, that the testator's brain had been "inoculated with the bacteria of faith taught by Indian swamis." Mrs. Bull had come to Hinduism seeking spiritual wisdom, Sherman Whipple argued. What she encountered was a "psychic conspiracy" of Hindu swamis who put her under a spell, coerced her into taking a variety of Indian drugs, and stripped her of her morals, her mind, and her money. According to testimony, Mrs. Bull chanted in Sanskrit, burned incense, and meditated. She traveled to India to pursue her spiritual goals, abandoning a dying granddaughter to be with her beloved swamis instead. In the "Raja Yoga" room at her Brattle Street home, she conducted "mystic meditations" before an altar adorned with images of Vivekananda and his guru Ramakrishna. Thanks to her talent for esoteric breathing exercises—and spirit communications with Swami Vivekananda after his death—Mrs. Bull reportedly became a yogi herself, hailed by friends as "Santi Sara" (Saint Sara).[3]

Apparently Mrs. Bull wanted to express her debts to Hinduism in death as in life, because she directed in her will that her corpse be cremated and her ashes spread by a courier on the grave of her husband in Bergen, Norway. In a letter written shortly after the will became public, Mrs. Bull's daughter complained bitterly about this postmortem plan. "Norway," she protested, ". . . is a Christian, not a heathen, country. A burial there must be in consecrated soil, and the scattering of human ashes by an expressman would hardly be recognized as a possible conception for a sane mind to tolerate."[4]

All this was front-page news from Portland to New York, but the most salacious testimony of the trial concerned neither brainwashing nor drug-taking but love and sex. Here the star witness was Mr. Nicola Ruberto, "a tall, handsome young Italian" variously described as a barber, a masseuse, a chauffeur, a billiard room operator, and a wine merchant. According to Ruberto, Swami Vivekananda taught an eight-stage practice of "Raja Yoga" that culminated in "an advanced stage of perfection and purity known as 'Bhakati.'" Those who attained that state, which Ruberto called "the acme of love," became gods themselves. Mrs. Bull, Ruberto continued, was a practitioner of *bhakti yoga*, which he described as "the attainment of super-consciousness through love." Some of what Ruberto had to say about "the delights of the love stage of yoga" so offended late-Victorian sensibilities that the judge heard it in closed session. And the transcript of what he said regarding Hindu "love rites" was sealed by the judge.[5]

One acquaintance testified that she believed Mrs. Bull's health declined after she was "attacked by malign influence which was sapping [her] life away." The daughter's attorney gave that "malign influence" a name—Hinduism—and placed the guilt for Mrs. Bull's mental and physical ruin at the feet of the Vedanta Society. "The mystic ritual of the 'Raja Yoga' cult," Whipple argued, "brought not only shattered health and loss of reason, but death to members of the band of Yogis and students who executed the psychic gymnastics in the home of Mrs. Bull." Whipple claimed that Swami Vivekananda had "died from excessive participation in the mysteries of the chamber of meditation," and he repeatedly invoked the case of Sarah Farmer, another American convert to Vedanta, who reportedly was "driven insane by the psychic orgies" and "had to be sent to an asylum because of psychic overindulgence." As for Mrs. Bull, she was coerced into taking "Hindu drugs" and other "oriental concoctions," which along with the "thought-viands, breathing-drills, wish-waves, malignant vibrations, incense incantations and orgies" of the Vedantist cult hastened her mental and physical demise.[6]

The motive behind the "incantations and orgies" of this psychic conspiracy was supposedly financial gain. Phony spirit messages—funneled through a London Vedantist called "Yum"—instructed Mrs. Bull to give money to Hindu swamis, and she complied by giving away tens of thousands of dollars in her lifetime. She was, Whipple argued, a "victim of spooks."[7] Her daughter was a victim too, robbed of her rightful inheritance and of her mother's affection.

Such anti-Hindu invective was spread not only by the daughter's counsel but also by newspaper reporters. Although the trial evidence amply demonstrates Mrs. Bull's debts to Spiritualism, Theosophy, New Thought, and Christian Science, journalists were fixated by her Hindu interests. In covering the case, the *New York Times* called Hinduism a "strange cult." Boston papers deemed Hindu rites "queer" and dismissed the icons in Mrs. Bull's home shrine as "pictures of fat swamis." The *Boston Herald* hit Hinduism particularly hard, sneering at the "psychic chaos of the Raja Yoga cult," the "psychic gymnastics of the Yogis," and the "weird doctrines of their creed." "Wealth is said to have no charm for the Yogis," it continued, ". . . but they appear to have practiced this only in books."[8]

In an editorial written toward the end of the trial, the *Herald* took Vedantist swamis to task for preaching "blissful fellowship with the divine" rather than educating Americans about Hinduism. "The Hindu ascetic in India," its editors wrote, "is for the most part a 'faker' as well as a fakir." "Real Hinduism in actual operation" was not about mystical union with God but about public prostitution, idol worship, antisocial ascetics, child brides, and the caste system.[9]

The Bull case concluded in late June 1911 with a stunning victory for the daughter. The attorneys for Mrs. Bull's estate knew they were faring poorly, in both the courtroom and the court of public opinion, so they agreed to a settlement that awarded virtually all of the estate to Mrs. Bull's daughter. Unfortunately, Olea Bull Vaughan did not savor her victory for long; she died of tuberculosis the day the settlement was announced.

SARAH FARMER AND "OOM THE OMNIPOTENT"

I first came across the Sara Bull case while I was teaching about the anti-cult movement, which began in the United States in the 1960s and ran its course by the 1990s. In that movement, evangelical Christians and their lawyers accused leaders of so-called "cults" (many influenced by Hinduism) of "brainwashing" their converts. Some anti-cult activists even kidnapped and "deprogrammed" converts, on the grounds that they were victims of "mind control." Anti-cultists also charged repeatedly that participants in new religious movements were sexual deviants, and that their leaders were motivated by material, not spiritual, rewards. Charges of religiously induced insanity did not begin with the anti-cult movement, however. In the mid-nineteenth century, dozens of Spiritualists were judged insane and confined to mental institutions.[10] And Hinduism itself stood at the center of lawsuits in two other cases that arose around 1911.

First, there was the case of Sarah Farmer, which was invoked repeatedly during the Bull trial. In the aftermath of the World's Parliament of Religions, Farmer established her spiritual retreat center in Eliot, Maine. Green Acre hosted a variety of speakers who had addressed the Parliament, including Anagarika Dharmapala, the Buddhist reformer from Ceylon, and Swami Vivekananda, the Vedantist from India. Many U.S.-born intellectuals also made their way there, among them the New Thought advocate Ralph Waldo Trine, the writer William Dean Howells, the photographer Jacob Riis, and the black educator Booker T. Washington. After Farmer became a Baha'i, she announced she would give much of her estate, including Green Acre, to the Baha'i community. Her heirs then got a doctor to declare her mentally incompetent and a judge to commit her to an insane asylum in Massachusetts. The Baha'is tried valiantly to reverse the order, but when the futility of that course of action became clear they took matters into their own hands, liberating Farmer from the facility in a daring night raid. After Massachusetts authorities decided not to pursue her, Farmer lived out her days in Maine.

Then there was the more notorious case of Pierre Bernard, a.k.a. "Oom the Omnipotent." Unlike Bull and Farmer, who were attracted to the nondualistic Advaita Vedanta philosophy of Ramakrishna and his disciples, Bernard gravitated to an esoteric form of Hinduism called tantra. Bernard reportedly traveled to India around the turn of the century. After settling in San Francisco in 1904 or 1905, he began teaching tantric practices through his Bacchante Academy, later known as the Tantrik Order in America. He also operated the Tantrik Press and published at least one issue of the *International Journal of the Tantrik Order in America*. In 1906, the San Francisco police (acting on tips by two women, both former followers) charged him with "soul charming" and morals violations.[11] The charges were later dropped.

After the San Francisco earthquake of 1906, Bernard moved from San Francisco to New York City. Once again, scandal pursued him. Newspapers investigating his reconstituted "Oriental Sanctum" reported hearing "wild Oriental music and women's cries, but not those of distress." In 1910, Bernard was charged again by two young women, who accused him of forcing them to serve as spiritual prostitutes. Dailies from the *New York Times* to the *San Francisco Chronicle* followed this scandal regarding the "wild orgies" of Bernard's "love cult." Although the "Omnipotent Oom" spent a few months in prison awaiting trial, this case too was dropped. Ultimately, Bernard's accusers refused to testify, leaving the papers to speculate that he had exerted some irresistible psychic power over them. "I cannot tell you how Bernard got control over me or how he gets it over other people," one of the women told reporters. "He is the most wonderful man in the world. No women seem able to resist him."[12]

FORMS AND VEHICLES FOR INTERRELIGIOUS ENCOUNTERS

Historians tell stories like this in part because they are entertaining, but our job is to make sense of them. My effort to interpret these three cases—of Sara Bull, Sarah Farmer, and the Omnipotent Oom—begins with the observation that all are instances of interreligious contact. For much of world history, religious traditions existed in splendid isolation. Modernity, however, has been characterized by raucous interactions among those traditions (as, it should be noted, were many pockets of the medieval and ancient worlds). Religions in practice do not respect the tidy boundaries we often assign to them in our books and courses. Hinduism, for example, is no longer simply a religion of

India. It is a North American religion, too. And it is practiced, as a *Time* magazine yoga cover of 2001 indicates, far outside the confines of Hindu institutions.

In my interpretations of interreligious interactions, I typically examine two factors: the form of the encounter and the vehicle for it. I see three dominant forms for interreligious encounters: *combination, collaboration,* and *conflict*.[13] Combination is a theme in my first book, *The White Buddhist* (1996), which explores the "Protestant Buddhism" of an early U.S. convert to Buddhism. Diana Eck's CD-Rom *On Common Ground*[14] celebrates collaboration: participants in interfaith projects who hold fast to their own religious identities even as they work with other people of faith to foster tolerance, build housing for the homeless, or combat AIDS. Finally, believers encounter one another in conflict—when members of the Nation of Islam denounce Jews as devils, or the pope warns Catholics of the dangers of *zazen*.

In considering interreligious encounters, I try to weigh the vehicle as well as the form of the interaction. Are practitioners of two different faiths interacting in person? Responding at a distance to each other's scriptures? Admiring (or destroying) each other's icons? Economists talk far more about distribution channels than do scholars of religion, but we too might be served by considering the channels through which religious traditions move across the country (and across the globe).[15] And so I like to speak of three vehicles for interreligious encounters: interpersonal, artifactual, and textual or, more informally, people, stuff, and books.[16]

Americans first encountered Buddhism, for example, in books. Sailors and travelers brought back artifacts from Buddhist countries, and a few missionaries met Buddhists abroad, but most Victorian Americans who knew anything about Buddhism got what they learned from the printed page. Ralph Waldo Emerson never met a Buddhist; his encounter with Buddhism (like the broader Transcendentalist encounter with Asian religions) was almost entirely textual. So there were no Buddhists around to correct him when he praised the Bhagavad Gita as a great Buddhist book. That began to change when Chinese immigrants came to the West Coast in the 1850s and Japanese immigrants, some of them Buddhist clerics, arrived in the 1890s.

Obviously, the quality of an interreligious encounter is quite different when it is mediated by a work of art as opposed to texts or persons—just as the experience of going to an art gallery differs from reading a book or engaging in a conversation. The "Boston Buddhists" of the late nineteenth century traveled widely in Asia, especially Japan, and encountered Buddhists there firsthand, but the artifacts they sent home (many of which made their way into the Museum of Fine Arts in Boston) enabled others to meet Buddhism artifactually—through Buddhist stuff.

The historian of religion W. C. Smith has argued that the study of religion should migrate from studying "isms" to studying persons. In fact, Smith has suggested that we accelerate that shift by banishing from our vocabulary words such as *Hinduism* and even *religion*.[17] There are many virtues to Smith's "personalist" approach, but it must be noted that in the past many people have encountered foreign religious traditions in "isms" alone, and never in the flesh.

My focus here is on interreligious conflicts that emerged during the first wave of immigration from India to the United States, which occurred during the quarter century between 1899 and 1924. The furors over Bull, Farmer, and Bernard arose in 1910 and 1911, just as the main vehicle for Americans' encounters with the Hindu tradition was shifting (because of immigration) from texts to persons, or, as W. C. Smith might have put it, as Americans were changing their focus from Hinduism to Hindus. It was the arrival of Hindus on U.S. soil, in other words, that prompted a flurry of Hinduphobia in print.

The anti-Hindu invective of the Sara Bull trial did not come out of nowhere, of course. There was already a substantial tradition of U.S. writing about Hinduism, stretching back through Mark Twain and Walt Whitman to the Theosophists and Transcendentalists. In order to understand why Hinduphobia proliferated in the first quarter of the twentieth century (and how it was related to Hinduphilia), it is necessary to review, however briefly, earlier U.S. encounters with the Hindu tradition.

A BRIEF HISTORY OF U.S. ENCOUNTERS WITH HINDUISM

Of all the religions of Asia, Hinduism has the longest history in the United States, and it initially came here via stuff. The *United States,* the first American ship to sail in Indian waters, initiated a vigorous trade between India and the United States upon its arrival in

Pondicherry in 1784. Soon U.S. traders were returning from the subcontinent laden with wares, some of which made their way to the East India Marine Society (established in Salem, Massachusetts, in 1799), whose collection of Indian artifacts became the first major U.S. collection of Asian art.

Of course, Indian artifacts were not widely distributed throughout the United States, and few Americans had the funds (or the stomach) to travel to India. So most Americans who learned about Hinduism got their information from books. Some scholarly texts touched on the subject, including Joseph Priestley's *Comparison of the Institutions of Moses with Those of the Hindoos and Other Ancient Nations* (1799) and Hannah Adams's *Dictionary of All Religions and Religious Denominations* (1817), but most Americans preferred more adventurous titles. Amaso Delano's *Narrative of Voyages and Travels* (1817), one of the first popular travelogues, set the stage for later interpretations of Indian religion by focusing on the exotic rather than the everyday, on practices rather than beliefs, and on popular rather than elite religiosity. Like many early interpreters of India, Delano wrote of hook swinging, widow burning, and cremation. He described Hindu priests as "immoral, ignorant, and cruel"—superstitious idol worshippers who had wielded far too much power over ordinary believers.[18]

Sea captains were not the only Americans to go to India, of course. In 1812, the American Board of Commissioners for Foreign Missions dispatched the first U.S. missionaries to the subcontinent. Soon Americans were reading missionary memoirs, filled with delicious details about the exotic religious rites of the "Hindoos" of India.

Another genre that alerted U.S. readers to India was the Oriental tale. Like the travelogue and the missionary memoir, the Oriental tale presented Hinduism as an object of both fascination and fear, reveling in the exoticism of the East while warning readers about its manifold dangers.[19]

Today the Transcendentalists are remembered as the first group of U.S. intellectuals to take Asian religions seriously, and Ralph Waldo Emerson, Transcendentalism's leading light, was surely one of the first Americans keenly interested in Hindu thought. Yet early in his life Emerson was more of a Hinduphobe than a Hinduphile. Influenced by popular Oriental tales such as Robert Southey's *The Curse of Kehama* (1810), he initially understood the Hindu tradition largely in terms of its practices rather than its beliefs, and he judged those practices to be despicable. Emerson wrote an undergraduate poem called "Indian Superstition," which a biographer has deemed "a jejune, xenophobic, condescending, even racist overview of Indic mythology from the vantage of European Christianity." The poem focused, however, less on myths than on rites—what Emerson called the "ostentatious rituals of India which worshipped God by outraging nature."[20]

Muhammad Ali once said that "a man who views the world the same at fifty as he did at twenty has wasted thirty years of his life." At least by this criterion, Emerson was no wastrel. Although never tired of disdaining "endless ceremonial nonsense" wherever he found it, he grew to love Hindu scripture. Late in his life, Emerson referred to Hinduism as "a simple & grand religion" and to his beloved Gita as a "venerable oracle"—"the first of books."[21]

Henry David Thoreau developed into even more of a Hinduphile. "I cannot read a sentence in the book of the Hindoos without being elevated as upon the table-land of the Ghauts," he gushed. "It has such a rhythmn as the winds of the desert, such a tide as the Ganges, and seems as superior to criticism as the Himmaleh Mounts." Like Emerson, Thoreau was attracted to Hindu texts rather than Hindu people. Unlike Emerson, however, Thoreau had something good to say about Hindu sannyasis. At the beginning of *Walden,* he seems to be perpetuating stereotypes "of Brahmins sitting exposed to four fires and looking in the face of the sun; or hanging suspended, with their heads downward, over flames; . . . or dwelling, chained for life, at the foot of a tree." But instead of sneering at these Hindu holy men, he redirects his readers toward the equally absurd austerities of his townsfolk in Concord. "These forms of conscious penance," writes Thoreau, "are hardly more incredible and astonishing than the scenes which I daily witness" among Concord's bedraggled "serfs of the soil." "The mass of men"—from Concord to Calcutta—"lead lives of quiet desperation," Thoreau famously observes. What is the difference whether one is chained to a tree or to a plow?[22]

One senses in Thoreau a reverence for religious virtuosi who vaccinate that desperation via austere living, and that suspicion is confirmed in an 1849 letter. There Thoreau writes, "The yogin, absorbed in contemplation, contributes in his degree to creation: he breathes a divine perfume, he hears wonderful things. Divine forms traverse him without tearing him, and united to the nature which is proper to him, he goes, he acts, as animating original matter." "To some extent, and at rare intervals," Thoreau concludes, "even I am a yogin."[23]

While the Transcendentalists were the first group of intellectuals in the United States to take Hinduism seriously, the Theosophists were the first organization to take Asian religions as their main cause. Helena Blavatsky and Henry Steel Olcott, who co-founded the Theosophical Society in New York City in 1875, both formally converted to Buddhism in Ceylon in 1880. Both saw all the great world religions as offshoots from the Hindu Vedas.

Yet the Theosophists and Transcendentalists alike mixed with their Hinduphilia large measures of Hinduphobia. The basic strategy in each case was to split Hinduism into two variants: one rooted in ancient scripture (call it "literary Hinduism"), the other in contemporary practice (call it "lived Hinduism"). Then they evaluated the ancient texts positively and the contemporary practice negatively, denouncing the popular Hinduism of the modern masses—the *bhakti* path of devotion—as heathenish while praising the elite Hinduism of ancient scriptures—particularly the *jnana* path of wisdom—for its lofty spiritual ideals. The Gita was, as Thoreau argued, better than Shakespeare. But Hindu rites were empty and the Brahmin priests who performed them were ignorant and superstitious. Or, to put it another way, even the Transcendentalists were Hinduphobes when it came to popular Hinduism. What they loved about the tradition was its past rather than its present, its texts rather than its rites, its great men rather than its ordinary believers. Emerson may not have changed his mind as much as we think.

HINDU INVASION

There are records of a man from Madras walking the streets of Salem in 1790, but Indian immigration did not begin in earnest until the turn of the twentieth century, when unskilled laborers from the Punjab (virtually all of them men) began to come to the West Coast to work on farms. By almost any measure, this influx was modest—a ripple rather than a wave. The pace quickened considerably after the turn of the century, but still, only 6,795 arrived between 1901 and 1920, taking up jobs in mines, in lumber mills, on railroads, and in agriculture.[24]

At the time, *Hindoo* was an ethnic rather than a religious designation. The term, first coined by British colonial administrators in the early nineteenth century, initially referred to all non-Muslims and non-European natives of India. In early-twentieth-century America, however, it meant anyone from India. The vast majority of the "Hindoo" immigrants to the United States in this period were Sikhs, and a considerable minority (perhaps as high as one-third) were Muslims. So at the time the Hindu tradition went on trial alongside Mrs. Bull, there were probably fewer than a thousand Indian-born practitioners of Hinduism in the United States.

Still, a host of critics saw this modest migration as an "invasion," denouncing "Hindoos" as practitioners of foreign faiths who were unwanted and unwelcomed in Protestant America. In 1910, the *San Francisco Call* ran an editorial cartoon called "A New Problem for Uncle Sam." The cartoon depicts three figures: Uncle Sam, the "Viceroy of India," and a man with bangles on his wrists, a turban on his head, a cigarette in his mouth, and a "Hindu" label on his pants. Uncle Sam is holding the "Hindu" (who is literally tagged incompetent and indolent) by the bottom and trying to pass him across the ocean to India. "Say! Take this impossible thing back! We don't want it over here!" The colonial administrator chuckles, "Ha! Ha! Not me."[25]

Echoing the *San Francisco Call,* white laborers derided these new immigrants, just as they had denounced the "Yellow Peril" from China and Japan. The Asiatic Exclusion League, formed in 1905 for "the preservation of the Caucasian race upon American soil," insisted that Hindoos, like the Chinese and Japanese before them, were unassimilable aliens. "From every part of the [West] Coast," the League argued, "complaints are made of the undesirability of the Hindoos, their lack of cleanliness, disregard of sanitary laws, petty pilfering, especially of chickens, and insolence to women." This bigotry graduated from words to action in 1907 in Bellingham, Washington, when an anti-Indian uprising forced hundreds of "Hindoos" working at lumber mills to flee for their lives into Canada. In 1917 it acquired the force of law when the U.S. Congress passed immigration legislation that severely restricted immigration from "barred zones," including South and Southeast Asia. Virtually all immigration from Asia came to an end seven years later, with the passage of the National Origins Act of 1924.[26]

In many respects, this abrupt resolution of the "Hindoo Question" mirrors what happened with the Chinese and the Japanese. But in one important respect this story differs, since the prevailing racial theories of the day classified Indians as Caucasians. While both the Chinese and the Japanese had been condemned as heathens, efforts to send them home had focused on race. Anti-Indian agitation, by contrast, emphasized religion. Even the most outspoken critics of Indian immigration admitted that the Hindoo was "a brother of our own race—a full-blooded Aryan." What distinguished him from other Americans was his faith.[27]

Around the time the Sara Bull case hit the the *New York Times*, a variety of books and articles appeared denouncing the "Hindoo invasion" as a religious threat to Protestant America. Rather than focusing on the dangers cheap Indian labor posed to white working men, these critics emphasized the dangers Hindu swamis posed to innocent women. In articles such as "Strange Gods of American Women" (1912) and "American Women Going After Heathen Gods" (1912), anti-Hindu activists penned modern-day versions of early American captivity narratives. But this time the innocents were taken captive by Indians from Asia.

In her article on "The Hindu Invasion of America" (1912), Mabel Potter Daggett rehashed standard complaints about temple prostitution, child marriage, and widow suicide in India. She built her piece, however, around the image of the seductive serpent. The Hindu swami was that serpent, and the American woman was his Eve. "It is not the worship of images of stone and wood that constitutes the gravest peril in the teaching of the Orientals," Daggett wrote. "It is the worship of men." She described American women as literally kissing the feet of their gurus, offering them their riches and, in many cases, their bodies and souls themselves. The relationships these women formed with their swamis separated them not only from true religion but also from their husbands and children. Citing explicitly the cases of Farmer, Bull, and Bernard, Daggett argued that American women were attracted to yoga by "the promise of eternal youth." What they got was "domestic infelicity and insanity and death."[28]

Elizabeth A. Reed reiterated these same themes in *Hinduism in Europe and America* (1914). Reed's book is particularly important, since she was widely respected at the time as a scholar of religion. Praised by the pioneering Indologist Max Müller for her prior publications on ancient Hindu and Buddhist scriptures, she was a member of the Royal Asiatic Society. But her standing in the new field of comparative religion did not prevent her from viciously attacking modern Hinduism. "The Guru," she wrote, "is a modern money-making invention." In India, ignorant Hindus blindly sell themselves, "body, soul, and mind," into "abject slavery." In the United States, swamis "creep into houses and lead captive silly women." Under "the hypnotic influence" of their gurus, who demand nothing less than "slavish devotion," these women become "helpless" and then "hopelessly insane."[29]

Scholars of the Americanist controversy in U.S. Catholicism now refer to Americanism as a "phantom heresy." The Hindu menace of the first quarter of the twentieth century may have been even more phantasmagorical. There were certainly no more than ten thousand Indian Americans in the country at the time, and probably only one or two thousand practitioners of Hinduism. The Vedanta Society, then the largest Hindu organization in the United States, was active in only a handful of U.S. cities, and in 1916 claimed only 190 members.[30] So it is worth pondering why Americans worried so much about "the tide of turbans."

Part of the answer lies in the prior history of Asian immigration to the United States. When it came to books, Hinduism preceded Buddhism in the United States. Americans were reading English translations of the Gita in 1785, while the first English translation of a Buddhist scripture did not appear until 1844. But when it came to immigrants, the Buddhists got here before the Hindus, and they came in far greater numbers. Chinese immigration began in force after the discovery of gold in California led to the famous gold rush of 1849. By 1880, over 100,000 had come to the United States, and roughly 10 percent of the California population was Chinese. The Japanese came next, and in larger numbers.

As a rule, Americans responded to these migrations from Asia with fear and trepidation. The black intellectual Frederick Douglass embraced the Chinese as true Americans, and Protestant missionaries defended them as Christians-in-the-making. But calls to "Keep California White" drowned out Douglass's plea for a "composite nation" of many races and ethnicities.[31] After the completion of the transcontinental railroad (much of it built by Chinese laborers) sent Chinese workers scurrying for work, nativism swelled. In 1882 U.S. legislators effectively ended Chinese immigration (and naturalization) via the Chinese Exclusion Act.

This process repeated itself with the Japanese, so when it came to the "Hindoo Question," Americans were able to draw on a longstanding tradition of anti-Asian nativism. Indian immigration mattered not because it was numerically significant—it was not—but because it raised the specter of another "Yellow Peril."

If this was one reason why Americans feared the "phantom menace" of Hinduism, it was not the most important. As I have argued, anti-Indian agitation differed from prior nativist campaigns in its focus on religion. The fear Americans exhibited regarding Hinduism was in my view more religious than racial. As a result, it took its clues more from Americans' fear of Catholics than from their fear of the Chinese or Japanese.

THE ANTI-CATHOLIC TYPE

Today there is reason to debate the religious character of the United States. One can reasonably argue that the United States is multireligious or secular, Judeo-Christian or Abrahamic. Throughout the nineteenth century and well into the twentieth, however, Protestants dominated the public square, first as evangelicals and later as liberals. De jure, the United States was secular, but de facto it was Protestant.

The anti-Hindu agitation of the 1910s and 1920s should be understood, therefore, as one episode in a broader story of the encounter of Protestant "insiders" with various religious "outsiders." In that story, the quintessential "outsiders" were Roman Catholics. So if Americans experienced a sense of *déjà vu* when reading about the Sara Bull and Pierre Bernard cases, what they were reliving was not so much the "Yellow Peril" as the "Roman Menace."

I cannot fully develop this argument here, but I can sketch its outlines. As I have already intimated, key themes in the anti-Hindu literature echo earlier captivity narratives about colonists and Americans kidnapped (and forcibly converted) by Native Americans and French Catholics. These parallels are worth exploring. But the parallels I want to highlight here concern the anti-Catholic furor that attended Catholic immigration from Europe in the mid-nineteenth century.

Americans who engaged Hinduism in the nineteenth and early twentieth centuries—Hinduphiles and Hinduphobes alike—almost always divided it into two parts: its ancient scriptures and its modern manifestations. Those who praised the tradition focused on ancient scripture, while those who condemned it emphasized modern manifestations. This basic strategy came in many variants, but typically American interpreters criticized Hindu rites far more than Hindu scriptures, and the priests who performed those rites far more than scholars of ancient texts. "Real Hinduism," a *Boston Herald* editorial contended, was not about Hindu thought (attaining "blissful fellowship with the divine"), as Vedanta Society swamis pretended.[32] It was about Hindu practice. Or, as other anti-Hindu literature of the time claimed, it was about:

- authoritarian religious leaders
- a superstitious, idolatrous, and dying faith
- mistreatment of women
- mind control
- illicit sex
- ill-gotten financial gain

What is striking about these themes is how closely they track nineteenth-century anti-Catholic literature. In a few cases, Hinduphobic writers explicitly compared Hindu and Catholic rites. Amaso Delano, for example, compared hook swinging with "the excesses of the Dominicans, the barbarities of the Inquisition."[33] But for the most part, the analogies were unstated.

Anti-Catholic tracts, sermons, novels, plays, and poems regularly described Popery (as they called it) as authoritarian and antidemocratic—a threat to individual autonomy and a destroyer of religious liberty. Still, anti-Catholic literature focused more on religion and morality than on politics and society. Or, to put it another way, while Catholicism was understood as an offense against democracy, republicanism, and individualism—what historian David Brion Davis called "an inverted image of Jacksonian democracy and the cult of the common man"—it was first and foremost an offense against Protestantism. In terms of theology, Catholics were idolaters, these texts argued, not Christians. True Christianity was biblical Christianity, but that form of religion had faded as Catholics hijacked the church, substituting idolatrous veneration of Mary for the true worship of Jesus. When it came to religious practice, Catholics were said to be superstitious.

The "hocus-pocus" of transubstantiation was to Catholicism's critics as nonsensical as the antics of Indian magicians. "What are your Eastern fire-eaters, sword-swallowers, and dervishes to a Popish priest?" one anti-Catholic writer asked (in another explicit connection between anti-Hinduism and anti-Catholicism). "Why, it would be easier to swallow a rapier, ten feet long, or a ball of fire as large as the mountain Orizaba, than to metamorphose flour and water into the *great and holy God.*"[34]

The dominant story line in these melodramas featured a lecherous priest seducing innocent women into illicit sexual relations. In a system as authoritarian as Catholicism, there was no saying no to a priest. Invoking the snake of Genesis, Protestant critics argued that Catholic priests were as cunning as they were lustful, "covering their hypocrisy with the cloak of *religion,* and with more than the serpent's guile, worming themselves into the confidence and affections of their unsuspecting victims." Some of these priestly seductions began in the confessional with Catholic lay women, but more often they were set in the convent, with nuns. In Gothic tales of Catholic horrors, such as *The Awful Disclosures* (1836) of Maria Monk, convents were "slave factories," "priests' harems," and "baptized brothels" where priests, under the cover of religion and oaths of celibacy, compelled innocent nuns to have sex with them. They were also dens of infanticide, since the most common fate of the children born of this priestly debauchery was supposedly murder in the convent dungeon.[35]

Along with sex and death, convents also produced insanity. In the summer of 1834, a nun named Elizabeth Harrison escaped from an Ursuline convent in Charlestown, Massachusetts. According to newspaper reports, life as a nun had driven Miss Harrison insane, so one night she fled to freedom in a nearby home. When she came back to the convent a few days later, however, newspapers reported that she had been coerced into returning, and was atoning for her sins in the convent's dungeon. The Harrison case was the lead story in Boston for a few weeks, until an anti-Catholic mob took matters into its own hands, marching on the convent and burning it down.

As we have seen, similar themes dominated the anti-Hindu literature of the early twentieth century. Instead of focusing on ancient Hindu texts, American critics focused on contemporary Hindu swamis, whom they described as authoritarian, anti-democratic, superstitious, deceptive, immoral, and greedy. The basic story line in almost all anti-Hindu literature featured a lecherous priest seducing innocent (and often wealthy) American women in order to gratify his own lust and greed. These seductions took place not in convents but in ashrams—in "Oom the Omnipotent's" "Oriental Sanctum," the Green Acre retreat center, and even Mrs. Bull's Studio House. In the end, Hindu swamis stripped these women of their autonomy, their virtue, and their money. They also made them idolaters, since these women supposedly came to worship their living saints as if they were gods. In some cases they even produced, in the words of the *Boston Globe,* "religious lunacies."[36]

The analogies between these two forms of nativism—the anti-Catholicism of the nineteenth century and the anti-Hinduism of the twentieth—are quite striking. Americans surely lashed out at Indian immigration because it reminded them of earlier waves of immigration from Asia. But most of the anti-Hindu fulminations were religiously rather than racially inflected, and they recalled more than anything else the anti-Catholic agitation of the nineteenth century. Whereas in the nineteenth century Americans accused Catholics of conspiring to overthrow the United States, in the early twentieth century they accused Hindus of conspiring to drive American women insane. If, as one nativist argued, Roman Catholicism was "the Mother of Abominations," anti-Catholicism was the mother of Hinduphobia.[37] It may also have been the mother of Hinduphilia, since much of what the Hinduphiles loved in Hinduism was framed in Protestant terms: its scriptures, its rejection of empty rites, its austerity, its ethics.

David Brion Davis has described anti-Masonic, anti-Mormon, and anti-Catholic literature as "both frightening and fascinating." Nativists, in his words, "projected their own fears and desires into a fantasy of licentious orgies and fearful punishments." Jenny Franchot has written of the "attraction of repulsion" in anti-Catholic literature—the thrill of reading these Gothic tales of intrigue, sex, torture, and escape. This same mixture of titillation and disgust can be found in the anti-Hindu literature, where the "attraction of repulsion" is also at play.[38]

CONCLUSION

For too long, scholars of U.S. religion have focused either on Protestantism or on pluralism. The way forward, in my view, is to attend to both. The history of Hinduism in the United States can be understood only in light of the Protestant dominance in the public square, which lasted in the United States at least into the 1920s. American reactions to Hinduism can be understood only in light of American reactions to other foreign faiths, most notably the quintessential foreign faith of Roman Catholicism. The contentious meeting of Protestantism and Catholicism, which came to U.S. shores with the first English, Spanish, and French settlers, is the *Ur*-encounter of U.S. religious history. All subsequent encounters—including the encounter with Native American religions—took place among a populace already well versed in Protestant-Catholic conflict. Hinduphobia erupted in the United States in 1911 just as the U.S. encounter with Hinduism was shifting from books to people—from ancient Hindu scriptures (which many Americans had praised) to contemporary Hindu practitioners (whom virtually all Americans disdained). Anti-Hinduism quickly found its voice because the Americans who employed it already knew the script.

Since World War II, and especially since the 1960s, anti-Catholicism has to a great extent abated in the United States, as Catholicism has joined Protestantism and Judaism in the "triple melting pot" described by Will Herberg.[39] Hinduphobia has largely faded, too. But the stereotypes conjured up in the Sara Bull trial are alive and well. In a study of American views of India and China, Harold R. Isaacs interviewed prominent Americans in an effort to understand their views of Asian religion and culture. One informant said Hinduism conjured up a picture of "sacred cows roaming the streets; mobs of religious fanatics hurling themselves into the Ganges; naked ascetics, scrawny fakiers on nails; the multiarmed goddess; the burning ghats; the skull-laden figure of Kali; Benares; obscene Hindu sculpture, phallic symbols and erotic carvings on the temples." *Gyn/Ecology* (1990) by the feminist theologian Mary Daly also traffics in blatant stereotypes, reducing Hinduism to suttee in an effort to judge the Hindu tradition guilty of what she calls the "Sado-Ritual Syndrome."[40]

Few Americans affirm such xenophobia. What endures from the days of Sara Bull is the tendency to mistake part of Hinduism for the whole, to split Hinduism into its good and bad halves and then (depending on whether one loves or hates it) to define "real Hinduism" accordingly. Americans who love Hinduism today feel few compunctions about jettisoning those parts of the tradition that make them uncomfortable—reducing Hinduism to hatha yoga exercises, for example, and in many cases utterly divorcing those exercises from Hindu theology.

The last time I taught my "Hinduism in America" course, I asked my Hindu students what they thought of the contemporary yoga craze. What, I asked, did Madonna and other popularizers of yoga owe to the Hindu tradition? My students responded with a minimal demand. They hoped only that U.S. borrowers would show Hinduism some respect, acknowledging the fact that yoga originated in India thousands of years ago. I think Americans owe the Hindu tradition a bit more: We need to be clear about how we are adapting its beliefs and practices to U.S. circumstances. In order to do that, however, we need to be honest about what Hinduism has been and what it is becoming. Although I understand why, for praise or polemics, Americans have whittled "real Hinduism" down to these beliefs or those practices, it is the job of scholars of religion to keep them honest. All religious traditions—at least all traditions that have survived over the centuries—rightly precipitate in us some measure of both fear and fascination. All harbor "texts of terror" alongside lofty ethical axioms.[41] All have sordid chapters in their histories, and brilliant episodes of which they are justly proud. To understand any of the world's religions we need to understand what they do well, and what they do poorly. We need to see Islam as a religion of both war and peace; we need to understand that Christianity has produced pacifists as well as warriors. We need to see how different religions have produced both insanity and the equally troubling propensity to find insanity in others.

All this is to say that scholars of religion serve their students and readers best when they steer clear of both Hinduphilia and Hinduphobia. As any observer of the Indian political scene can attest, Hinduism is not by nature as tolerant as I was once led to believe. But neither can it be reduced, as it was in the Bull case, to a series of techniques for brainwashing and seducing unsuspecting women. Like any great religious tradition, "real Hinduism" deserves to be understood for what it really is, not for what its lovers and haters wish it to be.

NOTES

1. "Says Psychic Plot Swayed Mrs. Bull," *New York Times*, 23 May 1911, p. 1; "Spirits Urged $25,000 Gift, Said Mrs. Bull," *Boston Herald*, 15 June 1911, p. 1.

2. "Looked at Pictures and Made Eyes Move," *New York Times*, 26 May 1911, p. 13; "Mrs. Bull's Indian Tonics," *New York Times*, 27 June 1911, p. 5;

"Sister Nevidita Disregarded Nurse's Order," *Boston Herald,* 27 June 1911, p. 1; "Mrs. Bull Was Insane, Says Yogi Ruberto," *Boston Herald,* 25 May 1911, p. 1; "Hindu Tonic for Mrs. Bull," *New York Times,* 2 June 1911, p. 6; "Tells Rites Observed in Bull Home," *Boston Post,* 24 May 1911, p. 1.

3. "Refuse to Make Bull Case Legal," *Boston Herald,* 13 June 1911, p. 8; "Masseur Tells of Bull Revels in 'Holy' Room," *Boston Herald,* 24 May 1911, pp. 1–2.

4. "Spirits Urged $25,000 Gift, Said Mrs. Bull," *Boston Herald,* 15 June 1911, p. 3.

5. "Masseur" (see n. 3 above), p. 2; "Hindu Love Lord in Bull Will Case," *New York Times,* 24 May 1911, p. 2; "Mrs. Bull Was Insane, Says Yogi Ruberto," *Boston Herald,* 25 May 1911, pp. 1–2.

6. "Swami Son of Ole Bull, Said Widow," *Boston Herald,* 27 May 1911, p. 7; "Eight Wills by Mrs. Bull in Evidence," *Boston Herald,* 26 May 1911, p. 7; "Says Psychic Love Plot Swayed Mrs. Bull," *New York Times,* 23 May 1911, p. 1; "Mrs. Bull's Wish About Ashes Unkept," *Boston Herald,* 28 May 1911, p. 4; "Says Psychic Love Plot Swayed Mrs. Bull" (see above), p. 1; "Mrs. Bull Inflamed by Hindu Drug," *Boston Herald,* 17 June 1911, p. 1; "Thorp Admits Drug was Given to Mrs. Bull," *Boston Herald,* 2 June 1911, p. 1; "Swami Son of Ole Bull" (see above), p. 1.

7. "Read Spirit Messages to Mrs. Bull in Court," *Boston Post,* 16 June 1911, p. 1.

8. "Bull's Cook Tells of Indian Drugs," *New York Times,* 17 June 1911, p. 5; "Tells Rites Observed" (see n. 2 above), p. 2; "Another Halt in the Bull Hearing," *Boston Globe,* 27 June 1911, p. 2; "Swami Son of Ole Bull" (see n. 6 above), p. 1; "Mrs. Bull's Wish About Ashes Unkept," *Boston Herald,* 28 May 1911, p. 4.

9. "Swamis and Others," *Boston Herald,* 2 June 1911, p. 6. See, however, "The Swamis Defended," letter to the editor, *Boston Herald,* 10 June 1911.

10. See William Sims Bainbridge, "Religious Insanity in America: The Official Nineteenth-Century Theory," *Sociological Analysis* 45, no. 3 (Fall 1984): 223–39. In the infamous Beecher-Tilton adultery trial of the 1870s, the husband of Mrs. Tilton accused the beloved Protestant preacher Henry Ward Beecher of brainwashing his wife. "I think she sinned her sin as one in a trance," he testified. "I don't think she was a free agent. I think she would have done his bidding if, like the heathen priest in the Hindoo-land, he had bade her to fling her child into the Ganges or cast herself under the Juggernaut" (quoted in Richard Wightman Fox, *Trials of Intimacy: Love and Loss in the Beecher-Tilton Scandal* [Chicago: University of Chicago Press, 1999], p. 114).

11. Quoted in Nik Douglas, *Spiritual Sex: Secrets of Tantra from the Ice Age to the New Millennium* (New York: Pocket Books, 1997), p. 195.

12. Charles Boswell, "The Great Fuss and Fume over the Omnipotent Oom," *True: The Man's Magazine* (January 1965), http://www.vanderbilt.edu/~stringer/fuss.htm; quoted in Douglas, *Spiritual Sex*, p. 195; "Wild Orgies in the Temple of 'Om': Police Get New Light on the Doings of Fakers of New York," *San Francisco Chronicle*, 5 May 1910; "Pierre Bernard, Oom the Omnipotent, Promoter and Self-Styled Swami, Dies," *New York Times*, 28 September 1955, p. 35; quoted in Paul Sann, *Fad, Follies, and Delusions of the American People* (New York: Bonanza Books, 1967), p. 190. After a few years in Manhattan, Bernard moved again, this time to Nyack, New York, where he set up an ashram of sorts known first as the Braeburn Country Club and later as the Clarkstown Country Club. There Bernard continued to teach his own brand of Tantra, affirming among other things that "love, a manifestation of sexual instinct, is the animating spirit of the world" (Pierre Bernard, "Tantrik Worship: The Basis of Religion," *International Journal, Tantrik Order* 5, no. 1 [1906]: 71). But in rural New York, Bernard came to be regarded more with love than with fear. In fact, he became "one of the most active and patriotic townspeople of Nyack" ("'Omnipotent Oom' Scents a Fraud," *New York Times*, 27 October 1922, p. 3)—the president of a local bank, the treasurer of the local chamber of commerce, the president of the Nyack Athletic Club, and the benefactor of an annual circus featuring his beloved Indian elephant "Mom."

13. My views of these matters have been shaped by a series of conversations with Catherine Albanese. See, e.g., her discussion of "religious interchange" in "Exchanging Selves, Exchanging Souls: Contact, Combination, and American Religious History," in *Retelling U.S. Religious History*, ed. Thomas A. Tweed (Berkeley: University of California Press, 1997), pp. 200–226.

14. Diana Eck, *On Common Ground: World Religions in America*, CD-Rom, rev. ed. (New York: Columbia University Press, 2002).

15. I am grateful to Colleen McDannell for pressing this point with me.

16. Over the last decade or so, Americans have begun as well to engage with other religious traditions over the Internet—in chat rooms, discussion groups, and through surfing the World Wide Web. So it makes sense to add to my interreligious *yanas* (vehicles)—the interpersonal, artifactual, and textual—a fourth vehicle: the online or *virtual* encounter.

17. See, e.g., Wilfred Cantwell Smith, *The Meaning and End of Religion* (Minneapolis: Fortress Press, 1991).

18. Quoted in Thomas A. Tweed and Stephen Prothero, eds., *Asian Religions in America: A Documentary History* (New York: Oxford University Press, 1999), p. 31.

19. Americans also learned about Hinduism from more scholarly books, including Joseph Priestley's *Comparison of the Institutions of Moses with Those of the Hindoos and Other Ancient Nations* (1799) and Hannah Adams's

Dictionary of All Religions and Religious Denominations (1817), though neither of these books was as objective as its author believed. See Tweed and Prothero, *Asian Religions in America*, pp. 44–48, 54–57.

20. Robert D. Richardson Jr., *Emerson: The Mind on Fire: A Biography* (Berkeley: University of California Press, 1995), pp. 8–9; Emerson quoted in Carl T. Jackson, *The Oriental Religions and American Thought: Nineteenth-Century Explorations* (Westport, Conn.: Greenwood Press, 1981), p. 48.

21. "Muhammad Ali: A Candid Conversation with the Greatest—and Prettiest—Poet in the World," *Playboy* (November 1975), http://www.sportsline.com/b/member/playboy/7511.html; Emerson quoted in Jackson, *Oriental Religions*, pp. 53, 45.

22. Thoreau quoted in Jackson, *Oriental Religions*, p. 64; Henry David Thoreau, *Walden* (New York: Thomas Y. Crowell Co., 1961), pp. 3, 4, 8.

23. Thoreau quoted in Jackson, *Oriental Religions*, p. 65.

24. Herbert R. Barringer, Robert W. Gardner, and Michael J. Levin, *Asian and Pacific Islanders in the United States* (New York: Russell Sage Foundation, 1993), p. 24.

25. "A New Problem for Uncle Sam," *San Francisco Call*, 13 August 1910, http://www.lib.berkeley.edu/SSEAL/echoes/chapter4/chapter4_1.html.

26. Ronald T. Takaki, *Strangers from a Different Shore: A History of Asian Americans* (New York: Penguin Books, 1990), pp. 201, 297.

27. Agnes Foster Buchanan, "The West and the Hindu Invasion," *Overland Monthly* 51, no. 4 (April 1908): 309. For a time, the courts seemed to agree. In landmark cases in 1910 and 1913, the courts ruled that Indian immigrants were Caucasians and, as such, were eligible for naturalization under a 1790 law restricting citizenship to "white persons." (Those rulings were overturned in 1923 in *U.S. v. Thind*, when the U.S. Supreme Court ruled that Indian immigrants, while Caucasian, were not "white persons" in the common sense of that term.)

28. Mabel Potter Daggett, "The Heathen Invasion of America," *Missionary Review of the World* 35, no. 3 (March 1912): 214, 211, 210.

29. Elizabeth A. Reed, *Hinduism in Europe and America* (New York: G. P. Putnam's Sons, 1914), pp. 117, 112, 133, 129, 131, 129. Indian Americans did not have the access to the many popular publishing venues enjoyed by scholars and missionaries, but they did respond to the critiques nonetheless. See Girindra Mukerji, "The Hindu in America," *Overland Monthly* 51, no. 4 (April 1908): 303–8; Saint Nihal Singh, "The Picturesque Immigrant from India's Coral Strand," *Out West* 30, no. 1 (January 1909): 43–54; Sudhindra Bose, "American Impressions of a Hindu Student," *The Forum* 53 (February 1915): 251–57. See also Swami Paramananda's *Message of the East*, which began publishing in 1912, in part in response to the Sara Bull affair. These apologies played into prevailing stereotypes by downplaying the

devotional Hinduism and emphasizing its wisdom traditions, and also by presenting Hinduism as anti-caste and for women's rights—in other words, as a tradition friendly to the Protestant social gospel.

30. Carl T. Jackson, *Vedanta for the West: The Ramakrishna Movement in the United States* (Bloomington: Indiana University Press, 1994), p. 108.

31. Frederick Douglass, "Our Composite Nationality," in *The Frederick Douglass Papers, Series One: Speeches, Debates, and Interviews, Volume 4: 1864–80*, ed. John W. Blassingame and John R. McKivigan (New Haven, Conn.: Yale University Press, 1991), pp. 240–59.

32. "Swamis and Others" (see n. 9 above), p. 6.

33. Quoted in Tweed and Prothero, *Asian Religions in America*, p. 30.

34. David Brion Davis, "Some Themes of Counter-Subversion: An Analysis of Anti-Masonic, Anti-Catholic, and Anti-Mormon Literature," *Mississippi Valley Historical Review* 47 (September 1960): 208; Ray Allen Billington, *The Protestant Crusade, 1800–1860: A Study of the Origins of American Nativism* (New York: Rinehart and Co., 1952), pp. 353–54. There is an extensive debate on the origins of anti-Catholicism in American life. In *Strangers in the Land: Patterns of American Nativism, 1880–1925* (New York: Atheneum, 1963), John Higham understands anti-Catholicism in socio-economic terms, while Davis sees it as largely ideological. Two more recent treatments are Mark S. Massa, *Anti-Catholicism in America: The Last Acceptable Prejudice* (New York: Crossroad, 2003), and Philip Jenkins, *The New Anti-Catholicism: The Last Acceptable Prejudice* (New York: Oxford University Press, 2003). For a provocative application of anti-Catholicism to a seemingly unrelated area, see Philip Hamburger, *Separation of Church and State* (Cambridge, Mass.: Harvard University Press, 2002).

35. Billington, *Protestant Crusade*, pp. 57, 366.

36. 1909 *Boston Globe* editorial quoted in Sara Ann Levinsky, *A Bridge of Dreams: The Story of Paramananda, a Modern Mystic, and His Ideal of All-Conquering Love* (West Stockbridge, Mass.: Lindisfarne Press, 1984), p. 116.

37. Billington, *Protestant Crusade*, p. 273.

38. Davis, "Some Themes of Counter-Subversion," pp. 208, 217; Jenny Franchot, *Roads to Rome: The Antebellum Protestant Encounter with Catholicism* (Berkeley: University of California Press, 1994), pp. 197–220.

39. Will Herberg, *Protesant, Catholic, Jew: An Essay in Religious Sociology* (Garden City, N.Y.: Doubleday, 1955). See, however, Jenkins, *New Anti-Catholicism*, and Massa, *Anti-Catholicism in America*, on the persistence of what they both term "the last acceptable prejudice." See also the proceedings of a conference on this topic held at Fordham University in May 2002, http://www.catholicsinpublicsquare.org/calendar/commonwealcalendar/fordham524.html.

40. Harold R. Isaacs, *Scratches on Our Minds: American Views of China and India* (White Plains, N.Y.: M. E. Sharpe, 1980), p. 259; Mary Daly, *Gyn/Ecology: The Metaethics of Radical Feminism* (Boston: Beacon Press, 1978), p. 136.

41. Phyllis Trible, *Texts of Terror: Literary-Feminist Readings of Biblical Narratives* (Philadelphia: Fortress Press, 1984).

Christianity, Judaism, and Islam and the Restoration of Justice in South Africa
JOHN W. DE GRUCHY

In 1993 my dear friend and mentor, Eberhard Bethge, wrote an essay on Bonhoeffer's theology of friendship for the volume on friendship in this series.[1] I am intrigued by the fact that whereas the theme was "friendship" ten years ago, the focus now is on the "stranger." Of course, the theme of friendship was more centered on personal relations, while that of the stranger is on the "stranger's religion" and therefore on intergroup relations. Still, I discern here a change in our historical consciousness from the heady days of the dawning "new world order" of the early 1990s, to the threatening days that have followed September 11, 2001. Perhaps this shift also reflects an altered religious situation. Then, we applauded the role of religious communities in bringing about the transition to democracy in countries such as Germany and South Africa. Now we fear that religion, especially that of the stranger, will shatter our dreams for a world at peace. Kosovo, with its "ethnic cleansing," was the turning point in this process, reminding us of how easy it is for neighbors and friends of different faiths to become strangers and enemies overnight.

Perhaps more than any other Protestant theologian in postwar Germany, Bethge awakened the conscience of the German church regarding its shameful responsibility for the Holocaust, and helped to initiate Jewish-Christian dialogue within his context. His witness was sensitive, far-reaching, and often courageous. Christians, he argued, had made Jesus a stranger to Jews and in doing so had turned Christianity into a "stranger's religion" to be feared by them. The consequences were only too apparent in the Holocaust. But, Bethge insisted, Judaism was not the religion of a stranger; it was the religion of Jesus our Jewish brother. Thus Christians who took their faith seriously had to recognize their obligation to Judaism and their kinship with Jews.

One issue increasingly perplexed and disturbed Bethge. He perceived that the Israeli-Palestinian question was adversely affecting the rebuilding of Jewish-Christian relations. While it was difficult for Bethge to grapple with this issue at the end of his life, he recognized its importance. For how can we pursue Christian-Jewish dialogue in isolation from what is happening in the Middle East, and therefore in isolation from Islam, the religion that has become such a source of fear and fascination in the West? Can two members of the household of Abraham remain friends if this means hostility toward the third, and if it leads to that member's deepening estrangement? Can two members overcome their estrangement without embracing the third?

The urgency of this issue is clearly apparent to us all in the wake of September 11. But it should not have required such a tragic event to make us aware of it. The situation in the Middle East, where Jews and Palestinians—both Muslim and Christian—have become strangers and enemies, is the greatest threat to world peace at this moment in history. The question facing us, therefore, is whether the family of Abraham will be a curse or a blessing to the nations of the world. The extent to which this question is becoming part of contemporary and even popular discourse can be seen from the main feature article in a September 2002 issue of *Time* magazine.[2] The article is appropriately realistic in its assessment of the situation and yet it also points to hopeful signs of understanding and even reconciliation.

My essay is a reflection on these issues but it focuses on the South African experience during both the apartheid struggle and the current era of national reconciliation and nation building. Before we explore the South African context, however, I will set its particularities within a broader historical framework.

A HISTORICAL FRAMEWORK AND SOME PERSPECTIVES

There have been times when Jews, Muslims, and Christians have lived together in relative harmony and peace. There were periods in medieval Spain, for example, when their interaction was remarkably productive, providing the textual resources and the creative spark that led to the flourishing of Western scholarship during the ensuing centuries. Tragically, this interchange was brought to a halt by the expulsions of Jews and Muslims from Spain in 1492, events which redefined the relationships among the three Abrahamic faiths in Europe and further afield for the ensuing centuries. Christendom, so it was argued within its citadels, could not be secure and stable as long as religious strangers dwelt in its midst. Consequently, Jews were expelled from Spain and scattered across Europe as perpetual aliens depending on the hospitality of others. In times of crisis they became the scapegoats for Christendom's woes, isolated in ghettos, while Europeans regularly sought a "final solution" to the "Jewish problem."

If Judaism was the internal threat, Islam became the external threat as Turkish armies of the Ottoman Empire sought to penetrate Christendom from the east. However, one of the grand ironies of European history is that even though Christendom tried to seal its borders against Islam, we have in our time witnessed the demise of Christendom in western Europe and the resurgence of Islam within its cities. And, whereas Jews were once the scapegoats for all that went wrong, Muslims now increasingly fulfill that role. Indeed, the stereotypical demonizing of Muslims too often provides the rationale for undermining human rights and for unleashing vengeful violence that threatens the future of the world. I recall Eberhard and Renate Bethge taking me and my wife to a Roman Catholic church in a small village in the Rhineland which contained a carving of the Virgin Mary holding the infant Jesus in one hand and the decapitated, bleeding head of a Turk in the other!

On the other hand, the Muslim onslaught on North Africa in the seventh century of the Common Era, and the later imperial expansion of the Ottoman Turks, were also extremely violent. And just as the so-called Christian West has often misrepresented Islam, Muslims frequently stereotype Christianity and Judaism. Current extremist Muslim attacks on Christians and others in Pakistan, Indonesia, and elsewhere are understandably causes for concern, as is the frightening escalation in anti-Semitic rhetoric and Holocaust denial on the part of certain Arab leaders and Islamic fundamentalist groups. The purposes of justice are not served if we fail to recognize culpability on all sides, even if we may regard one side as more seriously at fault than another in particular instances.

Given the history of alienation and aggression, the collective memory that sustains it, and the daily media reinforcing of stereotypes, it is essential that we develop strategies to help us overcome our estrangement. As attempts at interfaith dialogue around the world testify, this has been widely recognized. Such dialogue aims to lift the veil of strangeness and ignorance, but it also tries to deal with substantive issues that perplex, confuse, and divide. That is why it must be far more than a superficial "getting to know you" exercise. Hence Karl-Josef Kuschel describes an "Abrahamic *ecumene*" as "an *ecumene* of learning, studying, of spiritual exploration of one another's religion, culture, and civilization."[3] This is not unlike what occurred within Christian ecumenical circles in the context of the Faith and Order Movement. However, it cannot take place in a political vacuum, as though the historical context in which we live were remote and disconnected from our religious relationships. As we know from ecumenical experience, faith and order issues cannot be divorced from those of church and society, and vice versa.

Rowan Williams, the newly appointed Archbishop of Canterbury, wrote what is surely one of the best reflections on the events of September 11, entitled *Writings in the Dust*. In it, he makes perceptive comments on how religious perceptions and political power relations jointly impact our responses to the estranged "other." We all need, he says, "to assert some kind of control over the stranger, the other, by 'writing them in' in terms that could be managed and manipulated." "What happens," he continues, "is that the stranger is assigned a meaning, a value, in the dominant system. When, as with Christians and Jews in Europe, this is allied to a hugely disproportionate distribution of power, the effects are dreadful."[4]

Our perceptions of "religious others" and our actions toward them are too often shaped and determined by power relations, and therefore by political considerations rather than those of truth and justice. Attempts to overcome the legacy of estrangement between Islam, Judaism, and Christianity cannot be separated from current social and political realities. Islam in Cape Town, for example, cannot be separated from the social dislocation and poverty caused by apartheid, from the tension between economically competitive ethnic groups, or from the global awakening of Islam and its rejection of the hegemony of the West. Indeed, in this instance, as in most others, the local cannot be understood without reference to the global, just as the universal becomes reified unless it is grounded in the historically contextual.

We are also confronted with issues that are deeply rooted in the daily lives, culture, and identity of people. Consequently, the challenge facing us cannot be met simply at an academic level, or through dialogue between high-level representatives of the Abrahamic faith communities. Social and economic deprivation, cultural alienation, and alienation from sacred space and land directly impact well-being and social relations. Thus we need to keep firmly in mind the relationship between political and religious realities and praxis, on the one hand, and critical reflection and dialogue on the other; between grass-roots movements and the interaction of scholars. We need a profound change of consciousness, a radically new perspective on what it means to belong to the family of Abraham, and we need partnership in dealing with the social and political causes of alienation.

PARTNERS IN THE STRUGGLE AGAINST APARTHEID

The expulsion of the Jews and Muslims from Spain was coterminous with the beginnings of the Hispanic conquest of Latin America and the European colonization of Africa and Asia. Christopher Columbus set sail for the West Indies in 1492, the year of the Spanish expulsions, and Portuguese navigator Bartholomew Diaz "discovered" the Cape of Good Hope in 1488. This "discovery" led to the Dutch colonization of the Cape in the mid-seventeenth century, followed by the British in the nineteenth. Through these colonial adventures Christianity, but also Islam and Judaism, were planted at the Cape. And along with European colonization came Christendom's new attitudes of racial, religious, and cultural superiority that would eventually reach its climax in apartheid.

The first Muslims were brought to the Cape as political captives by the Dutch East Indies Company in the seventeenth century. Among them were distinguished leaders of resistance against Dutch conquest in the East.[5] Many of them became slaves in the service of the colonists.

Islam thus became a "slave religion" in South Africa, and its public practice at the Cape was prohibited on pain of death from 1642 until 1804. Even after religious freedom was promulgated in 1804, racial and religious oppression in the name of Christianity continued.[6] In addition, because Muslims were almost invariably classified as "coloured" or Indian by apartheid's ideologists, they also suffered as victims of apartheid.

The Jewish community was established at the Cape through immigration resulting largely from European anti-Semitism and pogroms. But Jews, especially those from Eastern Europe, were no more welcome at the Cape than they were elsewhere. The largely Christian citizens of Cape Town strongly opposed their coming, though in the end they could not prevent their disembarking. Prejudice was initially expressed in immigration laws and quotas, and in the many more subtle ways that operate in polite Anglo-Saxon society, but during the 1930s and 1940s there was a surge in virulent anti-Semitism fueled by the Nazi ideas of Afrikaner right-wingers.[7]

Numerically speaking, both Islam and Judaism are small in comparison with the dominant, though very diverse, presence of Christianity in South Africa. Though many Jews and Muslims have made significant contributions to public life, they have tended to live in their own ethnic and religious enclaves. Despite attempts to develop meaningful interfaith discussions in more recent times, such dialogues have been rare. At the same time, Jewish, Muslim, and Christian activists often found themselves united in protest and resistance during the struggle against apartheid, even if this comradeship did not involve interreligious dialogue. In the final years of apartheid, many progressive Muslims, Jews, and Christians united in their common commitment to justice and the ending of apartheid under the banner of the United Democratic Front, a front organization for the banned African National Congress. There was, however, little sense of being united within the family of Abraham as such. Indeed, many of those engaged in this way were critical of their faith traditions for lack of political commitment.

One reason for the relatively peaceful transition to democracy in South Africa, it has been surmised, is that the conflicting political parties were not divided by religious affiliation and conviction. If we compare the situation in South Africa with that of Northern Ireland, the

Middle East, or Kashmir, where religious differences reinforce the political divides, we soon recognize the truth and significance of this observation. Whereas in those instances Catholic and Protestant, Muslim and Jew, Hindu and Muslim, define the political identity of the opposing parties, Christians, Jews, and Muslims could be found on both sides of the apartheid divide in South Africa. Of course, at one level the struggle was religious and theological, as the slogan "apartheid is a heresy" so clearly indicated. Christians were divided over theological issues. But it was not a struggle *between* religions. Christians, Jews, and Muslims found each other either in defending the status quo, *or* in standing side by side as comrades, sharing the same prison cells, motivated by the same concern for justice, and rejoicing in the same victories.

The inauguration ceremony at which Nelson Mandela was installed as president of the new Republic of South Africa in May 1994 was a remarkable postmodern blend of the secular and the religious, and leaders of the three Abrahamic faiths played a prominent role in the proceedings. This dramatic change from the past, when the Dutch Reformed Church dominated similar events, signaled the birth of a new state that sanctioned religious pluralism. On one hand, South Africa had become a secular state rather than a quasi-religious one with Christian trappings, as in the past. On the other, religious communities and traditions were included rather than separated from the state as part of the process of national reconciliation and nation building. Constantine used the church to unify the Roman Empire; Nelson Mandela skillfully embraced religious pluralism in his endeavor to promote national reconciliation and build a new nation.

The transition to democracy in South Africa was not without struggle and pain, but it was hailed as something of a modern-day miracle and celebrated amid much euphoric jubilation. As most astute observers expected, however, the honeymoon soon ended. In addition to the problems that began to take priority on the national agenda, such as poverty, HIV/AIDS, and crime, South Africa had first to deal with its past and next to learn to live in accord with one of the most progressive democratic constitutions in the world. Integral to the first part of this process was the work of the Truth and Reconciliation Commission (TRC); integral to the second part were discussions and questions about how to develop a progressive multicultural and religiously pluralistic democratic culture within a secular state.

THE FAMILY OF ABRAHAM AT THE TRC

Whatever its shortcomings and failures, the Truth and Reconciliation Commission has been a significant signpost along the way of national reconciliation, as well as a catalyst for further reflection and action. Many have come from East and West, from North and South, to study the work of the TRC as a possible model for dealing with the past and achieving reconciliation. In doing so they have often remarked that the TRC seemed far more like a religious confessional than a court of law, led as it was by an archbishop and staffed by commissioners who were largely people of religious faith and conviction. What is not often noted, however, is that the TRC devoted three days of hearings specifically to faith communities as part of its attempt to ascertain the role played by key institutions during the apartheid era.

The TRC faith community hearings in November 1997 received submissions from leaders of all three Abrahamic faith traditions. These provide us with a good insider's overview of the record of Christianity, Judaism, and Islam during the apartheid years, and they are often frank in identifying failures and in highlighting the ambiguous role of the various faith communities.[8] Some in all three faiths supported apartheid, while others claimed neutrality, and others expressed opposition. None of these religions came off with an unblemished record; all were, in varying ways and to varying degrees, guilty. Whatever their criticisms of apartheid, they did not do as much as they should have to combat it. Because the majority of Christians in South Africa are black, and Muslims almost invariably "coloured" or Indian, many of the victims of apartheid were Christians and Muslims. This connection between the victims and especially black Christians was often evident during the TRC when those present sang hymns or offered prayers—a matter of some concern to those of other faiths who were also present.

For Jews, the TRC and the discussions surrounding it had a "parallel subtext running through their psyches that calls to mind the Holocaust and the Nuremberg Trials."[9] So perhaps it is not surprising that proportionally a significant number of Jews were involved in the struggle against apartheid. Still, many of these were secular and more identified with the politics of the left than with mainstream Judaism. The response of the Jewish religious communities was as ambiguous as that of the churches. As part of white South Africa, Jews were, after all, beneficiaries of apartheid.

In their submissions to the TRC the official representatives of the Muslim community acknowledged that some Muslims collaborated with the apartheid regime even though Muslims were also its victims.[10] The Muslim Youth Movement spoke of Muslims who were "silent accomplices to National Party rule."[11] But all the submissions detailed the extent to which Muslims were engaged in the struggle for liberation, many of them playing key roles and some giving their lives for the cause.

Much more could be said about how the three Abrahamic faiths dealt with their roles during apartheid, but we need to move beyond the past and consider how they perceived their future role in nation building. Here, once again, there was a similarity in their submissions. Virtually all representatives declared their readiness to work for justice and reconciliation in South Africa. But what is of particular significance for this essay is the way in which Muslim representatives described their commitment.

In its submission the Muslim Judicial Council stressed its commitment to the work of the TRC and emphasized the need to lay a "foundation for a new morality based on a culture of human rights."[12] Likewise, the Council of Transvaal Muslim Theologians called for religious and political tolerance, respect for the rights of others, social justice, and equality for all, "some of the core principles for national reconciliation and nation building."[13] Using language reminiscent of the struggle years and suggesting a degree of disenchantment with the TRC process, the Muslim Youth Movement insisted that reconciliation demands repentance on the part of oppressors and a fundamental redistribution of wealth and power. "It is our conviction," the submission declared, "that this is exactly what Islam would demand for reconciliation (*sulh*) between perpetrator and victim."[14] Reconciliation is founded on economic justice, and implemented with mercy and compassion, a task in which religious people should engage but, the Muslim Youth Movement warned, if "we fail in this responsibility, God forbid, it might well be administered with vengeance."[15]

In certain respects the submissions of the three Abrahamic faiths to the TRC reflected the position of their more progressive leadership and constituency that had been shaped by the struggle against apartheid. The language was that of both religious and human rights convictions, with a blurring of the boundaries between the two. Hence there was general support for the new and remarkably progressive constitution. Yet, as South Africa struggled with the realities of unemployment, HIV/AIDS, and an escalation of crime, conservative and fundamentalist sectors in each religion began to regroup in opposition to the secular nature of the state. Conservative Christians were concerned about the loss of their previous preferential status, but equally about what they perceived as an underlying anti-Christian bias in the new multicultural and religiously pluralistic policies. Conservative Jews and Muslims may have been pleased by the demise of Christendom, but they nonetheless equally feared the secular norms and values that were shaping government policy.

In some ways their reactions were the same, for conservatives in all three traditions were outspoken in their criticism of the abolition of the death penalty, the new laws permitting abortion, religious education school policies, and aspects of gender equality. At the same time, the situation in the Middle East and the war in Afghanistan polarized these groups in ways that ran counter to their participation in nation building in South Africa. This tension between global affiliation and local participation, between being a supporter of Israel and a South African Jew, or a supporter of Palestine and a South African Muslim, has already intensified national divisions and has the potential to threaten sharing together in nation building. This is further exacerbated by the fact that many Muslims view Christianity as the religion of the West, and they perceive the West as having embarked on a new crusade to destroy Islam. This is the context within which the family of Abraham in South Africa has to find a way to cooperate in restoring justice.

SECULAR SOCIETY AND GOD'S JUSTICE

Ahdaf Soueif's *The Map of Love* weaves the narrative of an unfolding love across the barriers of ethnicity and religion into that of the Egyptian struggle against British colonialism. At midpoint we find ourselves in Saint Catherine's monastery in the Sinai Desert. Anna's diary depicts the scene:

> The building is rather like a medieval Castle and was established in the Sixth Century and soon afterwards, as the Moslem armies advanced Westwards from the Arabian Peninsula, somebody had

the prescience to build a small Mosque in its courtyard to guard against it being burned or demolished. At the time of the Crusades it was the turn of the Monastery to protect the Mosque, and so it has been down the ages, each House of God extending its shelter to the other as opposing armies came and went.[16]

Synagogue, church, and mosque can and do come under attack, sometimes from each other, sometimes from within their own ranks, and sometimes from a hostile secular world. For many in each house of God today, the major threat is modernity and secularism, and the resultant collapse of moral value and virtue. But perhaps all would agree that the greatest danger of all, and one intrinsically related to the implosion of virtue, is global injustice, a danger that poses a particular challenge to the family of Abraham because of its covenant with the God of justice.

Each house of God is distinct, and the differences that divide the family of Abraham are real and often far-reaching. Yet these religions share a common legacy that shapes their identity and relates them to each other in meaningful ways. Each worships the God of Abraham alone. Each recognizes God's call to break with the idolatries of its culture and to embark on a journey of faith in dependence on the God of Abraham. And, to home in on our theme, each understands itself as being in a covenant relationship with the God of Abraham, which is aimed at the establishment of God's justice among the nations as the sole basis for lasting peace.

However, the family of Abraham is divided over the nature of God's justice, the way in which we discern God's will, and the means to pursue it. For while each of the three faiths traces its origins to Abraham, there are subtle and not so subtle differences in the way in which that story is told, and the way in which each tradition has historically unfolded. Abraham's faith is mediated through Torah, Gospel, and Qur'an with their distinct emphases and differences, as well as through Talmud, Tradition, and Sunnah. It is also expressed within a variety of cultural contexts, each shaped by a historical experience that influences the reading and living of the tradition. The relationship between Christians and Muslims in Egypt, Indonesia, or South Africa, or between Christians and Jews in Jerusalem, New York, and Cape Town, is not the same. Moreover, the divisions and differences are not simply between the three Abrahamic faiths; they also divide each faith into distinct tendencies, factions, and movements. All of these differences multiply the complexity we face in determining what it means to pursue God's justice above all else in a secular and pluralistic society.

Let us consider the very problematic case of the Nigerian woman Amina Lawal, who was sentenced by a Shari'ah court to death by stoning. Quite apart from the horrified reactions of non-Muslims, this has been a matter of considerable disquiet and embarrassment among more progressive Muslims as well.[17] Yet from the perspective of many Muslim leaders in Africa, including South Africa, the logic of the case is clear. Consider the response of Sheik Achmat Sedick, secretary-general of the Muslim Judicial Council, the same council that in its submission to the TRC stressed its commitment to the need to lay a "foundation for a new morality based on a culture of human rights."[18] Sheik Sedick supports the Shari'ah court's decision. The Shari'ah, he argues, is God-given, and therefore a Shari'ah court has the right and duty to decree the death penalty for adultery by stoning once certain criteria have been met. Christians and Jews, and other Muslims, may well react in horror, but the logic that moves from an infallible scripture, tradition, and law to moral prescription is intrinsic to traditional religion of all kinds. Moreover, it manifests itself particularly in times that are out of joint, and in places where the center has difficulty holding things together.

In his defense of Shari'ah law and its application in Nigeria, Sheik Sedick is expressing a widespread disquiet among conservative and traditional religionists, including African traditionalists, concerning a range of issues from abortion and the death penalty to public sex education and homosexuality. Hence, in his defense of the sentence of Amina Lawal to stoning (later overturned on appeal), Sedick criticized President Thabo Mbeki for passing critical judgment on the Nigerian Shari'ah court's decision, and more generally for the abolition of the death penalty in South Africa. Mbeki, he writes,

> knows for a fact that that Shari'ah allows the death penalty and the South African government has abolished the death penalty. It may be the prerogative of President Mbeki to astutely defend the South African standpoint, but he has no right to judge or pass judgmental remarks about the Shari'ah, whether it is in Nigeria or elsewhere.[19]

It is easy to criticize and condemn Sheik Sedick and others who share his views, but it is important to recognize the extent to which they and their respective communities feel threatened by the acids of modernity and the collapse of public morality. Sedick lives in a community that is torn apart by violent crime, rape and child abuse, drug addiction, poverty, unemployment, and HIV/AIDS, a community that is still trapped by many of the legacies of the apartheid era. When things are falling apart, it is natural to seek to restore and firmly uphold traditional norms and values and to oppose what is perceived to be the soft and secular approach of a progressive human rights culture.

For these and related reasons, a new interfaith coalition seems to be emerging among conservative Jews, Muslims, and Christians in South Africa. It strongly challenges both the norms and values of secular society, and aspects of human rights law on issues such as legalized abortion, gender equality, gay rights, and abolition of the death penalty, arguing that all of these policies are against God's justice as contained in the Bible and the Qur'an. There clearly are texts and passages that can be quoted in at least prima facie support of this claim. But equally clearly, the coalition has a political agenda that arises out of a shared conviction in the sovereignty of God's law, even though there are serious differences that theologically and politically divide them. Conservative believers, for example, do not agree on the questions of the authority of the Bible and the Qur'an, proselytism, or Israel-Palestine.

This conservative coalition is, in some respects, similar to the coalition which developed among progressive elements within the family of Abraham during the apartheid struggle, and which continues to exist in ecumenical circles. Divisive theological issues are set aside in the interests of a common political praxis. Just as during apartheid, representatives of all three faiths are to be found on both sides of the political equation, with much ambiguity in the middle and among the rank and file believers. The situation we face is also similar to that which has long existed within the Christian ecumenical movement. Even though conservative members of various confessions and denominations fundamentally disagree on substantive doctrinal issues, they have often found common cause in opposing those who are more progressive in their attitudes and convictions.

Although the dividing line is political, there is a deep theological and historical cleavage at the heart of the matter. Conservative religion reacts against any modernizing tendencies and the scholarship that goes along with them because it perceives them as threats against obedience to God. Bonhoeffer quotes the Muslim leader Ibn Saud with telling effect: "Europe is full of hatred and will destroy itself with its own weapons." This is why, so Ibn Saud argues, Islam may learn from the West but must never allow the West to destroy "the Arab soul" or undermine obedience to "the will of God."[20] Thus, even though all three traditions may confess their commitment to God's justice in society, what this means depends on very different ways of interpreting the sacred texts. Unless they have moved beyond the pale of their respective traditions, progressive scholars and believers take their sacred texts as seriously as their conservative co-religionists, but they read them differently. They would argue that human rights law, for example, has its origin not just in the Enlightenment but as much, if not more so, in trajectories within their own traditions.

At the heart of the debate between traditionalists and progressive believers is not the question of justice, but that of secularism. The Muslim concern about the West's captivity to secular norms is nothing new, and it is shared by Christians from Africa and Asia as well. For good reason, many Christians today, not least those in the "Third World," are unhappy about the identification of Christianity with the West and its captivity to secularism. But standing up for human rights is not falling prey to secularism. On the contrary, it is retrieving the best in the Abrahamic traditions through critical engagement with those who have justifiably challenged the traditions from the outside. For while it is true that many of the impulses for human rights originate in the prophetic tradition of the Abrahamic family, it has often been the critics that have forced us to return to the sources in order to critically retrieve our own legacy. This has certainly been the case in the struggle against racism and the struggle for gender equality.

The feminist challenge to established patriarchal religion was one of the most significant developments in the final decades of the twentieth century, and the issues surrounding gender and sexuality confront the family of Abraham in a way that is inescapable despite the defenses raised and widespread resistance. Fundamentalists of all three traditions reject gender equality, regarding it as an attempt by decadent Western secularism to undermine traditional values. Yet it is surely noteworthy that as Jews, Christians, and Muslims stood with each other in solidarity in the struggle against apartheid, it became evident that genuine liberation from oppression had to do not just with racism but also with sexism. This was part of the argument put forward by progressive Muslims associated with the Call of Islam in their critique of traditionalist interpretations of the role of women in Islam.

During the late twentieth century, significant gains have come about through interfaith dialogue or, as in the case of the struggle against apartheid, through joint engagement in political praxis. However, as Eberhard Bethge perceived, there is a real danger that we will be shipwrecked by the political events and social forces of our new century. Friends may become strangers again, and estrangement may lead to hostility and violence. Instead of becoming a blessing to humanity, the family of Abraham may well become the curse that many already think it is. For this reason it is imperative that those who have found each other in the family of Abraham renew their efforts to sustain and broaden their friendship, and to jointly counter the causes of the violence that is tearing the world apart. A return to the sources of our common tradition through engaging each other's Scriptures is surely one key way forward. But, I would argue from our South African experience, this has to be done by critically engaging secularism and struggling together for justice.

When faithful to their prophetic impulse, all three faiths seek to serve the just cause of the oppressed and to be critical of the powerful who oppress them.[21] But all three faiths are also called to challenge the idols of both our local and global cultures as we journey into the unknown in faith in the God who journeys ahead of us.

NOTES

1. Eberhard Bethge, "My Friend Dietrich Bonhoeffer's Theology of Friendship," in *The Changing Face of Friendship*, ed. Leroy S. Rouner, vol. 15 in Boston University Studies in Philosophy of Religion (Notre Dame, Ind.: University of Notre Dame Press, 1994), pp. 133–54.

2. "The Legacy of Abraham," *Time*, 30 September 2002, pp. 47–55.

3. Karl-Josef Kuschel, *Abraham: Sign of Hope for Jews, Christians, and Muslims* (New York: Continuum, 1995), p. 225.

4. Rowan Williams, *Writing in the Dust: Reflections on 11th September and Its Aftermath* (London: Hodder & Stoughton, 2002), pp. 66–67.

5. For a brief history of Islam in South Africa, see Ebrahim Moosa, "Islam in South Africa," in *Living Faiths in South Africa,* ed. Martin Prozesky and John de Gruchy (Cape Town: David Philip, 1995).

6. Ibid., p. 130; Transvaal Jamiatul Ulama, "Submission to the TRC," *Journal for Islamic Studies* 17 (1997): 95.

7. Milton Shain, *The Roots of Anti-Semitism in South Africa* (Johannesburg: Witwatersrand University Press, 1994); Patrick Furlong, *Between Crown and Swastika: The Impact of the Radical Right on the Afrikaner Nationalist Movement in the Fascist Era* (Johannesburg: Witwatersrand University Press, 1991), pp. 46ff.

8. See James C. Cochrane, John W. de Gruchy, and Steve Martin, eds., *Facing the Truth: South African Faith Communities and the Truth & Reconciliation Commission* (Cape Town: David Philip, 1999); for a personal account by one of the TRC Commissioners and a NGK (Nederduitse Gereformeerde Kirk) theologian, see Piet Meiring, *Chronicle of the Truth Commission* (Vanderbijpark, RSA: Carpe Diem, 1999), pp. 265ff.

9. Geoff Sifrin, "The Truth Commission: Jewish Perspectives on Justice and Forgiveness in South Africa: Introducing the Issues," *Jewish Affairs,* Spring 1996, p. 30.

10. Transvaal Jamiatul Ulama, "Submission," p. 95; Muslim Judicial Council, "Submission to the TRC," *Journal for Islamic Studies* 17 (1997): 101f.

11. Muslim Youth Movement, "Submission to the TRC," *Journal for Islamic Studies* 17 (1997): 106.

12. Muslim Judicial Council, "Submission," p. 104.

13. Transvaal Jamiatul Ulama, "Submission," p. 99.

14. Muslim Youth Movement, "Submission," p. 108.

15. Ibid.

16. Ahdaf Soueif, *The Map of Love* (New York: Anchor Books, 2000), pp. 213–14.

17. Sheik Achmat Sedick's position was critically challenged by another Muslim, Shafiq Morton—a Sunni in this instance—in a letter to the *Cape Argus,* 9 October 2002.

18. Muslim Judicial Council, "Submission," p. 104.

19. Sheik Achmat Sedick, "What We Can Learn from the Shari'ah," *Cape Argus,* 26 September 2002, p. 14.

20. Dietrich Bonhoeffer, *Ethics* (New York: Macmillan, 1965), pp. 382, 99.

21. Eqbal Ahmad, "Islam and Politics," in *The Islamic Impact,* ed. Byron Haines, Yvonne Yazbeck Haddad, and Ellison Findlay (Syracuse, N.Y.: Syracuse University Press, 1984), p. 18.

Mahatma Gandhi and Osama bin Laden: An Imaginary Dialogue
BHIKHU PAREKH

In this essay I briefly explore the nature and limits of political dialogue by imagining a debate between two individuals who, while sharing some concerns, could not be more different. History and the record of published speeches and writings make very clear what Gandhi stood for, what kind of person he was, and how he argued for certain positions; the record is far less clear for bin Laden. The debate that follows might also have been written as one between Gandhi and "an imaginary follower of bin Laden," or indeed, a follower of many others who have used terrorism as a means to their ends.

Both Gandhi and bin Laden, as I shall construct him here, are anti-imperialists and in revolt against the greatest power of their times. Both are as critical of the Western pursuit of global hegemony of their own societies, and believe that Western civilization does not represent the only way to lead the good life. Both men are deeply religious, ground their politics in their deepest religious commitments, and believe that religion should enjoy an important place in public life. Their views on human life, the good society, modes of struggle, and the relation between religion and the state, however, are wholly different. Gandhi rejected violence and trained his followers in the art of nonviolent resistance; bin Laden is an uncompromising champion of violence and set up al-Qaeda camps to train his followers in the dark arts of terrorism. Gandhi believed that every human being and society is a mixture of good and evil, that all systems of domination rest on an implicit cooperation between their perpetrators and victims, that the latter are never totally innocent or the former totally evil, that both alike are trapped within an exploitative system, and that our anger and struggle should be directed at the system rather than its beneficiaries; bin Laden takes a Manichean view of the world in which victims of history are innocent and enjoy the right to punish their irredeemably evil tormentors. Gandhi cherished his religion and thought he had both a right and a duty to enrich it by borrowing the insights of others; for bin Laden Islam is the definitive and final word of God whose purity he has a duty to safeguard. For Gandhi religion was the basis of human life and was too sacred and personal to be associated with the state; bin Laden thinks that its very centrality to human life requires that the state should be founded on and uphold it.

These and other basic differences inform their approaches to the political issues of the day. In this essay I shall use bin Laden's terrorist campaign to explore the interplay of these differences. Unlike a philosophical dialogue in which the participants can examine and debate an argument or a concept in isolation, a political dialogue has a holistic character. Every argument and opinion here derives its plausibility from a wider point of view, and hence the participants need to know where the other is coming from before they can understand and deal with each other's reasons and assumptions. I therefore articulate the dialogue between Gandhi and bin Laden in terms of broad statements of general positions. In each case I rely on their published speeches or writings and, when these are unclear or silent, on my constructions of what one would expect them to say in the light of their known views. In the early parts of the essay, I play the role of an advocate helping each make as strong a case for his views as possible. Toward the end I take on the role of an adjudicator, and explore where and why they disagree and which of these disagreements are amenable to rational resolution.

OSAMA BIN LADEN'S DEFENSE OF HIS ACTIONS

Ever since my followers attacked the U.S. embassy in Kenya, the U.S.S. *Cole* in Yemen, and more recently the World Trade Center in New York and the Pentagon in Washington, D.C., they and I have been demonized.[1] We are declared enemies of the civilized world, who can be killed at will. I was not surprised by the U.S. reaction, especially that of the Republican administration, because I expected nothing better of those who wish to dominate the world by force and are determined to put down anyone daring to challenge their evil designs. But I was surprised by the reactions of liberals in the United States, Europe, and other parts of the world, and also by those of my fellow Muslims who are now busy competing with each other in demonizing us.[2] I owe it to them to explain why we did what we did, why we remain unmoved by the calumnies heaped upon us, and why we would do it again at a time of our choosing. Since every political action occurs in a historical context and is unintelligible outside of it, I need to begin with a brief historical outline.

Islam is a great religion, continuous with and completing the other two Abrahamic religions. It accepts them as genuine and true religions, reveres their prophets, and has always been tolerant and respectful of them. Thanks to the force of its profound truths, Islam, a late historical arrival, was quickly able to win over the willing allegiance of hundreds of thousands of people in different parts of the world. It inspired its followers with such zeal and fervor that their armies chalked up conquests against all odds, making it the second most powerful world religion. Christians, who have long been jealous of its appeal and resentful of its power, tried to discredit and undermine it by mocking its beliefs, vilifying its prophet, and mounting crusades against it. Islam survived all these and built up large empires, the great Ottoman Empire being the last.

With the rise of modernity, Britain, France, and other European countries began to industrialize and form themselves into homogeneous nation states. Driven by the lust for power and profit on which their civilization was based, they conquered large parts of the world, built up vast empires, and set about reshaping their colonies in their liberal secular image. Since Muslim societies had betrayed their religious principles and become corrupt and degenerate, they fell an easy prey. Being infinitely better armed, the British and the French overwhelmed the Ottoman Empire, broke it up into artificial political units, set up corrupt rulers, played them off against one another, kept them weak and divided, and used them to consolidate and perpetuate their hegemony. After the Second World War, they deprived the Palestinians of their homeland, handed over large parts of it to the Jews, and created a lasting and festering source of injustice in the shape of Israel. Muslim societies have always included large Jewish communities and been protective of them. But giving them a state of their own, and that too at the Palestinian expense and right in the heart of the Arab world, was a highly provocative and grossly unjust act.

As the United States replaced the weakened Europeans in the 1950s, it continued the hegemonic project and designed a more subtle empire of its own. In the name of defending the "free world" against the Soviet threat, it set up and supported puppet regimes in many parts of the world, including and especially the Muslim societies of the Middle East, upon whose oil it had come to depend for its survival and prosperity. It was even more partial to Israel than the Europeans were, arming it and encouraging its expansionist ambitions. The collapse of the Soviet Union gave the United States an illusion of omnipotence and a sense of self-righteousness, and removed all external and internal restraints on its hegemonic hubris.[3] The United States today is determined to Americanize the world and restructure every society along secular, capitalist, liberal, and consumerist lines. Its troops are stationed in 120 out of 189 countries. It controls major international economic and political institutions, and uses them to pursue its interests. When that does not work, it resorts to bribe and blackmail to get its way. And when even that fails, it acts unilaterally in contemptuous disregard of international law and institutions. I am convinced that the United States today constitutes the greatest threat to global peace and human freedom. Although the current Republican administration is most unashamed in its imperialist design, the previous administrations including Clinton's were no better. They followed the same policy, albeit with greater subtlety and sophistication and relying more on economic and political pressure than on the threat of military might. This is why our struggle against the Americans goes back a long way.

Although U.S. imperialism must be fought in every part of the world, I am primarily concerned to liberate Muslim societies, not only because I belong to them but also because they constitute the weakest link in the imperial chain. My success there will inspire others. My goal is fourfold: to get the Americans out of Muslim societies, to destroy Israel as a separate Jewish state and create a free Palestine in which Jews can live as a respected minority, to remove corrupt U.S. stooges in Muslim societies and restructure the latter along truly Islamic principles, and finally to restore the earlier glory of Islam by uniting the *ummah* and ensuring Muslim rule in such erstwhile Muslim countries as Palestine, Bukhara, Lebanon, Pakistan, Bangladesh, Chad, Eritrea, Somalia, Philippines, Burma, South Yemen, Tashkent, and Southern Spain (Andalusia).[4]

Violence is the only way to achieve these goals because this is the only language the United States understands. Our violence, further, has to be terrorist because the militarily ill-equipped Muslims can never match the U.S. might in open combat. Although the terrorist violence is primarily directed against what I call the "icons of US military and economic power," one cannot be so fastidious as to exclude civilians. The United States itself has never spared civilians in its wars on us, including killing nearly half a million innocent children by imposing sanctions on Iraq.[5] American citizens have freely elected their governments, often supported their policies—or at least failed to protest against and dissociate themselves from these—and are directly or indirectly complicit in their government's deeds.[6]

Since our terrorist violence is systematically misunderstood, I should make two additional points. First, it is reactive. We are only responding to the terrorist violence of the United States. As I have said repeatedly, "We are only defending ourselves. This is defensive jihad. We want to defend our people and our land. This is why I say that if we don't get security, the Americans too would not get security. This is a simple formula that even an American child can understand. This is the formula of live and let live."[7] Americans rob us of our wealth and oil, attack our religion, trample upon our dignity, treat us as pawns in their global game of chess, and have the moral impertinence to call us terrorists when in fact we are only defending ourselves against their own terrorism.

Second, I distinguish between "commendable" and "reprehensible" terrorism.[8] Terrorism to abolish tyranny, external domination, corrupt rulers, and traitors belongs to the first, and one that imposes or perpetuates these evils belongs to the second category. Ours clearly is of the commendable kind. My followers neither kill like cowards nor make personal gains from their actions. They give up ordinary pleasures of life, careers, families, and even their lives, and show by their supreme self-sacrifice that they are guided by the highest of motives. Our terrorism thus is moral and religious. Nothing could be more perverse than to equate it with ordinary criminal activities. Our consciences are clear, and I say to my fellow Muslims that "to kill the Americans and their allies—civilian and military—is an individual duty for every Muslim who can do it in any country in which it is possible to do it."

Terrorists need training. And I also want to make sure that they are kept on a tight leash and do not go about settling their own personal scores. I therefore set up al-Qaeda al-Subah to train a committed and disciplined band of *jihadis* and to plan and monitor their activities. We screen our recruits most rigorously, ensure that they are inspired by the highest religious and moral ideals, provide them with a mutually sustaining communal ethos, and inspire them to die as disciplined martyrs. In this way I channel the intense anger and desperation of millions of Muslims in a proper direction, and prevent an otherwise certain wave of indiscriminate and infinitely more damaging acts of terrorism.

GANDHI

Listening to you, my brother Osama, I was strongly reminded of my dialogue with my terrorist countrymen, which began in London in 1905 and continued almost until my death.[9]

As I did in their case, I admire your bravery, spirit of self-sacrifice, and commitment to the oppressed, but find your reasoning totally confused and your glorification of violence evil.[10]

Whether you realize it or not, you think and talk like an imperialist. You present a highly sanitized picture of Islamic history. All conquests and empires involve bloodshed, oppression, and injustice, and yours were no different. Muslim conquerors and even some Muslim rulers in India destroyed Hindu temples, looted Hindu property, and converted vast masses by a combination of inducement and force. They destroyed traditional African cultures and social structures and sought to obliterate their collective memories of their pre-Islamic past. And although they treated Christians and Jews better, they never granted them equal citizenship. Since all this occurred a long time ago, there is no point in lamenting it and apportioning blame, but we do have a duty to acknowledge the full truth of the past and resolve never to repeat it. You do not do this, and are even determined to revive Muslim rule in the countries you mention. You attack European imperialism because it ended yours, and the Americans because they are preventing you from reviving it. An imperialist yourself, you have no moral right to attack the imperialist designs of others and you are just as immoral and dangerous.

You keep talking about the truly Islamic society whose glory you want to revive and in whose name you condemn the Americans. I do not find it at all appealing, and neither do your fellow Muslims. You want to combine a centralized state, an industrialized economy, nuclear weapons, and so on, with a set of Islamic values and practices. This is an incoherent enterprise. Once you opt for the economic, political, and other institutions of modernity, you cannot escape their inherent logic. You would increasingly become more and more like a Western society and get sucked into a process of globalization and thus into the U.S. empire. Furthermore, these institutions cannot be sustained without creating an appropriate culture, radically transforming social, educational, and other institutions, and undermining the very religious and moral values you cherish. As far as I can see, you are only interested in creating economically and militarily powerful Muslim societies that are capable of standing up to the West. If you are really serious about creating a truly good society, you should stop measuring yourself against the West. You should start instead with the great values of Islam, relate them to the circumstances and aspirations of your people, and assimilate such Western values and institutions as enrich yours and can be assimilated without much difficulty.

As you rightly admit, Muslim societies have become degenerate, but your explanation for this is wholly wrong. They are degenerate because they are static, hidebound, inegalitarian, patriarchal, averse to change, and lacking the spirit of scientific inquiry and individual freedom and the capacity for collective and cooperative action. In these areas we have much to learn from the West. With all its limitations, Western civilization has developed many values that we need to imbibe, not in a spirit of slavish imitation nor to become modern, but because they are worthwhile values and will vitalize our societies. I have myself been a grateful student of the West, learning much from its liberal, Christian, and socialist traditions, and suitably integrating it into the Indian ways of life and thought. A crude division of the world into West and East is profoundly mistaken because it homogenizes each and obstructs a mutually beneficial dialogue.

You say that the West is spiritually empty and repeatedly refer to its citizens as infidels. Although the West is consumerist and militarist, many of its members have a strong social conscience. The concern for the poor, the welfare state, the desire to create a just society, and the pressures for global justice and humanitarian intervention are all examples of this. Religion matters a great deal to many in the West, and some of them are keen to enter into a dialogue with and borrow generously from non-Christian religions. You are wrong to think that Muslims have a monopoly on spirituality. Indeed, their spirituality, like that of my own people, leaves a good deal to be desired. Spirituality is not about how regularly you pray, fast, and visit the mosque, but about serving your fellow humans and living by the great virtues of humility, benevolence, tolerance, and universal love. I see little evidence of this in you and your society or in mine.

I am particularly disturbed by your desire to base your society on truly Islamic principles. A religion can be interpreted in several different ways, and no interpretation can claim to be final and incorrigible. It calls for sincerity of belief, and thus rules out coercion. It is ultimately a matter between the individual and God, and must leave the believer free to decide how she wishes to obey her God. Religion also needs to be adapted to changing circumstances and made to address contemporary issues. You, bin Laden, violate all these. You claim to know the true principles of Islam better than anyone else, and brook no dissent. You rule out their creative adaptation to a world vastly different from the one in which they were first articulated. And by asking the Islamic state to impose them on its subjects, you deny the latter their basic religious freedom. This is the surest way to corrupt both your religion and the state and to arrest the moral and spiritual growth of your people. Like you, I am a deeply religious person. God matters to me more than my daily food, and I have striven all my life to craft a soul worthy of Him. A truly religious person wants to live by the values and beliefs of her religion. If the state has to enforce them on her, then clearly her religion has ceased to have any meaning for her. A religiously based state is a sacrilege, an insult to God and to the human soul. It introduces coercion in areas where the latter has no role, and gives the state the authority to interpret sacred texts which it is inherently unequipped to exercise.[11]

You make these and other mistakes because your analysis of the causes of Muslim degeneration is shallow. You keep blaming the Europeans and the Americans and never yourself for your sad predicament. You forget the simple truth that no outsider can get a direct or indirect foothold in a society unless it is itself rotten, just as no human body succumbs to a disease unless it has lost its regenerative resources. Stop blaming others, and concentrate your energies on radically rebuilding and revitalizing your societies by patiently educating and organizing the masses. You are right to say that many Muslim rulers are corrupt stooges of external powers, but you forget that our rulers are not an alien species but a magnified version of ourselves. We create them in our image, sustain them by our actions, and are responsible for who and what they are.

It took me some time to realize this, but once I did I devoted all my energies to building up a mass movement dedicated to the task of fighting the ugly social practices of my society, building up cohesive local communities, fostering the habits of self-help and cooperation among my people, and training them to stand up against widespread economic, social, and political injustices. You, Osama, have no patience, no plan of social regeneration, no desire to deal with the deeper causes of social decay. You rely on a small and tightly knit group of religiously minded activists to transform society, and that simply will not work. Once in power, they too will become corrupt, arrogant, and dictatorial. And since they will claim to have God on their side, they will be even more intolerant and repressive. Soon someone like you will come along and seek to replace them with others no different. As I said earlier, society and state are simply their members writ large. Unless ordinary men and women are empowered, reformed, fired with a fierce desire for individual freedom and collective self-determination, all societies remain vulnerable to a takeover by corrupt rulers.

While repeatedly attacking the Americans, you also keep condemning the Jews and talking of a Zionist conspiracy. I could not disagree more. Unlike you, I have worked and lived with them and know them and their history well. Some of them became my closest friends in South Africa, and one of them bought a farm where we set up my first experiment in communal living. I once called them the "untouchables of Christianity." Although they are an integral part of the Judeo-Christian tradition, they were for centuries ostracized, shunned, humiliated, and subjected by Christians to degrading treatment, of which the Nazi atrocity was a most horrendous example. Christians treated them the way my people treated the untouchables, and both have much to atone for.

I well know that the victims of yesterday can easily become the oppressors of tomorrow, and use their past suffering to excuse and even legitimize their brutal treatment of others. Israel in recent years has behaved in an unjust manner with the connivance and support of the United States. Its misdeeds must be exposed and fought, but you must not be insensitive to what their past suffering has done to the Jews. They are prisoners of their bitter historical memories, feel profoundly insecure, and sometimes find it difficult to trust even the well-meaning outsiders. They have at last found a home and understandably feel intensely possessive about it. Their new home rendered the Palestinians homeless and caused them immense suffering. We need to find ways of doing justice to both. I was keen on a binational state of Jews and Arabs, just as I would have liked a united India. In spite of all my efforts to stop it, India was partitioned. I accepted it in the hope that once the two quarrelling brothers set up their separate homes and got their hostilities out of their systems, they would not only learn to coexist in peace but even perhaps revive their deeper bonds and draw closer. You, Osama, must accept the existence of Israel, give it the sense of security it needs, and work patiently toward getting it to appreciate the justice of the Palestinian cause. As long as you threaten it, you frighten its people and drive them into the arms of its reactionary and militarist leaders. Sensible Israelis know that they have to live in the midst of Arab societies, and that the latter will not for long remain backward and divided. If you allow Israelis to relax and lead normal lives, they will one day be compelled by the logic of their history, geography, and demography to become peaceful members of the wider Arab world.

Finally, I would like to turn to your terrorist methods. I find them wholly unacceptable on both pragmatic and moral grounds. They cannot drive away the Americans, who will use their enormous might to smash your terrorist camps and networks, as they have done in Afghanistan. As you say, they do not mind disregarding international law and institutions and even their own constitutional procedures, and you have no hope against such a determined opponent. Even if they were to go, your methods would not be able to defeat their indigenous collaborators, let alone revitalize Muslim societies. There is not a single example in history of terrorists creating a humane and healthy society. Reasons for this are obvious. A society is ultimately sustained by the willing allegiance and support of its members, and these cannot be secured by terrorist means. Furthermore, once a group gets used to terrorism, it falls into the habit of resorting to it every time it encounters opposition, making a stable social order impossible. Today, Osama, you use terrorism against the Americans and Muslim rulers; tomorrow your own people will use it against you and claim the same justification for it. When will this vicious circle end?

As I said, I also have moral objections against your method. Human life is sacred, and taking it is inherently evil. Besides, however fallen a human being might be, he is never so degenerate that he cannot be won over or neutralized by organized moral pressure. Furthermore, human beings do evil deeds because they are in the grip of evil ideas, or are driven by hatred, or because of the structural compulsions of the wider social system which often disposes them to do things they might personally disapprove of. Violence does not address any of these, and only makes the situation even more intractable.

Evil must certainly be resisted. Indeed, not to do so is to be complicit in its continuance. As I have shown by example, organized nonviolent resistance is the only moral and effective way to fight evil. It appeals to the opponent's sense of shared humanity, awakens his temporarily eclipsed conscience, reassures him that he need fear no harm, and mobilizes the power of public opinion. It also allows time for tempers to cool and reason to work, lifts both parties to a higher level of relationship, teases out what they share in common, avoids false polarization, and leaves behind no lasting legacy of mutual hatred. Don't play your opponent's game and remain trapped in the chain of action and reaction, dear Osama. Take upon yourself the burden of his evil, become his conscience, appeal to his shared humanity and sense of decency, and transform both the context of your conflict and the quality of your relationship. I call this the surgery of the soul, purging the poison of prejudice and hatred and releasing and mobilizing the moral energies of the opponent.

Take the case of Palestinians. They have so far used violence. Israel has countered it with even greater violence. The result is an increasing brutalization of the two societies and an ever-growing burden of hatred and bitter memories. Now consider what would happen if the Palestinians were to follow my advice. They would eschew all threats to Israeli citizens, acknowledge them as their brothers, appeal to their sense of decency and long history of humiliation, and get them to appreciate both the enormous suffering they are causing to the Palestinians and the considerable damage they are doing to their own psyche and society. The Palestinians would also invoke the collective memories of shared life in the past and the great Jewish tradition of concern for the oppressed. If necessary they would mount well-organized acts of nonviolent resistance and civil disobedience to highlight their injustices and dare the Israeli government to do its worst.

I cannot imagine that any Israeli government, not even that of Ariel Sharon, would kill unarmed and peaceful protestors with the whole world watching. If it did, it would not only incur universal condemnation, including that of the diasporic Jewish community, but also divide its own people. Some of its morally conscious citizens would disown its actions; and those who have been hitherto passive and indifferent would be forced to ask themselves if they wish to be a party to the slaughter of innocent people. I am convinced too that even some of the Israeli soldiers would disobey government orders, as some are already doing and as was done by their Indian counterparts during my struggle against British rule. Peaceful protests by Palestinians would also trigger an agonized debate in Israel, help them link up with its peace activists, build common bonds with ordinary Israelis, and create a climate in which the two peoples can conduct a sensible dialogue. Things are not, of course, so simple. A frightened and brutal Israeli government might try to put down your protests by force, and some would die. However, they are dying anyway. Unlike the current wave of violence, peaceful protests have the great advantages of delegitimizing Israeli violence, mobilizing world opinion in your favor, raising the morale and moral stature of Palestinians, and ending the futile cycle of violence.

You might say, as some of your associates have sometimes done, that nonviolence comes easily to Hindus and is alien to the Islamic tradition. This is not true. Hindus have a long tradition of violence, and are by temperament as violent a people as any other. It was only after a long educational campaign and examples of successful nonviolence that I was able to bring them round to accepting it. As for Muslims, you should know that they too have a long tradition of nonviolent resistance and martyrdom. The ferocious Pathans of the North West Frontier Provinces of what is now Pakistan embraced it with great success under the guidance of my good friend Abdul Gaffar Khan. No religion is inherently for or against violence. It is up to a religion's leaders to interpret it appropriately and guide its followers accordingly.

OSAMA BIN LADEN

I must confess that I never had an occasion to read your writings or follow your life. You are not as popular or even known in Muslim countries as you are in the West, and all I had heard about you was that you were a Hindu leader of India who could not command the loyalty of the Muslims and who fought against the British by a passive and rather feminine method. I was sufficiently fascinated by some of the things you said to read and reflect on your life and work. While I now see the situation a little differently, on the whole I remain unpersuaded.

You misrepresent your Indian experience and, like all moralists, extend it illegitimately to societies where it does not apply. Since British forces did not occupy your country, they had to depend on local support, which naturally placed considerable constraints on them. The British people were ambivalent about the empire, and some of them were opposed to it. You could therefore always count on a sympathetic body of British opinion and the Labour Party to represent and press your case for independence. By the time you came to dominate the Indian political scene, the British were exhausted, initially by World War I and then by the Great Depression. The events leading up to World War II and that war itself debilitated them yet further. You were therefore in the fortunate situation of confronting a weak opponent who had neither the will nor the means to continue to rule over your country. The British were also a reasonably decent people and never unleashed massive violence against what you call your "nonviolent army" of women, children, and the elderly. Had they done so, you would have had no chance of success. You should also remember that you lived at a time when there were several centers of power, each regulating the others, and none—including the vast British empire—enjoying such overwhelming military and economic superiority as to dominate the world.

The historical context in which I have to operate could not be more different. It is dominated by a hyperpower with a global reach and an overwhelming military superiority over the rest of the world put together. It feels triumphant after its victory over a well-armed enemy of fifty years, and thinks that it can now do what it likes. It is controlled by corporate capitalism driven by an insatiable appetite for profits and the concomitant desire to turn the whole world into a market for U.S. goods. Although its political system is dominated by money and selfish pressure groups, and although it incarcerates more people than any other advanced country, has a larger class of the poor than any other advanced nation, has launched more clandestine, proxy, and open wars than any other, and so on, the United States considers its form of government to be the best in the world, and insists without the slightest embarrassment that it has a right and a duty to export it to other countries. This formidable combination of self-righteousness, missionary spirit, national self-interest, moral myopia, and overwhelming power in a single country has radically transformed the world. Your ideas, Mr. Gandhi, belong to a world that is dead, and are of no help to those fighting against current injustices.

The Americans have to be checked in the interest of global peace, stability, and justice. This requires not just military power but a better civilizational alternative, a superior vision of society that satisfies the deepest urges and aspirations of the human soul. Europe cannot achieve the goal of stopping U.S. hegemony because it is part of the same Western civilization and because it is all too keen to share the spoils of the U.S. empire. Only Islam offers a superior alternative. It has the right vision of a truly good society and the will to realize it. It is also endowed with the requisite wealth, strength of numbers, and long historical experience of ruling over a multiethnic and multireligious world. It is therefore vital that Muslim countries should unite, acquire nuclear weapons, take control of their wealth—above all, their oil—and lead the rest of the world in the right direction. You call this imperialism. I understand your fears and assure you that we do not seek to impose our views on others, let alone run their societies. We want to restore the Islamic civilization in the erstwhile Muslim countries and are confident that its moral and spiritual vision will, over time, win the allegiance of the rest of the world. The Cold War was dominated by a clash between the two materialist global ideologies of capitalism and communism. Since Islam provides a superior alternative to both, the future belongs to it.

You say that my vision of a truly Islamic society is muddled. You reject modernity; I do not. The modern world is here to stay and has much to be said for it, and anyone opting out of it is doomed to impotence. I do not want an alternative to modernity as you do; I want an alternative modernity, a society that uses modern technological resources—such as nuclear weapons, the modern state, and industrialization—in the service of Islam. Without these resources my people would remain at the mercy of the Americans. However, I do not want the modern secular, egalitarian, and liberal culture with all its attendant evils of pornography, confused gender roles, promiscuity, homosexuality, selfish individualism, consumerism, and so on. The cultural synthesis I envision, which gives modernity an Islamic soul, is possible and well worth fighting for. I appreciate the dangers you see in it, and would guard against them. You are right to say that I do not yet have a blueprint. This is partly because I have not had the time to work it out, partly because I need to be vague to broaden my support, and partly because I believe in fighting one battle at a time.

You condemn my terrorist violence. Unlike you, I do not consider violence inherently evil. I take a purely instrumental view of it and judge it on the basis of its goals and its ability to realize them. As you should know, your nonviolence did not always work. From time to time your desperate followers resorted to acts of violence, and you defended these as "understandable" and "excusable." Your nonviolent struggle was also constantly shadowed by terrorist activities, which frightened and weakened the British and must be given as much credit for Indian independence as your own nonviolence. Every method of struggle requires certain conditions for its success. Nonviolence requires a decent opponent, freedom to mount protests, and an impartial media. You had all three; I do not. We do not have the civil liberties you enjoyed. If we resorted to nonviolent protests, the Americans and their despotic stooges would infiltrate our ranks, create divisions, spread false stories, and, if all this failed, use force to mow us down. They would then use the pliant global media to manipulate public opinion in their favor. Don't you see how cleverly they misreported, suppressed, or explained away the deaths of over half a million children caused by the ten-year-long economic sanctions against Iraq?

If you need further proof, look at the ways in which the Americans and the British justified and continue to justify the recent war on Iraq. They solemnly announced that they had incontrovertible proof that Iraq had weapons of mass destruction, and they still cannot find them. When Hans Blix introduced a note of caution, he was vilified. When the French president said that the arms inspectors should be given more time, he was grotesquely misrepresented as being against the war altogether and was threatened with dire consequences. We are not even told exactly how many Iraqi civilians died in the war. We are told little about the daily atrocities committed against Iraqi civilians by the U.S. soldiers, and none of the latter have so far been tried, let alone punished. A similar blanket of silence is thrown over the systematic Israeli humiliation, harassment, and murder of Palestinians in the occupied territories. In the light of all this, there is absolutely no chance of success for our nonviolent protests. The world would not even know what humiliations and atrocities were inflicted upon us, let alone exert pressure on our behalf. You, Mr. Gandhi, had no answer when Martin Buber asked what advice you would give to the Jewish victims of Hitler's concentration camps. As he rightly pointed out, where there is no witness, there is no martyrdom, only a pointless waste of life.

You have an acute sense of the power of tradition, and need hardly be reminded that every society has its characteristic moral rhythm. We can inspire it to great deeds only by appealing to its native idioms and images. Islam takes a more charitable view of violence and sanctions than does Hinduism and even enjoins it under certain circumstances. The prophet himself used violence, and so did his followers and other great Muslim religious and political readers. Even if I were to plead for nonviolence, which I would not dream of doing, it simply would not cut much ice with my fellow Muslims. The Pathan followers of your friend Abdul Gaffar Khan used it only for a while, and then abandoned it in favor of violence. I simply see no other way to shake the might and weaken the arrogance of the Americans than to use violence. And since we cannot even remotely match their might, violence has to take a terrorist form.

This was how we got rid of the Soviets in Afghanistan. Americans understood this and gave us all the help we needed. And it is precisely because of this that they are now scared of the same methods being used against them. As I have said on several occasions, the struggle against the Soviets was a profound "spiritual experience" for me and my fellow fighters, and represented a decisive turning point in our ways of thinking.[12] It gave us enormous self-confidence, expanded our political horizon, helped us build a global network, and enabled us to move beyond narrow and largely ethnic Arab nationalism to the vision of a wider Islamic unity. I would rather stick to the method my followers and I have found successful than try out yours. You keep telling me that I should not lower myself to the level of my opponent and should act on higher principles. Why should I? If others hit me, I hit back. If they harm me or my people, I harm them. This is justice or reciprocity, and it is morally right. I don't see why I should endure the suffering involved in being my opponent's redeemer. I am a follower of prophet Mohammed, not Jesus Christ; and even the Christians do not much care for nonviolence and turning the other cheek.

GANDHI

Let me sum up your basic arguments and tell you where and why I disagree. You advance the following four propositions. First, Americans are embarked on an imperialist project and want to dominate the world. Second, Muslim societies should be reconstructed on the basis of the true principles of Islam. Third, this cannot be done without getting the Americans out of your societies and overthrowing their native collaborators. Fourth, only terrorist violence can achieve these goals.

As for the first argument, I see a little more clearly than before why you take this view. Although you have a point, you are wrong to homogenize the United States. Some groups there fit your description; others do not. Many Americans are highly critical of what their government is doing in their name, and have protested against the recent war on Iraq. Some of those who support the present administration do so because they have built up a fear psychosis after the events of 9/11. Their belief that their country was invulnerable against foreign attacks has been shattered, and they live in the constant fear of similar attacks. Bush reassures them that his global war on terrorism will give them the security they desperately crave, so they go along with him. As long as you keep talking the way you do, you reinforce their paranoia and ill-conceived support for Bush's policy. Talk the language of peace, link up with the progressive forces in the United States, and you have a better chance of success.

As for your second argument, I could not disagree more. Identifying religion and state corrupts both. Religion has a legitimate place in public life and is an important source of people's commitments and motivations. But that is wholly different from saying that the state should be based on, enforce, or be guided by religious principles. The state is based on coercion, religion on freedom, and the two simply cannot go together. In your case the situation is made infinitely worse by the fact that you take a static, self-righteous, and intolerably dogmatic view of religion. This necessarily commits you to a tightly knit politico-religious party supervising all areas of individual and social life, the surest way to destroy religion, create a terrorist state, and turn human beings into soulless automata. Have you learned nothing from the disastrous experiences of Iran and Saudi Arabia, both of which now appreciate the need to separate religion and state?

As I said earlier, your third proposition is only partially true. Following our earlier discussion, I studied the history of U.S. interference in the affairs of Muslim societies closely. I appreciate better your view that you cannot achieve significant changes in your society without ending U.S. influence, and wish you well in your anti-imperialist endeavor. However, getting Americans physically out of Muslim countries does not mean that you will be able to get rid of U.S. values and views of life. You can fight ideas only with ideas, and need a clearly worked-out alternative that your people will find attractive. Furthermore, as long as your society remains deeply divided, unjust, unequal, and devoid of a strong sense of freedom and cohesion, it will remain too weak to resist external manipulation and domination. There is simply no shortcut around the massive and painful task of educating the masses and revitalizing your society. Terrorist attacks achieve nothing lasting. You need to build a cadre of reformers and activists, work among the masses, open up spaces of action by judicious acts of protest, and create a broad-based popular movement with the power to reconstitute your society. Once your society develops a collective sense of identity and a strong spirit of independence, Americans will not be able to stay in it even for a day.

Finally, you make a serious mistake in rejecting nonviolence. Braving all the brutality of the Southern states, Martin Luther King used nonviolence to achieve civil rights for black Americans and to give them a sense of pride and self-confidence. Iranians too used it successfully against the Shah. The more his troops killed innocent protestors, the faster was the dissolution of his regime, with even some of his troops deserting him. You say that my own countrymen used violence and that I sanctioned it. Some of my countrymen from time to time did resort to violence when they were provoked beyond endurance. Although I said that it was understandable, I continued to condemn it in the strongest possible terms, fasted in a spirit of atonement, and even apologized to the colonial rulers for it. To condone isolated acts of violence by desperate individuals is one thing; to make violence the central principle of struggle is totally different.

You rightly say that martyrdom requires witness and that the role of the media is crucial to its success. However, you are wrong to homogenize them. Some sections of the media are biased, but others have a strong professional conscience. Had that not been the case, we would not have known of the atrocities committed by the coalition forces during and after the war on Iraq. You should not exaggerate the power of the media either. Ordinary men and women are not fools. They well know that the media are biased and tell lies, and make appropriate allowances for that. Had this not been the case, so much of the opposition to the war on Iraq would be inexplicable. By exaggerating the power of the media and giving up on them, you fall into the trap set by your opponents. They want you to despair of the media and resort to desperate acts of terrorism so that they can demonize and destroy you and distract attention from your genuine grievances. If your cause is just and is pursued in a courageous and humane manner, it is bound to command attention. Truth cannot be suppressed for long. My long political experience bears this out. And in any case, for deeply religious persons like us, this has to be our basic article of faith.

Even if you do not approve of nonviolence, you should know by now that your methods have done an incalculable harm to your people. You have discredited a great religion. Millions instinctively associate Islam with violence and destruction. You have also deeply divided the *ummah,* subjected your followers to torture and degradation, and rendered the lives of many innocent diasporic Muslims miserable. You have given the Bush administration an excuse to unleash extensive violence and pursue an imperialist project. It is about time you gave up violence, if not for moral then at least for pragmatic reasons.

CONCLUSION

It is not difficult to imagine how Osama bin Laden would reply to Gandhi and how the dialogue would go on. Assuming that both are open-minded and willing to learn from each other, their differences should narrow. Both should be able to agree that the current U.S. policy has an imperialist thrust and needs to be fought, as also that the United States speaks in many voices and should not be homogenized. Bin Laden cannot deny the obvious fact that many Americans are deeply uneasy about what their government is doing in their name, and that in a democracy a government's policy is best fought by mobilizing its domestic critics. Both Gandhi and bin Laden would agree that Muslim societies desperately need to be revitalized and restructured, and that this is a painful and prolonged process requiring education of the masses and a cadre of social activists. They would disagree about the basis of the good society, Gandhi wanting to separate religion and state, and bin Laden insisting on their fusion. Even here bin Laden should be able to appreciate the force of Gandhi's arguments, and see the need for at least some degree of separation between the two.

Even on the crucial question of the justifiability of terrorist violence, differences should narrow, though they would not disappear. Given his moral theory, Gandhi would not see violence in purely instrumental terms and would remain implacably hostile to terrorism. However, he would agree that some form of nonterrorist violence cannot be ruled out. When they are provoked beyond endurance and see no other alternative, desperate and humiliated people tend to resort to violence. If a political leader were to refuse to have any truck with it, he would be disowned by his people, and leave a vacuum that the terrorists would fill. As for bin Laden, he is unlikely to be persuaded by Gandhi's moralistic attitude to nonviolence, especially its underlying belief that one should take upon oneself the burden of another's evil and act as his or her higher self. Bin Laden believes in fighting violence with violence, and sees no reason why he should take the moral high ground. This is a fundamental difference of moral attitude, and it is difficult to see how it can be resolved. However, he should be able to appreciate Gandhi's pragmatic case for nonviolence. Given his view of human life, he would remain suspicious of its efficacy, and given his view of Islam, he would be skeptical about his people's willingness to accept it, but he should be able to see that it has something to be said for it and deserves a try.

The fact that Gandhi and bin Laden would continue to be divided by deep moral and political differences does not mean that their dialogue is pointless. It helps them and their followers appreciate each other's point of view, and see where and why they disagree. Such an increase in mutual understanding is an important gain. The dialogue also enables each to see the deeper assumptions and biases of his point of view, and adds to his self-understanding. Finally, it offers each participant new practical and moral insights and a new way of looking at the contemporary world and at human life in general; and it encourages them to develop a richer and more balanced perspective on the issues in question. In so doing the dialogue opens up the possibility of self-criticism and self-enrichment.

The dialogue between Gandhi and Osama bin Laden is not limited to them alone. Two important groups are silent partners to it. There is a large Muslim constituency whom both are seeking to influence and whose response would decide which arguments will ultimately prevail. If large sections of it were to be persuaded by or at least feel sympathetic to Gandhi's analysis, bin Laden would be isolated and forced to either change his tune or become irrelevant. Citizens and governments in the West form the second constituency. Their willingness to understand why bin Laden and his followers think and act the way they do and to take a critical look at themselves is an equally important factor in determining the outcome of the dialogue. The responses of the two constituencies are dialectically related and both shape and are shaped by each other. A political dialogue has its own politics and is never a purely intellectual exercise. Its outcome depends as much on the participants as on the audience. It is therefore not enough that the participants are open-minded and guided by a sense of justice and fellow feeling; their audience too should display these virtues.

NOTES

I am most grateful to my good friend Leroy Rouner for several long conversations on the subject. I am also grateful to Douglas Allen, the discussant for the lecture, and David Lyons and Robert Cohen for their helpful comments.

1. For good accounts of the ideas of Osama bin Laden, see Yussef Bodansky, *Bin Laden: The Man Who Declared War on America* (New York: Random House, 2001); Peter Bergen, *Holy War, Inc.: Inside the Secret World of Osama bin Laden* (London: Weidenfeld and Nicolson, 2001); and the audiotapes of bin Laden's broadcasts and interviews. See also Stephen Schwartz, *The Two Faces of Islam* (New York: Doubleday, 2002); Graham E. Fuller, *The Future of Political Islam* (London: Palgrave Macmillan, 2003); Daniel Pipes, *Militant Islam Reaches America* (New York: Norton, 2002).

2. "The Quest for Sanity: Reflections on September 11 and the Aftermath" (London: Muslim Council of Britain, 2003), pp. 18ff.

3. "The collapse of the Soviet Union made the U.S. more haughty and arrogant, and it has started to look at itself as master of the world and established what it calls the New World Order" (Osama bin Laden, cited in Bergen, *Holy War, Inc*, p. 21).

4. An audio message by Osama bin Laden broadcast on al-Jazeera on 11 February 2003.

5. "The name of Clinton or that of the American government provokes disgust and revulsion. This is because [it] . . . directly reflects in our minds . . .

the picture of the children who died in Iraq" as a result of the economic sanctions (Osama bin Laden, cited in Bergen, *Holy War, Inc.*, p. 23). See also *Nidaul Islam*, October–November 1996 (http://www.islam.org.au).

6. "The American and British peoples stated widely that they support their leaders' decision to attack Iraq. This means that all individuals of these two nations . . . are belligerent people. . . . They are enemies to us, whether they are involved in direct fight against us or pay their taxes" (Osama bin Laden, cited in Bodansky, *Bin Laden*, p. 369). Those Americans are exempted who "object to the American government's policy" (bin Laden, cited in Bergen, *Holy War, Inc.*, p. 24). See also bin Laden's interview with Hamid Mir in *Dawn*, 10 November 2001 (www.dawn.com/2001/11/10/top1.htm).

7. Osama bin Laden, interview with Hamid Mir in *Dawn*, 10 November 2001.

8. Osama bin Laden, interview with Tayseer Alouni in October 2001 (CNN transcript, 5 February 2002). See also the interview with some of bin Laden's followers in May 1998 (www.pbs.org/wgbh/pages/frontline/shows/binladen/who/interview.html).

9. For Gandhi's views on the subjects discussed here, see Raghavan Iyer, ed., *The Moral and Political Writings of Mahatma Gandhi* (Oxford: Clarendon Press, 1987), vol. 3, sec. 2; and V. V. Ramana Murti, ed., *Gandhi: Essential Writings* (New Delhi: Gandhi Peace Foundation, 1970), secs. 1, 4, 9, and 10. See also my *Gandhi's Political Philosophy: A Critical Examination* (London: Macmillan, 1989), chap. 6; and *Colonialism, Tradition, and Reform* (New Delhi: Sage, 1989), chap. 4.

10. For a discussion of Gandhi's dialogue with Indian terrorists, see chap. 5 in my *Colonialism, Tradition, and Reform*.

11. For a good analysis of the different interpretations of the Qur'an and the debates between them, see Joshua Cohen and Ian Lague, eds., *The Place of Tolerance in Islam* (Boston: Beacon Press, 2002).

12. "I have benefited . . . greatly from the *jihad* in Afghanistan. . . . What we benefited from most was [that] the glory and myth of the superpower was destroyed not only in my mind but also of all Muslims" (Osama bin Laden, cited in Bergen, *Holy War, Inc.*, p. 63).

PART II

Understanding Difference

Other Peoples' Religions, Other Peoples' *Kama* and *Karma*
WENDY DONIGER

THE ARGUMENT FOR COMPARISON

The modern comparative study of religion was in large part designed in the pious hope of teaching our own people that "alien" religions were like "ours" in many ways. The hope was that if we learned about other religions, we would no longer hate and kill their followers. Emmanuel Levinas argues that the face of the other says, "Don't kill me,"[1] and the comparative enterprise strives to illuminate this face. A glance at any newspaper should tell us that this goal has yet to be fulfilled in the world at large. But the academic world, having gone beyond this simplistic paradigm, now suffers from a post-postcolonial backlash. In this age of multinationalism and the politics of individual ethnic and religious groups, the assumption that two phenomena from different cultures are "the same" in any significant way is regarded as demeaning to the individualism of each, and is viewed as a reflection of the old racist attitude that "all wogs look alike." At the other end of the anticolonial continuum, seeing correspondences between cultures is regarded as politically retrograde for different reasons. As Annie Dillard discovered in China in 1983, "Mao said that there is no such thing as 'human nature'; there is only class nature. To talk about human nature is, then, to undermine the theoretical basis of socialism. . . . That people, despite differences in culture, have feelings in common . . . was, as recently as four months ago, a somewhat risky statement in China."[2] In many politically sensitized academic cultures in the United States, it is still risky.

Moreover, in the present climate of anti-Orientalism, it is regarded as imperialist if a scholar who studies India, for instance, stands outside (presumably, above) phenomena from different cultures and equates them. The present trend is to study only one cultural group or only one gender and, indeed, to study *one's own* group or gender. This is a trend fueled in large part by disciplines, such as feminism and cultural studies, that argue or imply that their subject matter (racism, sexism, the class struggle, genocide) has such devastating human consequences that there is no room for more than one answer (there goes interdisciplinary studies); moreover, they imply that the experiences (more particularly the sufferings of injustice) of the particular group are unique and therefore not comprehensible to anyone who has not "been there." (There goes comparative studies—indeed, area studies in general, taking "non-Western civ" with it on the way down.) I would challenge the trend of limiting those who study any group to those within the group—women studying women, Jews studying Jews—a trend which, if followed slavishly, would automatically eliminate my tiny, precious world of cross-cultural comparison as well as the more general humanism of which it is an essential part. This sort of identity politics has led to attacks on a number of leading scholars of Hinduism, including myself, by Hindus whose argument is that I have no right to tell anyone my ideas about Hinduism because I am not a Hindu. To complicate the matter, they have also attacked several other scholars of Hinduism who *are* Hindus but who use Western ideas in their scholarship. Freud and Marx are perceived as the enemy, unacceptable in the mind of a non-Hindu scholar of Hinduism and even more threatening in the head of a Hindu.

This is the bigoted version of the more thoughtful academic program that Wilfred Cantwell Smith introduced at Harvard half a century ago, a tradition that I used to mock as the "take a Buddhist to dinner" school of thought. This tradition reigned for many years at the Center for the Prevention of World Religions, as it was known in certain circles when I was there in the late 1950s and early 1960s. The other extreme was represented by the Chicago school that I later joined. It argued that the last person in the world one would want to ask about Buddhism is a Buddhist, not merely because of possible emotional bias but simply because there are so many different sorts of Buddhists, so that no one Buddhist could have the wide-angle lens that a properly educated scholar of Buddhism should have. Neither extreme now dominates either of these two institutions, but they are more broadly influential, there and elsewhere, than I would want them to be.

I want to argue for a parallax, a double fix on the distant universe, that would combine the view of the insider, expressed in texts and by living informants, with the approach of the outsider—ourselves and our living and dead colleagues.

In terms of academic theory, the emphasis on individual cultures tends to generate an increasingly narrow focus, eventually making it impossible to generalize even from one moment to the next. Nothing has enough in common with anything else to be compared with it even for the purpose of illuminating its distinctiveness; each event is unique. The radical particularizing of much recent theory in cultural anthropology, for instance, seems to deny any shared base to humanity at large and often even to members of the same culture.[3] But if we start with the assumption of absolute difference, and the belief that each culture can only be understood from the inside, then there can be no conversation. We find ourselves trapped in the self-reflexive garden of a Looking-Glass ghetto, forever meeting ourselves walking back in through the cultural door through which we were trying to escape.[4] While extreme universalism means that the other is exactly like me (a distortion that must indeed be avoided, and that scholars such as Talal Asad have taught us to avoid), the extreme nominalism of identity politics means that the other may not be human at all. Many of the people who argued (and continue to argue) that Jews or blacks or any other group defined as "wogs" were all alike (that is, like one another) went on to argue— or, more often, to assume—that they were all different (that is, different from us white people, us Protestants). This latter argument easily led to the assertion that such people did not deserve the same rights as the rest of us. Essentialized difference can become an instrument of dominance; European colonialism was supported by a discourse of difference.

Indeed, the members of a single cultural "group" may be very different, and it is just as insulting to say that all Japanese are alike as it is to say that the Japanese are just like the French. (The essentialism of time can be just as harmful as the essentialism of place; we cannot explain Shakespeare simply by understanding "the Elizabethan age.") The culturally essentialized position is indefensible and politically dangerous. Yet it is often assumed in "culturally contextualized" and historically specific studies: "Let me tell you how everyone felt at the *fin de siècle* in Europe and the United States." A monolithic focus on the class or ethnic group can become not only boring, but racist. My aim is an expansive outlook on inquiry, one that enhances our humanity in both its peculiarity and its commonality.

If we assume that cultures are incommensurable so that we can understand any phenomenon only in terms of its cultural context, we make it impossible to leave one context and enter into another. Yet while two cultures are never *entirely* commensurable, one can, nevertheless, "mense" them together. They are, if not co-measurable, at least what I would call co-mensable, co-thinkable; and then we can move on to the criterion that keeps castes together (and apart) in India: commensality. We can, I hope, dine with other cultures. Commensality is very much what a pluralist education is about: sitting down together at the same table.

Flawed though it is, cross-cultural comparison is an extremely useful way of understanding the world. To borrow the Zen koan, we cannot hear the sound of one hand clapping; we cannot hear sameness. But through the comparative method we can see the blinders that each culture constructs for itself. We can use a phenomenon from one culture to reveal to us what is *not* a similar phenomenon from another culture, to find out the things not "dreamt of in your philosophy" (as Hamlet said to Horatio).[5] Moreover, we can use comparative work to test theories about our own culture. Comparison defamiliarizes what we take for granted. We can only see the inflection of a particular phenomenon when we see other variants.

THE JOYS OF COMPARISON

Comparing our religion with that of someone else forces us to come to terms with the Other, the one both different from us and the same as us. The challenge lies in choosing an Other as different from us as possible, perhaps one whom we do not like or understand at all at first and have to work hard to like or understand. The comparison that chooses an Other in which the initial likeness is more immediately apparent is more ethnocentric; it is easier, and ultimately it proves less.

But what aspects of the Other define the Otherness? My colleague David Tracy, the Catholic theologian, is fond of engaging in dialogues with Buddhists. I used to chide him that he was taking the easy way out by choosing the reasonable, ethical Buddhists; to dialogue with Hindus would be the real test—all those gods, all those arms and heads.

Not at all, he replied; Buddhists are far more Other than Hindus for a Catholic theologian since they have no god at all, whereas the Hindu challenge of too many gods is mediated by the multiplicity of Catholic saints.[6] But for historical reasons Judaism poses even greater problems for a Catholic who wishes to engage in dialogue—even though it is monotheistic, and hence at least on that level less Other than the atheism of Buddhism or the polytheism of Hinduism. Because Judaism has served as a projection for Catholics for so many years, the Jews are too close and too tangled with Catholic history to be seen by many Catholics as they really are. Unlike the Buddhists, the Jews must be retrieved from Catholic projection and acknowledged in their real Otherness before the conversation can even begin.[7]

Indeed, the minor differences between two subgroups within a single culture often inspire far more bitter and passionate antagonism than the more obvious differences between one culture and another. The centuries-old struggle between Catholics and Protestants in Northern Ireland has been more destructive than the many clashes between Christians and Muslims. Also consider the bloodiest encounters: Shi'ite and Sunni, Jew and Muslim (within the Semitic world), Yankees and Rebels in the U.S. Civil War.[8] We react against what we find extremely strange in another religion because we think people who believe and act like that must be crazy and irrational; but we react more violently against what we find only slightly strange in religions closer to us because we think that such people have made the wrong rational choice, thereby betraying us. It is in part for this reason that historians of religions in recent decades have turned their lens back on their own cultures, to study not merely the Orientals, the distant Others, but Christians and Jews, the near Others.

On the other hand, a false sense of familiarity with a religion that is actually quite unfamiliar to us may prevent us from discovering, and coming to terms with, that religion's genuine otherness. For this reason, the false Orientalist stereotypes in kitsch movies of the *Temple of Doom* variety (mindless Hindu mobs, romantic desert Arabs, and so forth) give us the mistaken belief that we know something about these religions, and prevent us from actually learning about them. These stereotypes are to genuine interreligious understanding what *faux amis* are to the genuine understanding of a foreign language. (*Faux amis* ["false friends"] are words that sound or look just like English words but in fact have very different meanings, such as taking the French *pain* ["bread"] to mean "pain" in English. The still closer false friends between British and American English are even more disconcerting: Does "first floor" mean one-up, or ground? Is the "boot" the trunk of the car or footwear?) Unlike the linguistic false friends, the stereotypes in interreligious understanding may cost many lives.

If we choose to use a less dichomotizing word than "same" for the Other in our comparison, such as "similar," we might construct a Venn diagram of shared ideas. There will be a set of categories that interlock like chain mail, with various degrees of resemblance or "family likenesses" (to use Wittgenstein's useful term). As the themes overlap, it becomes apparent that there is no actual center to the group, no single indispensable or defining theme. This emptiness in the center suggests that the figure might better be named a Zen diagram. In this way we can replace polarized grids with infinitely fluid continuums. But whatever word we choose to use for the same/like/similar/resembling pole of the comparison, we must come to terms with the other pole, the pole of difference. We may start with an initial assumption of similarity, but we must go on to end up with difference.[9]

Moreover, similarity must not be allowed to be normative. It is to an extent inevitable to assume one's original stance and to assume that the Other is "like me." But this assumption must immediately be qualified by both difference and a shift of center. One must go on to say, "I am like you," "I will be able to understand you because I am like you," and then, later, "I see ways in which you are in fact not like me." For instance, one who already knows the *Iliad* begins reading the Sanskrit epic, the *Ramayana*, by saying, "It's like the *Iliad*" (in part because European scholars have called both works epics, already a problematic step which we will not debate here). But then the reader must shift the ground to notice how the *Iliad* is not like the *Ramayana*. It is natural but not good to be ethnocentric. Acknowledging that we are is the first step but it must not become an excuse. We have to go on to see how the rest of the world is. There is no value-free comparison, but we do the best we can.

The initial, assumed comparison is always between us and the Other. This happens whenever we confront a single phenomenon from another culture. The comparative insight prevents an interpreter from glossing any particular phenomenon *only* in terms of the specific cultural context. For instance, a Cinderella tale in India may very well be told in terms of the caste system (Cinderella treated as an Untouchable), but once one knows that it also occurs in other cultures that have no caste system it cannot be explained *only* in terms of the caste system. The key to the game of cross-cultural comparison lies in selecting questions that might transcend any particular culture. Some people think that there are no such questions, but some think, as I do, that worthwhile cross-cultural questions can be asked.

Claude Lévi-Strauss said it best and most boldly: "In proposing the study of mankind, anthropology frees me from doubt, since it examines those *differences and changes* in mankind which have a meaning for all men, and excludes those peculiar to a single civilization, which dissolve into nothingness under the gaze of the outside observer."[10] Thus, difference itself becomes a basis for comparison because the comparison is possible only if we assume that difference has "a meaning for all men" (and, presumably, for all women). In other words, one of the ways in which we are all alike is in our shared interest in our differences. This seems to me to be a very good place at which to start the work of comparison.

THE SAME AND THE DIFFERENT: THE *KAMASUTRA*

I hope I have now persuaded you that other peoples' religions are, to borrow Lévi-Strauss's famous phrase, good to think with. Let me illustrate the benefits of thinking with other peoples' religious ideas by considering the *Kamasutra* and the theory of karma.

Let us consider the ways in which we can and cannot think, or feel, with the *Kamasutra*. Working on a new translation of the *Kamasutra*, I became aware, time and again, of how the foreign cultural assumptions of the text simultaneously enlarged my own vision of what was possible, illuminated the invisible arbitrary walls that my own culture had used to veto certain possibilities even before they could be considered and rejected, and revealed a common denominator in human nature. Some of it, like the magic formulas, remains truly foreign to us:

> If you coat your penis with an ointment made with powdered white thorn-apple, black pepper, and long pepper, mixed with honey, you put your sexual partner in your power. If you make a powder by pulverizing leaves scattered by the wind, garlands left

over from corpses, and peacocks' bones; or pulverize a female "circle-maker" buzzard that died a natural death, and mix the powder with honey and gooseberry, it puts someone in your power. If you mix the same powder with monkey shit and scatter the mixture over a virgin, she will not be given to another man.[11]

A comparison with Viagra is superficially useful, but it does not enable us to take this paragraph seriously on its own terms. The commentary on the first verse is far from helpful: "Do this in such a way that the woman you want does not realize, 'A man with something spread on his penis is making love to me.'" This text inspired one of my students to remark, "Any woman who would let you make love to her with all that stuff smeared on you would have to be madly in love with you already."

Other bits of the text become accessible only through rather distant analogies. Betel, for instance, is a delicacy concocted from a betel leaf rolled up around a paste made of betel nuts, cardamom, lime paste, and other flavors, sometimes including tobacco or other stimulants (even, sometimes, cocaine). The finished product, shaped rather like a stuffed grape-leaf, is eaten as a stimulant, to redden the mouth, and to freshen the breath. Throughout the *Kamasutra,* lovers give one another betel, take betel out of their own mouths, and put it in their lover's mouth. This basic part of the erotic scene in ancient India can best be understood by non-Indians through an analogy with the overtones that champagne or the postcoital cigarette has in Europe. It evokes the cigarette foreplay of Bogart and Bacall in *To Have and Have Not* and *The Big Sleep* or the cigarette sublimation shared by Bette Davis and Paul Heinried in *Now Voyager.* Magic and drugs, betel, the life in the harem, the world of courtesans—these parts of the *Kamasutra* make one think, "How very different these people are from us."

But then we come across this passage in a section about courtship and flirtation, providing advice for a young boy who wants to make a young girl notice him: "When they are playing in the water, he dives underwater at some distance from her, comes up close to her, touches her, and dives underwater again right there" (3.4.6). Here we are in familiar territory. For me, this passage immediately evoked the summers of my early teens, spent in various camps in the Adirondacks, where the boys did precisely this whenever we swam in the lake. It is also easy to recognize the man who tells the woman on whom he's set his sights "about an erotic dream, pretending that it was about another woman" (3.4.9), and the woman who does the same thing (5.4.54). Sometimes the unfamiliar and the familiar are cheek by jowl. The culture-specific list of women the wife must not associate with (including a Buddhist nun and a magician who uses love sorcery [4.1.9]) is followed in the very next passage by the woman who is cooking for her man and finds out, "This is what he likes; this is what he hates; this is good for him; this is bad for him"—a consideration that surely resonates with many contemporary Anglophone readers, cooking for someone they love, balancing the desire to please (perhaps with a béarnaise sauce?) with concern for the rising cholesterol level. This constant alternation of the familiar and the strange teaches us a great deal about human nature.

COMING TO TERMS WITH KARMA

Let us turn now from *kama* to *karma* (people often mix them up). My relationship with the theory of karma has changed in major ways over the half century since I first encountered India. In my book *The Origins of Evil in Hindu Mythology,* published in 1975, I argued that the theory of karma was not regarded as an adequate explanation of evil even in its own country, as evidenced by the fact that the Hindus developed many other approaches to evil, including the myths that I wrote about in that book. In the preface to the second edition of *The Origins of Evil,* I remarked that I had come to respect the karma theory more, in part by editing a 350-page book about it, *Karma and Rebirth in Classical Indian Traditions* (1980); and in 1986, in *Other Peoples' Myths,* I took it very seriously indeed.[12] I gradually came to think with and then to feel with the karma theory.

The karma theory *tells* us that we have lived other lives, that our souls have had other bodies. But how can we *feel,* as well as accept intellectually, the reality of those other lives if we cannot remember them? Plato constructed his own version of this theory in the myth of Er in Book 10 of the *Republic,* but Platonism did not become an integral part of Western thinking about death. It is easier for Hindus to *feel* the theory of rebirth, as they feel themselves to be a part of a larger human group in a way that we do not. They believe that they are joined in nature, as well as in culture, not only with the people in the past and the future to whom they are related (people whom we, too, regard as part of our physical substance) but also with the other people with whom they have present contact (people whom we do not generally regard as physically connected with us). But what about those of us who are not Hindus? For us, the previous incarnation unrecalled has no existence.

Reincarnation is generally regarded as a fresh start, but the *tabula* is not always quite so *rasa* as it is cracked up to be. Indian philosophy generally locates memory, which does not transmigrate, in the *manas,* a combination of mind and heart. The *manas* blurs the Cartesian distinction between mind and body. Like the heart, *manas* is a physical organ in the body; like the mind, it is where we learn calculus; and like both mind and heart, it is where we fall in love. Some branches of Indian philosophy locate memory in the soul, but they do not totally divorce it from the body. Thus, although the transmigrating soul in Hinduism usually loses its memory as it crosses the boundary of rebirth and sheds its body like the soul in Plato's myth of Er, some particularly gifted and/or lucky people can remember their previous births.

Even in Plato's myth, our transmigrating souls retain some sort of magnetic attachment to our old bodies and, with them, to our old personalities, like Eeyore to his detached tail. For before our minds are washed clean as we drink the waters of Lethe, we choose who to become in our next life, but we choose to become the same sort of person we were before, or, as the case may be, the very opposite of the sort of person we were before. One way or another, the force of our previous personality constrains and skews our rational choice:

> The choice was both laughable and amazing, since most people chose according to the habits of their former life. The soul that had been Orpheus chose to be a swan, because he so hated the race of women—at whose hands he had met his death—that he did not want to be conceived and born of them. And Er saw a swan changing into the life he chose as a man. When all the souls had chosen their lots, they went to the Plain of Oblivion and drank from the River of Forgetfulness, and then they all fell asleep.[13]

Plato describes many similar cases, each choice based on the experience of a previous life: Atalanta, seeing the great fame of an athlete, was unable to resist the temptation; the jester Thersites chose the form of a monkey; and so forth. (Orpheus's choice of a swan may have been influenced by Plato's knowledge of the importance of that animal in Indian theories of transmigration.)[14] Even if we cannot remember who we were, we are reborn in the shadow of that previous personality. The soul gets typecast.

This belief is also expressed in Hindu texts, which imagine the reincarnating soul meditating on its next life not on the far shore of Lethe but in the womb of the soul's future mother, where it (not yet he or she) remains fully conscious and remembers its previous lives in agonizing detail:

> Then it begins to remember its many previous existences in the wheel of rebirth, and that depresses it, and it tosses from side to side, thinking, "I won't ever do *that* again, as soon as I get out of this womb. I will do everything I can, so that I won't become an embryo again." It thinks in this way as it remembers the hundreds of miseries of birth that it experienced before, in the power of fate. Then, as time goes by, the embryo turns around, head down, and in the ninth or tenth month it is born. As it comes out, it is hurt by the wind of procreation; it comes out crying, because it is pained by the misery in its heart. When it has come out of the womb, it falls into an unbearable swoon, but it regains consciousness when it is touched by the air. Then Vishnu's deluding power of illusion assails him, and when his soul has been deluded by it, he loses his knowledge. As soon as the living creature has lost his knowledge, he becomes a baby. After that he becomes a young boy, then an adolescent, and then an old man. And then he dies and then he is born again as a human. Thus he wanders on the wheel of rebirth like the bucket on the wheel of a well.[15]

Chagrin at the memory of previous mistakes, and despair at the realization that they will make them all again in this life, too, make babies cry as they enter the world. Mae West once said that if she had her life to live over again she would make all the same mistakes, but she would make them sooner. The *Laws of Manu,* the code of Hindu social law, composed early in the Common Era, promise many upwardly mobile transmigrations, but not for everyone. Most of us make the same mistakes, sooner or later: "Through the repetition of their evil actions, men of little intelligence experience miseries in womb after womb in this world."[16]

The body remembers some things, and the mind remembers others. But memory is not all there is. There is also a reality of unrecalled experience that gives a kind of validity to our connection with lives that we do not recall. The karma theory recognizes the parallel between events forgotten within a single life—the events of early childhood, or the things that we repress or that (in Indian mythology) we forget as the result of a curse[17]—and the events forgotten from a previous life. It also recognizes a similarity in the ways in which we sometimes half recall these events. We remember a lost past through the power of the invisible tracks or traces they leave behind on our souls. (A similar concept of physical traces on the transmigrating soul may be seen in Plato's *Gorgias* 524, in which a man who has been whipped bears the marks of the whip upon him when he is judged after his death.) Hindus call these traces perfumes (*vasanas*), scents that are "the impressions of anything remaining unconsciously in the mind, the present consciousness of past perceptions."[18] They have a force that accounts for our sense of *déjà vu*, the sense that one sometimes has, on seeing someone or some place for the first time, that one has seen them before. These are the "impressions of lingering emotions" that a certain king, who has been cursed to forget the woman he loves, has in mind when he says:

> Even a happy man may be overcome by passionate longing when he sees beautiful things or hears sweet sounds.
> Perhaps he is remembering something he was not conscious of before that moment,
> the loves of a former life, firmly rooted in the impressions of lingering emotions.[19]

In the Hindu view, these are the karmic memory traces. They are bits of experience that cling to our transmigrating souls even in new bodies, loose threads trailing not merely from a "former life" within this lifespan, but from a previous incarnation. (One commentator remarks that it is impossible to shake off these impressions even after thousands of lives.)[20] These unconscious memories of past lives predispose the transmigrating soul to act in one way or another in its new life. In many ways the *vasanas* that return to the reborn soul correspond to aspects of the unconscious as we have come to understand it, more particularly to the repressed unconscious that *returns*, in Freud's formulation. The signals that we send to ourselves from our former lives are wake-up calls, like the message that the Chippendale Mupp, one of the creatures in *Dr. Seuss's Sleep Book*, sent to himself: at bedtime, he bit the end tuft on his *very* long tail, so that the pain would work its way up the whole tail and, finally, wake him up in the morning.[21]

Such "perfumes" also correspond in many ways to the social chemosignals that Martha McClintock has studied. These chemosignals are olfactory clues to social behavior that are handed down genetically (which is, in a sense, through rebirths), generally unconscious clues that influence our emotions. Appropriately, McClintock named one group of these chemosignals after the *vasanas* of Hindu philosophy:

> Social chemosignals are remarkably similar to the medieval Sanskrit term *vasanas*. *Vasana*, the singular noun, is derived from the Sanskrit term *vas*, meaning "to perfume." . . . The term is used to explain why a person has a tendency to react to a situation in a particular way. We find it useful to adopt this philosophical term in our classification of human social chemosignals because both its etymology and its functional definition are so close to the findings from our empirical psychological data. . . . Vasanas are those unconscious chemosignals whose functional effects are related to or predicted by their odor qualities when they are experienced consciously. . . . The power of subconscious odors to evoke emotional memory-derived experience in humans is widely recognized. . . . Because they are not necessarily conscious, the term *vasana* may be more appropriate than "unconscious odors," which is an oxymoron.[22]

I find these parallels convincing and meaningful. They bring to mind the taste (so closely related to smell) of Proust's Madeleines from Combray, which bring back to him the rich memories from a forgotten childhood.

Social chemosignals aside, belief in reincarnation has long appealed to non-Hindu consciousnesses. In his magnum opus, *Human Personality and Its Survival of Bodily Death*, Frederic Myers "thought up the notion of 'subliminal consciousness', a model in which the mind is never entirely present to itself, but constantly impelled by inaccessible memory layers. This was a material conception, not an idea of the soul."²³ Karmic thinking continues to surface in New Age circles, in Hollywood (both in films and in the personal beliefs of stars like Shirley MacLaine), and in what might be called American folk belief. An advertisement for a book entitled *Understanding Homosexuality through Reincarnation,* by Numa Jay Pillion, claimed: "A gay man reveals the past lives of himself and other gays through Life Readings to understand homosexuality."²⁴ Most scholars of Hinduism and Buddhism tread lightly upon the karma theory for reasons of intercultural tact (or raging relativism, depending on your point of view); some (including myself) go further, and grant the theory some degree of useful wisdom, at the very least as a powerful metaphor. But a more critical stance is taken by scholars such as Robert P. Goldman, who accused me of being "coy" in my appreciation of karma and who questions my "scientific stance" and "scholarly distance."²⁵ I find myself, therefore, fighting a war on two fronts: against Hindu critics who accuse me of being insufficiently sympathetic to the Hindu view, and against Freudians (and Marxists, but that is another story) who criticize me for being *too* sympathetic. I take heart here from a comment by my old friend Ernest Gellner, who told me that the greatest compliment he had ever been paid was the statement, made by an angry colleague: "Come the revolution, *both* sides will shoot you."

For his part, Goldman has characterized the karma theory as "nonsense." He asks, "What is going on here? What could possibly induce intelligent and well-educated people to take this nonsense seriously?" Then he exhorts us to ask down-to-earth questions about it: How do events in our real, as opposed to imaginary, pasts affect our later lives? What is our responsibility for events to which we were unwilling or even unwitting parties? What are the constraints upon our ability to recover clear memories of our early years? Central to these concerns are the issues of memory—its distortion, loss, and recovery—and guilt—its assignment and displacement.²⁶

His answer begins with a perceptive discussion of the connection between repressed childhood memories and the alleged memories of former lives:

> The feelings and the terrible anxieties they generate are nonetheless real. What better way to partially confess to the former while at the same time fractionally discharging the latter than to ascribe the aggression to someone who both is and is not oneself?

If these dark feelings are the result of real events in one's past life then by all means let us push the boundaries of our past back beyond our childhood into the shadowy realm of "past lives."[27]

"Someone who both is and is not oneself" is a fine statement of the ambivalence of the many people who do believe in the karma theory.

Another tenet of the karma theory also explains a kind of psychological projection: karma can be transferred from one person to another.[28] Goldman finds it preposterous to assert, as the theory does, that "we live in a strange and morally blind universe in which our own actions may see their rewards in the lives of other people while we must content ourselves with the fruits of the actions of still others."[29] Yet it needs no South Asian come from the grave to point out the relevance of this truth to our own lives, from the most tragic level to the most trivial. Caught up in the great Rube Goldberg machine of human causation, we enjoy the shade of trees planted by other people generations ago, and we miss our plane because some idiot rear-ends another idiot on the freeway. The karma theory exaggerates and dramatizes a situation that is entirely banal. It expresses the intuition that the things that happen to us now, and that make us who we are, in large part consist of forces from the past that we cannot control and may not even be aware of.

The karma theory, however, goes on to add the less obvious assertion that the other people who take the guilt or credit for our deeds, or for whose deeds we take the guilt or credit, are forms of ourselves. As Goldman notes, they are people "who—we must take it on faith—were somehow identical with us. We cannot even expect to know exactly what it is 'we' have done."[30] And the prime candidates for this role are, of course, our parents. The theory asserts both an identification and our ignorance of that identification. The identification sits well in a traditional society like Hinduism, which regards a son as his father reborn, but it goes against the grain of American individualism. Even an American, however, will acknowledge that a parent's crime may ruin the life of his or her child precisely because they are, in some significant sense, the same person. The ignorance (of the identification) also sticks in the American craw. Yet even within one life, we are, more often than not, ignorant of the precise deeds committed by the people (usually our parents) who have made us what we are. We are ignorant of them either because we have forgotten (or repressed) them or because they took place before we were born. After all, we all forget many of our former selves—the infant, much of the child, some of the adolescent, or the former marriage, the pain of childbirth, and so forth. One door opens and another shuts; we awaken from one dream not to full wakefulness but only to fall into another.

Hindu thinking does not regard the parents as the only, or even the primary, source of karma. Instead, the transmigrating soul is said to mix its inherited karma with the karma of each of the new parents to form the cumulative karma of the new child.[31] But parents are, I think, the best way to translate the Hindu theory of karma into something that makes sense for people who do not believe in the rebirth of the soul after death. From unknown episodes in the lives of our ancestors, we get not only the shape of our noses but our susceptibility to certain diseases and, perhaps, to certain sorts of people. There is a long continuum of parental influence: closest are the things we remember that our parents did for/to us relatively recently, then the things that they did when we were so little that we cannot remember them clearly or at all, then the things (like smoking or contracting AIDS) that our mothers did to us while we were in the womb, then the things that our parents did before we were born, and finally both the genetic stock and the cultural memories transmitted from earlier generations (events during the pogroms in Russia, traumas suffered during the Depression). The weight of these influences, the realization that we are not and never were a tabula rasa on which we can inscribe ourselves as we would wish to be, is one of the insights that drive the karma theory.

Parents are the key to Goldman's understanding of the karma theory, too, which explains karma by using Freud's idea of the Oedipus complex. All South Asians were abused by their parents and bamboozled by Brahmins, who profited from the naiveté of people overwhelmed by guilt and anxiety as a result of believing the karma theory.[32] He argues:

> What could that complex of emotions plausibly be other than the desire in fact to kill one's father and the powerful mixture of guilt and devastating anxiety that that desire must generate especially in a social milieu in which the father and his surrogates are both abusive and menacing to their sons? ... It is a natural response to emotional and physical abuse suffered at the hands of adults. Such anger, in a culture like India's, can only be turned inward. ... Such an emotional climate, widely pervasive in most cultures but

heavily institutionalized and thinly disguised in traditional India, easily gives rise to a situation where the victim of abuse is encouraged to revere, even worship his abuser.[33]

My emphasis on the role of parents in the karma theory differs from Goldman's in several ways, but most significantly I reject his assumption that the parental influence will be negative and produce anxiety and guilt. It may indeed be and do all of that. (Philip Larkin said it best: "They fuck you up, your mom and dad; they do not mean to, but they do.") But it also accounts for the transmission of talents, positive memories such as those stirred by music and art, and, above all, irrational love, or the ability to fall in love at first sight, generally with a highly inappropriate person who either is or most definitely is not just like our father or mother.[34]

For those of us who lack the imagination to perceive the infinity of our lives in time, it might be possible to perceive the infinity of our lives in human space. Again, the Indian texts tell us that we are karmically linked to all the other people in the world; they *are us*. I have known and respected this theory for a long time, though I have not always believed it. But for one important moment, I did believe it.[35] It was at a time when I was feeling rather sorry for myself for having only one child. I wished that I had had lots of children, and now it was too late. I felt that having six children would have meant having an entirely different life, not merely six times the life of a woman with one child, and I wanted that life as well as the life that I had. This thought was in my mind as I wandered on a beach in Ireland, and saw a woman with lots and lots of children—very nice children, too, and at their best, as young children often are on a beach. Normally I would have envied her, but this time I enjoyed her children. I was happy to watch them. And suddenly I felt that they were mine, that the woman on the beach had had them for me so that they would be there for me to watch them as they played in the water. Her life was my life too. I felt it then, and I remember it now. The idea of my karmic identity with other people had been a mere idea to me until then, but now it became an experience. I was able to live her life in my imagination.

One way of interpreting my epiphany of the woman on the beach was by saying that this realization of my connection to her—and to every other woman who had ever had or ever would have children—meant that my brief lifespan was expanded into the lifespans of all the other people in the world. This is a very Hindu way of looking at one's relationship with all other people. Woven through the series of individual lives, each consisting of a cluster of experiences, was the thread of the experience itself—in this case, motherhood. That experience would survive when her children and mine were long dead.

I felt then that all the things that one wanted to do and to be existed in eternity. They stood there forever, as long as there was human life on the planet Earth. They were like beautiful rooms that anyone could walk into, and when I could no longer walk into them, they would still be there. They were part of time, and though they could not be part of me for much longer, part of me would always be there in them. Something of me would still linger in those things that I had loved, like the perfume or pipe smoke that tells us that someone else has been in a room before us. This is the same "perfume," the same karmic trace of memory, that adheres to the transmigrating soul. And through my connection with the woman on the beach, I would be the people in the future who sensed the perfume that I had left behind in that room, though (unless I was a gifted sage) I would not recognize it as my perfume. Perhaps, since I am not a Hindu, that is as close as I can come to believing that I can remember my other lives. And perhaps it is close enough.

NOTES

1. Emmanuel Levinas, *Totality and Infinity: An Essay on Exteriority*, trans. Alphonso Lingis (The Hague: Martinus Nijhoff, 1979 [*Totalité et Infini*, 1961]), pp. 198–99.

2. Annie Dillard, *Encounters with Chinese Writers* (Middletown, Conn.: Wesleyan University Press, 1984), pp. 20, 71.

3. I am indebted to Sarah Caldwell for this cogent summary, in her introduction to my lecture at Ann Arbor on February 7, 1997.

4. Lewis Carroll, *Through the Looking-Glass and What Alice Found There* (New York: Macmillan, 1885), chap. 2.

5. Shakespeare, *Hamlet* 1.5.

6. Personal communication from David Tracy, August 1995.

7. David Tracy, *The Analogical Imagination: Christian Theology and the Culture of Pluralism* (New York: Crossroad, 1981), pp. 449–50; and *Dialogue with the Other Other: The Inter-Religious Dialogue* (Louvain: Eerdmans, Peeters Press, 1990), pp. 4–6.

8. This perceptive observation was made by Peter Hawkins in his excellent response to an earlier version of this essay, presented at Boston University on March 19, 2003. In this context, the clash between myself and my cousin Robert P. Goldman, far more tenacious and substantive than the clash with critical Hindus whom I have never met, is instructive. The karmic resonances between us become stronger when you know that Bob Goldman is my cousin—by marriage, I hasten to add: his father's sister was my father's brother's wife.

9. I am indebted to conversations with Bruce Lincoln for the ideas in this paragraph.

10. Claude Lévi-Strauss, *Tristes Tropiques*, trans. John and Doreen Weightman (London: Jonathan Cape, 1973), p. 58, italics mine.

11. Wendy Doniger and Sudhir Kakar, trans., *The Kamasutra of Vatsyayana* (London and New York: Oxford World Classics, 2002), 7.1.25–30.

12. Wendy Doniger O'Flaherty, *Other Peoples' Myths: The Cave of Echoes* (New York: Macmillan, 1988; University of Chicago Press, 1995), pp. 14–15.

13. Plato, *Republic* 10.613–20.

14. Urwiek, *The Message of Plato*, 213, cited in Paul Shorey, Loeb Library edition of Plato's *Republic*.

15. *Markandeya Purana* (Bombay: Venkateshvara Steam Press, 1890), 10.1–7, 11.1–21.

16. Wendy Doniger with Brian K. Smith, trans., *Manavadharmasastra* [Laws of Manu] (New York: Penguin Classics, 1991), 12.74.

17. Robert P. Goldman, "Karma, Guilt, and Buried Memories: Public Fantasy and Private Reality in Traditional India," *Journal of the American Oriental Society* 105, no. 3 (1985): 413–25.

18. Sir Monier Monier-Williams, *Sanskrit-English Dictionary* (Oxford: Clarendon Press, 1899), p. 947, s.v. *vasana*.

19. *Abhijnanasakuntalam* of Kalidasa, with commentary by Raghava (Bombay: Nirnaya Sagara Press, 1958), 5.2.

20. *Raghavabhatta* 9, cited in Goldman, "Karma," p. 423.

21. Dr. Seuss [Theodore Geisel], *Dr. Seuss's Sleep Book* (New York and Toronto: Random House, 1962).

22. Martha McClintock et al., "Pheromones and Vasanas: The Functions of Social Chemosignals," in *Evolutionary Psychology and Motivation* (vol. 48 of the Nebraska Symposium on Motivation), ed. Jeffrey A. French et al. (Lincoln: University of Nebraska Press, 2001), p. 99.

23. Frederic Myers, *Human Personality and Its Survival of Bodily Death* (New York: Longmans, 1903), cited in Marina Warner, "Into Thin Air," review of *The Invention of Telepathy* by Roger Luckhurst, *London Review of Books*, 3 October 2002, p. 14.

24. The advertising line appeared in an advertisement from "First Books" in *New York Times Book Review,* 1 September 2002, p. 13.

25. Goldman, "Karma," p. 415, referring to my introduction to *Karma and Rebirth in Classical Indian Traditions,* ed. Wendy Doniger O'Flaherty (Berkeley: University of California Press, 1980).

26. Goldman, "Karma," p. 416.

27. Ibid., p. 425.

28. Doniger O'Flaherty, "Karma and Rebirth in the Vedas and Puranas," in *Karma and Rebirth in Classical Indian Traditions.*

29. Goldman, "Karma," p. 424.

30. Ibid.

31. Doniger O'Flaherty, "Karma and Rebirth in the Vedas and Puranas."

32. Goldman, "Karma," p. 424.

33. Ibid., p. 425.

34. Sigmund Freud discusses sexual overvaluation in *Totem and Taboo,* trans. A. A. Brill (New York: Vintage, 1918), pp. 14–15, 20–21. See also his "A Special Type of Choice of Object Made by Men," in *Standard Edition of the Complete Psychological Works,* ed. James Strachey (London: Hogarth Press, 1958) 11:163–76.

35. Doniger O'Flaherty, *Other Peoples' Myths,* pp. 14–15.

Holy Otherness: Religious Differences Revisited
ELIOT DEUTSCH

There has been a great deal of philosophical discussion over the last few decades regarding the nature of absolutism, relativism, and pluralism in science, ethics, political theory, and other areas of cultural concern—and, most recently, regarding religious beliefs and practices. In the more straightforward philosophical areas, some form of relativism or pluralism seems to be the order of the day. The situation in religion, on the other hand, appears to be somewhat more murky. The reasons for this are perhaps connected with persistent Western theistic claims for an absolutistic, true system of belief; the increasing encounters among, and cross-cultural awareness of, different religious traditions; and the intrusion of religious authority in civil societies in many places today.

    The terms *absolutism, relativism,* and *pluralism* have come to acquire various meanings. To avoid confusion, let me indicate roughly the meaning of these terms that I will assume in my discussion. The absolutist upholds the universality of one true system of beliefs or values. This unique system then serves as the standard by which all other systems may rightly be judged. The relativist, on the other hand, claims that all beliefs and ideas are culture-bound and historically grounded and thus always subject to change in the light of new forms of experience and understanding. Most relativists are convinced that this implies that one is never in a position to make sound critical judgments about other culturally informed beliefs and values, for one must always offer such judgments within the framework of one's own cultural presuppositions and values. The pluralist agrees with the relativist that there are valid alternative ways of thinking and thereby opposes any kind of absolutism. No idea or belief can claim infallibility; all ideas and beliefs must stand the test of experience. However, the pluralist nevertheless opposes relativism, insofar as she affirms that there are criteria available that enable us to make meaningful critical judgments about the beliefs of the other.

The title of my presentation is "Holy Otherness: Religious Differences Revisited." The "Holy" is a take-off from the theologian's "the wholly other," defined by the distinguished theologian and philosopher of religion Rudolf Otto as "that which is quite beyond the sphere of the usual, the intelligible, and the familiar, which therefore falls quite outside the limits of the 'canny', and is contrasted with it, filling the mind with blank wonder and astonishment."[1] In opposition to the rather austere dualistic orthodoxy implicit in this definition, I will affirm a kind of pluralism in the context of a nondualistic metaphysics that upholds a primordial oneness of being. This kind of pluralism makes it possible to celebrate religious differences but at the same time to set forth criteria for appraising diverse religious beliefs and practices.

I

The most expansive and controversial affirmation of religious pluralism on the scene today has been put forth by the noted theologian and philosopher of religion John Hick. In his attempt to develop an account of diverse human responses to the divine reality, Hick argues for what initially appears to be a nondualistic ontology. In his magisterial book *An Interpretation of Religion*, Hick states that "the Real is the ultimate Reality, not one among others; and yet it cannot literally be numbered; it is the unique One without a second."[2] But he further argues that this (Kantian-like) Real *an sich*, Reality in itself, cannot be directly experienced. Reality, "the divine noumenon," becomes "a necessary postulate of the pluralistic religious life of humanity."[3] The religious traditions of the world are viewed as cultural constructions, conceptualizations of that inexperienceable transcendent ground of all religious experience and practice. Knowingly or not, each and every religious tradition becomes a response to and an expression of that divine oneness.

I have argued elsewhere that for all of its generous comprehensiveness, Hick's religious ontology is precisely contrary to a nondualistic understanding.[4] While employing nondualistic designations (at times, Vedantic *nirguna* Brahman; at other times, Buddhist *sunyata*), which in their own contexts are intended to point to experiential oneness, Hick argues that they point only to that which is "postulated."

What, then, we may ask, is the spiritual power or reality of a *postulate* necessary to make intelligible "the pluralistic religious life of humanity"? Just as many anti-realists believe that *a* world is no longer necessary to make sense of *many* worlds, a theist might well argue that a nonpersonal Reality that is not experienceable in itself is superfluous. One God or many gods would seem to suffice.

I would suggest therefore that Hick's whole metaphysics is designed—perhaps unwittingly but, nevertheless, essentially—to provide a basis for an exclusive *theistic* religious pluralism. He argues that various gods of the world's religions are "both idealized projections of the character of . . . worshipers *and* manifestations of the Real."[5] Perhaps so, but how do we know this if we are unable to experience the Real as such? Nondualistic, nonpersonalistic religious experience holds that Reality is the very content of spiritual experience, whereas theistic, dualistic, personalistic experience holds, even in its most liberal, generous reading, that the nondualistic is only another kind of experience among others and is as much influenced by cultural forms and traditional factors as is the theist. Is there not, in the last analysis, a basic incompatibility between the two?

In order to make sense of religious otherness we need a more robust pluralism—one that recognizes that not all religious paths lead to the same spiritual end and that supports critical engagement across religious differences. I will first outline, in rather abstract epistemological terms, a conception of rationality that underlies such a pluralism. I will then apply this conception to the matter of religious differences and their philosophical and religious significance.

II

In the context of explicating his notion of virtue, Aristotle states that

some [actions and passions] have names that already imply badness, e.g. spite, shamelessness, envy, and in the case of actions adultery, theft, murder. . . . It is not possible, then, ever to be right with regard to them; one must always be wrong.[6]

Following Aristotle's lead, we can convincingly argue that in the context of moral judgment we have what I call "exclusionary principles" at work. They exclude certain kinds of behavior from the arena of positive moral value because such behaviors violate core values, including human dignity and freedom.[7] The torture and enslaving of another person cannot possibly have inherent moral worth. The same holds for certain epistemic practices: by their very nature they could not possibly be truth-knowledge-producing, and they are thus void of cognitive value. Exclusionary epistemic principles set the boundaries between the rational and the irrational and, like Aristotle's rejection of certain moral practices, they do function universally.

One such principle is the logical law of noncontradiction: both P and not-P cannot be true. We cannot intelligibly assert that it is and it is not raining outside now. This logical law is—or at least strongly appears to be—foundational for rationality because any rational practice must abide by it. If self-contradiction were not prohibited, there would be no way to distinguish the true from the false.

However, as is widely recognized, the principle of noncontradiction and other "laws of logic" tell us nothing regarding what statements are materially true or false. They function like the skeletal structure of a building that needs to be filled out with walls, windows, doors, and the rest in order for the building to become livable—and livable in many different ways. With respect to any particular epistemic practice (nomic explanation, instrumental determination, justification of actions), one always needs to understand those general principles of thought or action which must be adhered to if that particular rational undertaking is to be possible. One would be irrational if one claimed to be playing a truth/falsity–conducive game but was dwelling cognitively in the realm of what is necessarily excluded.

Although it might sound somewhat disquieting to speak of irrational explanations or beliefs as incapable of being true or false rather than as simply false, this way of speaking has the advantage of enabling one to see truth and falsity across a continuum within the rational. For a belief to be false (or lack truth to whatever degree) it must be formed in such a way as to be capable, at least in principle, of being true. Exclusionary principles that preclude ways of thinking and acting from entering the arena of the true and false altogether thus differ from various rules that regulate particular rational practices, the violation of which would only lead to falsehood or inadequacy.

Holy Otherness 103

Exclusionary principles are of two kinds: the *foundational* and the *operational*. We must adhere to foundational exclusionary principles to even get started in any rational practice whatsoever (for example, again, we must accept the law of noncontradiction). As we have noted, although laws of logic are not by themselves productive of substantive knowledge, their rejection would simply and effectively shut one off from the possibility of attaining ordinary cognitive truth or knowledge and therefore from the domain of the rational. Operational exclusionary principles, on the other hand, demarcate rational practices. While they might be taken to be universal at any one time, they are in principle subject to historical revision under changing circumstances. Foundational exclusionary principles are invariant—we cannot imagine epistemic situations in which they would not be effective; operational exclusionary principles are historically variant, since we can imagine situations where some of the principles could be subtracted from the set while others could be added.

For example, for us, today, any set of operational exclusionary principles concerning beliefs would surely include coherence and falsifiability. A belief must in principle cohere with a web of beliefs that is otherwise sustainable as a background corpus of knowledge. One would be irrational if one were to affirm—rather than simply suspend judgment regarding—a belief that was utterly incompatible with everything else one felt justified in believing. Rationality calls for at least the possibility of systematic order in experience.

A belief must also be framed in such a way that it might be revised or even rejected (falsifiability). It must, in short, be fallible. Although one might rightly hold to the initial validity of one's perceptions/conceptions, one must acknowledge the possibility that they might be false, and accept that they are open to revision in the light of future experience. By this exclusionary principle we would regard it to be epistemically irrational for X to hold a belief Y when, for whatever psychological factors, X is compelled to hold Y and would accept nothing to count against it. Avoiding the so-called "genetic fallacy," we would have to allow that Y might be true. However, because X is in no position to justify Y and in this instance would not be thinking rationally in affirming it, his belief Y would still be epistemologically irrational.

These operational principles are universally binding for us at this time, but they are nevertheless susceptible to alteration and elimination under very different epistemic situations. For instance, it is conceivable (albeit barely) that falsifiability might be dispensable in some possible world because the state of knowledge in that world was so complete that all beliefs held there were incorrigible.

In this actual world, criticizing or evaluating beliefs is a two-stage affair. First, we examine the belief and reasons allegedly supporting a belief by seeing if it violates the foundational and operational principles of the rational. This examination determines whether a belief could be true (or adequate or right) by ascertaining whether it violates the conditions that are accepted as defining the practice as rational. Second, on the basis of various positive criteria adhered to by a given community of practitioners, we determine to what degree a claim is warranted. Here we discover the degree of truth (adequacy or rightness) of the belief, asking whether it fulfills the set of conditions that are accepted by the appropriate community as necessary for truth attainment within the context of various general criteria.

After the first stage described above, the pluralist is strongly inclined to look primarily toward the possibility that alternative procedures within different cultural perspectives are indeed genuinely "alternative." That is, they are potentially offering new and valuable insights and sources of knowledge, and are not just objects of negative criticism. However, the pluralist might still recognize inadequacies in the other's rational practices and show how one's own way of thinking and acting might be better than the other's way. This is so because where universality obtains on the exclusionary side, various positive aims or general purposes will emerge, and they will set ideal standards of rightness for specific practices, although they are always open to revision in the light of future experience. As Stephen Toulmin notes:

> A collective human enterprise takes the form of a rationally developing "discipline," in those cases where men's shared commitment to a sufficiently agreed set of ideals leads to the development of an isolable and self-defining repertory of procedures; and where those procedures are open to further modification, as to deal with problems arising from the incomplete fulfillment of those disciplinary ideals.[8]

This enables us to respond to the relativist's argument. He argues that because we can justify a particular model of rationality only by using criteria already presupposed in that model, it is impossible to judge between it and another model in any proper way, that "truth," in short, can only be determined according to the norms of *our* culture. We respond by bringing exclusionary principles into the picture and showing how different ensuing models may each attain, or fail to attain, a rightness appropriate to them.

Genuine criticism may also be directed to the basic moral values that centrally inform a culture's rationality or style of reasoning. Once again, on the exclusionary side, one is certainly entitled to challenge another culture's actual moral practices and ideals (indeed, it might be argued that one is morally obliged to do so) when they appear to violate the very possibility of human flourishing by betraying the primary values of human dignity and freedom (with the understanding, of course, that our own cultural practices and ideals are open to the same criticism from others).

III

Let us apply this conception of pluralism to religious differences. It ought to be apparent to everyone today that there are many significant and oftentimes incompatible differences between the beliefs and practices of the historical religious traditions (both internal to the particular tradition and external among them) as well as the many contemporary new religious movements that have transformed the traditional religious landscape. I think we would further have to allow that there may indeed be fundamental differences in the core values and aims between these traditions and movements. Some strive for an impersonal contemplative life; others for a transformative experience that may bring about an intense emotional engagement with a personal divine being; and so on. On the immediate practical level, we are also compelled to see in the world today that institutional religion still has its historical capacity to engender the worst forms of hatred and animosity in human beings and to justify the release of the most barbaric behavior imaginable among its various adherents. In almost every part of our planet today we witness—while of course taking into account other social, economic, and political factors—what journalists and pundits everywhere refer to as "religious wars."

But before we attend to religious differences and their giving rise to pernicious religious otherness, let us ask what significance we attach to differences in general. We still continue to hear much from our

Gallic cousins about *différance*—where everything seems to get defined in terms of what it is not. In English, however, we deal with differences in a rather less esoteric manner. We recognize easily enough that there are various kinds of difference (the kinds themselves making for interesting differences). For example, there are differences in simple qualities within a rather restricted range of possibilities (a red pencil, a yellow pencil); in species-defining characteristics (that which differentiates a dog from a worm); in complex qualitative determinations that are rather open-ended (what distinguishes, value-wise, one work of art from another); and so on. Differences of various kinds are always noted relative to our interests and are weighed accordingly. They are also noted relative to our knowledge. A physician or medical researcher looking in her microscope might very well see an important difference between two specimens which a layman, if he saw it at all, would regard as without significance. Getting another person to "see the difference" is thus seldom a matter of just pointing at it.

Some feminist writers have made much of the idea that difference (in this case, between the sexes) does not imply a better or worse situation; biological differences mean just that and no more. Logically, this is surely correct, but psychologically it is very difficult to sustain; our perceptions, as we know, are informed by many factors, including some that are hierarchical modes of evaluation. The moment I see that one thing is different from another thing, I have already brought value considerations of some kind or other into play. One ought, I think, to turn this otherwise discriminatory situation into an opportunity for enhanced discernment and richness of perception—especially with respect to religious differences.

With religion, perhaps more than any other cultural phenomenon, we tend to turn perceptions of difference into attitudes of extreme otherness, regarding that which is different as something which cannot be assimilated into the field of one's potential appropriation. The different becomes the incomprehensible, the alien, the "stranger's religion." In astonishment, one asks: How could someone believe and act like that?

And yet that which is incomprehensible and alien does provide a certain fascination. Rudolf Otto, whom I quoted earlier, once suggested that any phenomenological account of theistic religious experience as such needs to include the manner in which the believer, in her encounter with the divine numinous, feels at once a withdrawing from its overpoweringness and a special fascination with it. "The qualitative *content* of the numinous experience," he writes, "to which the 'mysterious' stands as *form,* is in one of its aspects the element of daunting 'awefulness' and 'majesty' . . . ; but it is clear that it has at the same time another aspect, in which it shows itself as something uniquely attractive and *fascinating*."[9]

Let us go back now to the issue of pluralism and ask: What philosophical basis do we have to engage religious traditions (others and our own) critically? How can we transform negative alienation (even when it embodies a certain fascination) into a genuine pluralism of "Holy Otherness" that allows, when possible, for the positive recognition of various religious truths and values? We need, I think, to answer these questions within at least two of the primary domains of religious life, namely, religious belief and faith, and the experiential ways of attaining spiritual being—what Hick called achieving "Reality-centredness" in place of "ego-centredness."

Our model of rationality has the closest application within the framework of creedal belief, for at the minimum this model enables us to distinguish credible from incredible beliefs, and to recognize different possible degrees of truth and rightness among credible beliefs. It is not my intention to rule out the nonrational in spiritual experience and understanding; quite the contrary. I am arguing only that when religious beliefs are put forward as true propositions they must, if they are to be credible and possibly true, meet certain rational criteria which I have briefly spelled out.

With the possible exception of those who insist, Tertullian-like, that "I believe because it is absurd," I think we can allow that no religious tradition is likely to fail the foundational exclusionary test that I outlined earlier. In other words, basic religious beliefs are unlikely to be self-contradictory. Foundational exclusionary principles are those which believers must accept if they are to even get started on any rational practice whatsoever.

Operational exclusionary principles, on the other hand, might very well be at play. As previously noted, these principles demarcate rational practice but are, in principle, subject to historical revision under changing circumstances. We called attention to two such operational exclusionary principles that we apply to beliefs today, namely, coherence and falsifiability. If someone affirmed a religious belief (say, that God quite literally created the world ten thousand years ago) that was utterly incompatible with other beliefs she holds regarding the natural world (e.g., those derived from geological data and fossil records), we would consider that person irrational. We would further hold that it would be irrational for someone to hold to such a belief in a manner that no evidence whatsoever would be allowed to count against it. Fallibilism is the rule for the rationality of our human beliefs. To be rationally held, a belief pertaining to any state of affairs must always be acknowledged to be open to revision in the light of present and future experience.

Let us assume, then, that a given set of religious beliefs did pass both foundational and operational exclusionary criteria and thus was entitled to enter the arena of the credible—to be, in principle, a bearer of truth (and falsity). As pointed out before, it must then be subject to a second stage: On the basis of various positive criteria adhered to by a given community of practitioners, we would determine to what degree a belief or set of beliefs is warranted.

At the outset, of course, one faces the difficulty of identifying just who is a party to the community of religious practitioners. In the paradigm case of science, some gray areas exist, but there seems to be a well-established consensus as to who can rightfully claim membership in the scientific community and what conditions must be fulfilled for hypothesis formulation, testing, verifying, theory making, and so on. In the case of religion, we do not have such a well-established consensus. Nevertheless, would we not expect that anyone claiming participation in the community of religious belief-making would be sufficiently rational to have some keen sense of the criteria for warranting credible beliefs?

This is not the occasion to try to spell out the general features of those criteria. Here I merely call attention to the role of our expectations in this matter. If they were not satisfied, we would feel justified in regarding the stated belief to be false; if they were satisfied, we would look closely and sympathetically to determine as best we could what truth values might indeed be present, especially in the face of doctrinal incompatibilities. We would engage in a hermeneutical openness to what was being said in its full religious context, questioning our own deep-seated presuppositions and culturally shaped attitudes in the process, and we would aim at overcoming cognitive dissonance in what hermeneutics sometimes rather dramatically refers to as a "fusion of horizons." In short, we would move from an initial logical or critical undertaking of judgment to a more artful hermeneutic effort of understanding and appreciation.

I turn now to religious faith, which, following Wilfred Cantwell Smith and others, I will characterize simply as the endeavor to live in such a way as to realize a set of fundamental religious values, values which one has accepted on the basis of either a commitment to a particular religious tradition and community or one's own particular spiritual orientation and experience. Religious faith, then, is not essentially a matter of belief, a claim regarding cognitive truth. It is rather the intense commitment to realize what one sees and understands to be the most important way of participating in spiritual being.

Now it is certainly clear to anyone who is not hermetically sealed into her own faith commitment that there are a multiplicity of religious faiths abroad in the land. Indeed, within any one of the historical traditions, be it Judaic, Christian, Muslim, Buddhist, Hindu, and so on, one finds many different paths to spiritual attainment. In the ever-popular Hindu text, the Bhagavad Gita, several *yogas* or disciplines for achieving spiritual liberation and fulfillment are set forth, and they are designed, as it were, for persons of different temperaments and capacities.

Do different faiths, different paths, necessarily or inevitably clash? Are there any criteria available to us to judge the relative rightness or efficacy of a particular faith?

The answer to the first question would seem rather straightforward. From the standpoint of someone who adheres to the absolutistic idea that the way to salvation proffered by his or her own tradition is uniquely right—who, say, adheres to the old exclusivist dogma *Extra ecclesiam nulla salus* ("No salvation outside the Church")—a fundamental incompatibility, if not outright conflict, between that faith and the faith of another would indeed be the order of the day. On the other hand, from the standpoint of someone who recognizes many faiths as a historical reality and religious imperative, a diversity of faiths may not only be tolerated but celebrated. A nondualist is certainly inclined toward the latter standpoint. Any faith, being on this side of reality, is stamped with contingency and finitude; nevertheless, any faith that is grounded in spiritual values can potentially be spiritually fulfilling.

John Hick writes:

> It has been self-evident, at least since the axial age, that not all religious persons, practices and beliefs are of equal value. Indeed

the great founders and reformers were all acutely dissatisfied with the state of religion around them. Their criticisms have been either metaphysical (as in the case of Gautama, who rejected the prevailing *atman* doctrine) or theological (as in the case of Muhammad, who rejected the Arabian polytheism of his day) or, much more often, moral.[10]

Hick goes on to say that

behind all these criticisms, ethical, metaphysical and theological alike, there lies a soteriological concern. Gautama's rejection of the *atman* doctrine was basically soteriological: for the liberation to which he pointed is liberation from all that flows from the illusion of an enduring self. The Hebrew prophets were concerned to reject the understanding of God as valuing burnt offerings more than justice and so to open their hearers to a different way of salvation. . . . Accordingly the basic criterion must be soteriological. Religious traditions and their various components . . . have greater or less value according as they promote or hinder the salvific transformation.[11]

I tend to agree with Hick that the most general criterion for judging religious faith is soteriological. With some important qualifications, I also agree with his notion that the available criteria for determining "when that transformation has taken or is taking place . . . will be those that have developed within the [various religious traditions]." "Some of these," Hick states, "are tradition-specific. . . . But in addition to such confessional tests tradition also operates with the idea of the spiritual and moral fruits of true as distinguished from merely conventional religion. This is more promising inasmuch as the 'fruits of the spirit' are universally recognized and respected whereas the value of creedal and communal loyalty presupposes the accident of birth at some one particular time and place."[12]

The answer to the question, Are there any criteria available to us to judge the relative rightness or efficacy of a particular faith, one's own as well as others? is yes. There are indeed such criteria which, apart from "confessional tests," focus on the "fruits of the spirit." The achieving, in varying degrees, of the enduring values of Buddhist compassion (*karuna*), Hindu *dharma*, Christian *caritas,* and so on, in transformed spiritual consciousness—and the peace, serenity, and gladness of heart that appear everywhere as its content—testify at once to the universality of these values as expressed in a plurality of "Holy Otherness."

The entire business of judging, though, is existentially somewhat misleading. In our intense religious commitments, we do not merely sit down and coolly appraise different faiths or paths and then choose one among them for ourselves. Faith is an ongoing process of our total response to our being in the world, and it is formed and shaped by historical and cultural factors as well as by personal conditions, experiences, and creative self-makings. We are chosen by our faith as much as we choose it.

Religious pluralism on the side of faith, as I understand it, thus becomes fundamentally an attitude of openness, an un-self-consciousness that recognizes what is potentially valuable and fruitful in the other's tradition and experience and which may deepen one's understanding of the possible richness of human experience. The religious pluralist is not some kind of connoisseur who objectively tastes bits and pieces of various traditions, liking some and disliking others; rather, he is dynamically engaged with different traditions and expects that the engagement will alter his own deep-seated presuppositions and open up new possibilities of experience.

In closing, let me also say that we should not be so deadly solemn about all this. In the end, I believe, religious faith is a kind of creative play, an engagement, a way of being spiritual, that is carried out for its own sake, without expectation of anything in return. Faith here becomes a surpassing love that informs every dimension of one's being. "Holy Otherness" becomes spiritual togetherness—and when it is achieved by anyone, we may rightly rejoice therein.

NOTES

1. Rudolf Otto, *The Idea of the Holy*, trans. John W. Harvey (New York: Oxford University Press, 1958), p. 26.
2. John Hick, *An Interpretation of Religion: Human Responses to the Transcendent* (New Haven, Conn.: Yale University Press, 1989), p. 249.
3. Ibid.
4. See my feature review of Hick's work in *Philosophy East and West* 40, no. 4 (October 1990).
5. Ibid., p. 266.
6. Aristotle *Nicomachean Ethics* (trans. W. D. Ross) 2.6.9–14.

7. See my *Creative Being: The Crafting of Person and World* (Honolulu: University of Hawaii Press, 1992), chap. 11, "A Creative Morality."
8. Stephen Toulmin, *Human Understanding* (Oxford: Clarendon Press, 1972), 1:359.
9. Otto, *Idea of the Holy*, p. 31.
10. Hick, *Interpretation of Religion*, p. 299.
11. Ibid., p. 300.
12. Ibid., pp. 300–301.

Toward a Theology of World Religions: The Existential Threats
ROBERT CUMMINGS NEVILLE

I

At present, when specialization has defined academic excellence, with the legitimation of boundaries between disciplines by so-called methodological differences, the Boston University Institute for Philosophy and Religion, under the leadership of Leroy Rouner, has struck an alternative course. For Rouner, the important topics are not defined by the evolution of disciplinary agendas in philosophy, theology, or religious studies. They are defined rather by enduring human issues of both chronic and acute urgency. For their understanding and resolution, the issues themselves determine what disciplines are relevant, how, and where. Speakers in these Institute series need to be public intellectuals, responding to the shape of the issues, rather than disciplinary experts who say only what their home discipline might contribute. Although some of us might intend modesty in attempting to limit work within the boundaries of an academically accredited discipline, this in fact would be the hubris of preserving purity while the issues go unaddressed. True humility in the life of the mind is to let the issues dictate the needs for disciplinary inquiry.

The consequence is that we must keep our repertoire of disciplines in a constant state of revision, with sensitivity to the issues at hand as well as to the history of their evolution, and we must think collaboratively with colleagues who can insist on the highest standards of inquiry in disciplines where we can only borrow expertise. Moreover, we must always be aware of the limitations in the integrity with which we address issues, not that we should fear bastardizing our disciplines, but that even with the most sensitive integration of disciplines at our disposal we still might miss the core of the issues at hand.

By framing the Institute series as he has over these many years, Leroy Rouner has led an anti-Kantian counterrevolution. Kant's famous "Copernican Revolution" was to abandon the response of curiosity to nature and affirm "that reason has insight only into that which it produces after a plan of its own, and that it must not allow itself to be kept, as it were, in nature's leading-strings, but must itself show the way with principles of judgment based upon fixed laws, constraining nature to give answer to questions of reason's own determining."[1] Although Kant attempted to justify a generous and universal sense of reason, in practice his philosophy has said that nature must be constrained to fit into what our methodologically defined disciplines can represent: what cannot be represented in those disciplinary terms can be dismissed as unreal. Kant intended to say only that it is necessary to explain things causally within the disciplines of science in order to distinguish that part of our consciousness which is objectively real from that which is mere fantasy.[2] Nevertheless, dismissal as mere fantasy is dismissal into irrelevance. Thus one part of Kant's legacy is that the treasure of brilliantly imaginative disciplines of inquiry developed from the Enlightenment to our own day has been turned into a plague of reductionisms: one discipline says "if it isn't frogs, it doesn't count"; another says "if it isn't flies, it doesn't count," or "if it isn't boils, it doesn't count," or "if it isn't hail, or locusts, or red tide in the river, or the death of the firstborn."[3] We have had astrophysical, biological, sociological, anthropological, psychological, economic, historicist, literary critical-theory, and phenomenological reductionisms, and then philosophical reductionisms to justify all the rest. What should be an enormously rich and varied set of continuously evolving and interacting self-critical tools of inquiry had become an array of separated disciplines by mid-twentieth century, and each was depreciating the method/subject-matter links of the others because they were not harnessed to the leading strings of its own rational constructions. These barriers have been battered down considerably now by the consequences of their own silliness, by fatigue in the fad of doing micro-studies in so many fields that made a virtue out of blindness to external questions, and by renewed interest in systematic connections of kinds of knowledge. Nevertheless, we cannot reintegrate disciplines by thinking about the disciplines themselves. It must come from engaging the issues of existence, including intellectual issues, whose very shape can dictate cooperation and congruence among modes of inquiry.

Another part of Kant's legacy is that the focus on disciplines blinds us to realities for which we have no disciplinary leading strings, until the realities ruin the world we thought we understood. Then we realize that we should have looked around with more curiosity and wonder, and less ambition to constrain nature with our rational constructions. Although Kant believed in pure science for its own sake, we know that science costs money and that money comes mainly from agencies who want to know for the sake of some interest. We do not have to agree with postmodern or Nietzschean critiques of Western culture to see that rational constructions, the questions we force upon nature, serve human interests, noble and otherwise.

II

What I have just said might seem a long and irrelevant introduction to a talk on theology of world religions, but it is not. One of the most comprehensive and disastrous reductionisms of our time is theological. By *theology* here I do not just mean academic theology, although that has been reductionistic enough. I also mean the theologies of our leaders in government and business, of ordinary religious people, of our intellectual elites, and of people for whom religion means little or nothing. For all these groups, the terms of their own religion constitute the leading strings by which they register the religion of others. Even people who reject the religion of their ancestral culture are constrained by the terms of that religion when they try to understand religion in general. Of course there are exceptions to this reductionism in all the groups mentioned. Nevertheless, it is shocking how parochial even sophisticated people in business, government, or the academy can be about the religions and cultures of people different from themselves. In a moment I will say why this is so.

Reductionism in theology is not Kant's fault, of course. It antedates him by centuries, and flourishes in cultures around the globe that have been little affected by Kant or the interests of the Enlightenment until recently. But Kant's exhortation to constrain nature to the leading strings of our rational constructions explains how theological reductionism works: the religions of others are recognized only insofar as they conform to one's own religion's categories.[4]

Theological reductionism is not simple ignorance, although ignorance can cause reductionism. Rather, theological reductionism consists in a privileging of one's own religion's categories for defining what is important in religion and for determining what other religions must be saying, meaning, and doing. The privileging, of course, comes from believing that one's own religion is true, or that one's ancestral religion is the important one to reject. Many forms of this privileging exist. A common way to catalogue them comes from the simplistic distinction between exclusivist, inclusivist, and pluralist theologies of religions.

Exclusivists believe that only their religion is true. This belief itself has many forms. The most common and unsophisticated form adopts some kind of internal authority, such as a scripture that proclaims an exclusive truth, and then concludes that the other religions simply can be ignored for all religious purposes. All that is necessary to know about the other religions is that they miss the truth of one's own. Sometimes more knowledge is required if the others need to be combated, and often much more knowledge of the others is required if one wants to convert them to one's own. Many Americans on the religious right are exclusivists in something like this sense. The great missionary movements of the late nineteenth and twentieth centuries found this kind of exclusivism hard to abide, however. Inquiry into other religions for the sake of converting their adherents led in fact to respect for the others and recognition of many kinds of difference. Indeed, sophisticated kinds of exclusivism can actually engage in a more or less thorough review of the alternatives and conclude that one is in fact best, adopting it as one's own. Sometimes sophisticated exclusivism can be of a conservative bent; think of the spiritual odyssey of Cardinal John Henry Newman. At other times it can be radically liberal, as in those religious movements that reject all others as pedestrian, authoritarian, or war-mongering. One thinks here of some mystical movements, some Anabaptists, some Unitarian Universalists, or some Baha'is. Cultural elites who like to be spiritual though not religious are often liberal exclusivists. Of course these left-wing exclusivists are syncretistic and include many elements of other religions, but their main regard for the other religions is negative and dismissive. Insofar as sophisticated exclusivism does in fact engage with the other religions before making a judgment, it is not reductionistic in principle.

Inclusivism is the view that one's own religion includes the whole or best truth and that other religions have partial or alternative versions of this truth, combined with a positive regard for those other religions. The classic example is the Muslim theological position toward Judaism and Christianity, which are regarded as having partial though valid revelations. Theologians of the Second Vatican Council of the Roman Catholic Church became inclusivist in regarding Protestants and Orthodox as "separated brothers and sisters," and found people in other faiths to be "anonymous Christians." This was offensive both to Protestants and Orthodox who thought it was Rome that had gone wrong, and to people of other faiths who had no desire to be Christians of any sort. Nevertheless, it allowed Roman Catholicism to say that significant truth exists in other religions and that they are all true in important ways that Catholic theology can express.

The difficulty with inclusivism is that it is nearly always viciously reductive. One's own religion dictates the criteria for truth that are fulfilled in other religions, at least in part. Judaism and Christianity are true within Islam because their sacred texts are also sacred with the Islamic canon. Roman Catholicism finds Christian-like traits in practitioners of other religions, and so on. When in a generous mood, most of us are anxious to find what we know to be true (on our own terms) in the faith of other people through analogies of belief and practice. All these are reductive practices because they ignore elements in other religions which do not register in one's own theology but which *are* important in the other's.

The major exception to the claim that inclusivism is generally reductive is the position that all religions really are about the same thing, that they differ in the historical evolution of their symbols, and that they agree to the extent that they address the ultimate reality with symbols that transcend historical differences. John Hick is famous for maintaining such a position in our own time, yet the whole tradition of perennial philosophy holds to this point. From the ancient Neoplatonic lineage in the West to Huston Smith—with parallels in Indian philosophy continuing to Ramakrishna's version of Vedanta, and in Islamic philosophy from Jabir to Sayyed Hossein Nasr—perennial philosophy has claimed that reality has a hierarchy of levels. On the lower levels, historical differences are undeniably important. On the higher levels obtainable by mystical experience and transcendent philosophical reflection, however, the different religions testify to the same truth. Perennial philosophy does not use any single religion's theology for rational constructions with which to interpret the rest; it uses its dialectical method to interpret all religions. Perennial philosophy is reductive on its own terms, therefore, when the valuation implicit in its hierarchy of levels of reality trivializes elements that are mightily important in specific religious traditions. Concern for Jerusalem or Benares does not register as important on the perennial scale, though they are very important indeed for some religions.

Pluralism is the theology of religions that says they are all true somehow. Being "true somehow" means that each religion gets to define truth in its own terms. Pluralism exhibits a generous spirit of tolerance by holding that every tradition with a significant history must have a handle on some important religious truth and therefore is to be respected and honored for that. People often come to a pluralist theology of world religions by participating in interfaith dialogues with deep thinkers of other faiths and finding that they have more in common with them than they do with the "schlubs" of their own tradition.

Pluralism is nearly always a reductive theology, however, because it says that in principle serious disagreements are not about matters of truth. While claiming to avoid an inclusivist claim to a common core of truth among religions, it also avoids claiming that differences among religions can be over matters of serious truth. The exception would be positions that have thoroughly studied all religions, found that they are all unique, and that each is true in its own way. Although this is an ideal for many scholars of religion, at this point in time it is absurd because there is as yet no scholarly basis for it. The world religions are only barely comparable, let alone analyzable in terms of detailed criteria of different areas of truth.

Pluralism is absurd at an even more obvious level. I have never met a Christian who believes that all forms of Christianity are equally true. Jewish theology is no more unanimous than Israeli politics. Islam is notoriously split into factions. Six orthodox schools exist in Hinduism, plus many others, each claiming that its interpretation of the Vedas is correct. Buddhism is divided into competing schools. Daoist religious sects dispute about their scriptures. Confucians have at least two main schools in China with multiple variants in other national cultures, such as Korea, Japan, Vietnam, and California. If none of these "Big Seven" religions is even unified theologically within itself, how can pluralists say they all have their own truths? The only way to do so is to impose some inclusivist model of what counts as true and use this to interpret what is really important in each religion, which of course reduces away the very elements that have led to diverse and frequently bellicose denominationalism within the various traditions.

In point of fact, the distinctions between exclusivism, inclusivism, and pluralism are formal to the point of being pernicious rather than helpful. They treat religions as if they were homogeneous bounded entities that can be represented by the terms "a religion" or "a tradition." Nothing in reality corresponds to conceptions of religions as homogeneous bounded entities, except perhaps the religion of some tribe that has no neighbors and has never been discovered by scholars. All the religions of the world have interacted with others, borrowing and transforming themselves in the process, while influencing the others at the same time. Moreover, religions are not static ways of life lived for their own practices and beliefs. Rather they are ways of practice and belief that engage the realities of life, constantly being transformed by reinforcement or negation in that engagement, constantly in competition with neighboring ways of life for the direction of engagement. The categories of pluralism, inclusivism, and exclusivism are pernicious because they deny that religions are constantly alive. The categories essentialize living existential realities. They identify religions through mere themes rather than engaged life. They reduce living religions to static positions on some chart whose x and y axes are defined by one's own religion, by some superior conception of what counts as religion (which amounts to one's own religion), or by a genial nominalism that says that any religion that claims to be a religion is acceptable on its own terms.

III

We need to abandon the formalistic categories of exclusivism, inclusivism, and pluralism and take a new approach to a theology of world religions. Yet we can learn from the difficulties of formalistic classification.

The first thing a new approach needs is a better way to study the boundaries of world religions, to identify in what they consist and how they differ. I recommend a historical approach based on the analysis of core texts and motifs.[5] I propose that we study the emergence of key religious ideas from the prehistoric past, their expression in core texts, and the different ways those texts have been interpreted and reinterpreted throughout history, interacting with interpretive traditions formed by other core texts and motifs. The ancient Vedas, for instance, evolved through perhaps a fifteen-hundred-year history before taking the oral form expressed in the written forms we now have. Their older elements were interpreted by the Upanisadic movements that systematized them into a way of life quite different from the cultures of their origins. Buddhism and Jainism arose as revolutions against the authority of the Vedas, soon collecting their own canons of the teachings of their founders, of the schools of interpretation, of debates among schools of interpretation, and so forth. Meanwhile, heirs of the Upanisadic traditions reorganized into what we now call Hinduism to reaffirm the authority of the Vedas. As I mentioned, there are six orthodox schools of Hinduism: Nyāya, Vaiśesika, Sāmkhya, Yoga, Pūrva Mīmāmsā, and Vedanta, the last having three main branches associated with the leadership, respectively, of Śamkara, Rāmānuja, and Madhva. Meanwhile the resurgent Vedic tradition interacted with the older, pre-Aryan forms of Indian religion to produce the textual tradition of the Bhagavad Gita and the religious practices focusing on the worship of Śiva, Krishna, and a host of other deities. All of these traditions evolved in continuing debate with the many diverging and ramifying branches of Buddhism until the latter was virtually eradicated in India, moving to Tibet and China. By studying how the ancient texts were used and interpreted differently, and whose fortunes led to the divergence of different schools, it would be possible to see how the current religious situation has been formed by different roots, entangled and divided at crucial points in history. The real identity of any contemporary religious group needs to be understood in terms of the complex history that has led to it.

When Buddhism came to China, it was first in a popular form, in which the Buddha was added to Chinese deities on Daoist funerary vessels, according to our earliest records. Elite Buddhism came to China with its Sanskrit texts, which were translated into Chinese with a Daoist vocabulary. Nestorian Christianity came to China a few centuries later with the same translation vocabulary: the Gospel of John began, "In the beginning was the Dao. . . ." China tempered the factionalism of Indian Buddhism with the need for bureaucratic harmony that came from imperial success; for nearly eight hundred years, Buddhism was a major player in imperial politics, sometimes overshadowing the more ancient Chinese traditions of Confucianism and Daoism. Indeed, the Chinese schools of Confucianism and Daoism came to self-consciousness as Chinese in response to the foreign religion of Buddhism, and as different from one another only with the arising of Neo-Confucianism in the Song Dynasty. The meditative practices of Song Neo-Confucianism owe more to Buddhism than to antique Confucianism, and its metaphysical concerns about Principle and Material Force, and the opposition to Nothingness, owe more to the debates between Daoists and Buddhists than to the texts of Confucius, Mencius, or Xunzi. To understand contemporary Confucianism requires understanding that evolving history, in which India with its (rejected) Vedas was almost as important as China with the splintered legacy of the Yijing (I Ching).

If we are to understand the West Asian religions of Judaism, Christianity, and Islam, we cannot limit ourselves to the Hebrew Bible, New Testament, and Qur'an genealogy. Prophetic apocalyptic, as interpolated into Isaiah, came from the dualistic Zoroastrianism the Jewish exiles encountered in Persia. Did Asoka's Buddhist mission, which reached Egypt in the fourth century, inspire Ecclesiastes? How much of the metaphysics of Wisdom in Proverbs and Sirach came from Hellenistic thought? Paul's view of Jesus as a demigod had its origins in paganism rather than in the anti-idolatrous Levitical code, which abhorred the touching of corpses only slightly less than the appearance of resuscitated ones. Christmas was the Roman Saturnalia and Easter a Norse goddess. Good history allows us to identify the roots of religions and the reasons in dialogue, debate, and historical influence for their current shape; it blows apart the essentialist definitions of wholesale religious traditions required for the exclusivist, inclusivist, or pluralist discussion.

A new approach to theology of world religions also needs to develop fair and stable comparative categories. Theological reductionism manifests itself most in the academic study of religion by defining religion and its important elements according to European Enlightenment models, which are mainly deistic and derived from Christian and Jewish sources.

To develop proper comparative categories is the responsibility of the academic community, and it should treat candidates as hypotheses to be tested for their neutrality and friendliness to the religious elements being compared.[6] Three stages in the development of proper comparative categories must be distinguished. First, we need to develop properly vague categories, categories that have some historical baggage—no other kind exist—but that are redefined so that they are not biased toward one kind of religion rather than another. The process of the purification of vagueness is complicated and requires the criticism of proposed definitions of the categories from the sides of those positions that feel themselves to be distorted or marginalized by the categories. A vague category, properly understood, tolerates instantiation by specific instances that might contradict one another. The category of ultimacy, for instance, tolerates representations of highly anthropomorphic gods as well as highly abstract notions such as the Dao. The second stage of developing comparative categories is in fact to instantiate or specify them with the positions to be compared. The category of ultimacy has instantiations across a wide spectrum, from anthropomorphic polytheism to monotheism, to what some scholars call "henotheism" (the dominance of one god over a pantheon), to Advaita conceptions, and to Shangdi the Chinese sky god, Heaven, the Dao, and abstract Principle/Material Force in Neo-Confucianism. The category of ultimacy also needs to register the Madhyamika Buddhist complaint that nothing at all is ultimate in an ontological sense, and that concerns for ultimacy are the root of human suffering. Once the vague category of ultimacy is specified in a multitude of ways, it is possible to say just how those ways agree, disagree, overlap, or are irrelevant to one another. This is the third stage in the development of a comparative category: the laying out of the similarities and differences among the positions compared. The positions are not wholesale religions, but specific manifestations of them. Each religion might have a wide spectrum of such manifestations. Commonalities along the spectrum of representations of ultimacy might cross religious boundaries rather than reinforce them.

Typological comparisons of religious positions are not enough for a theology of religions, although they are necessary to get the enterprise started. We also need a procedure for identifying how theologies can be true or false. For this part of the project I recommend a program I call theology of symbolic engagement. The phrase *symbolic engagement* refers to the fact that people engage the religious dimensions of life by means of symbols. Symbols shape their thinking as well as their perceptions and behavior. They structure what people take for granted, and how they negotiate the differences between foreground objects of attention and the background that gives them meaning. Symbols are the principal vehicle by which tradition is passed down from generation to generation. Religious symbols are the means by which we identify religious belief and behavior: intellectual symbols for theologies, verbal for religious texts and their various uses, liturgical for shaping personal and communal religious practice, moral as precepts for living, and symbols of dress, movement, gestures, definitions of social roles, goals, and authorities for a host of other things. The analysis of symbols is vastly complex, but these lists indicate something of its range. The symbols direct how people engage the religious dimensions of life. The definition of the religious dimensions of life is itself a difficult theological topic, but for our current purposes we can leave it relatively undefined. It probably has to do with how we live before ultimate matters, but that is a topic for another time.[7]

The general rubric for understanding symbolic engagement is interpretation. "Interpretation," like "symbol," is a very broad notion.[8] In cognitive interpretation, we take a symbol to stand for its object in a certain respect, and that "taking" results in or has the form of an intellectual claim. Interpretation takes the form of action, however, when we take the object to call for a response, as when we interpret a joke with a smile, or duck when something is symbolized as threatening. Emotions, enjoyments, sufferings, queries, and many other human responses are interpretations of objects by means of symbols that we take to stand for the object in a certain respect. At any given time a human being is making a very large number of related interpretations. Our kinesthetic interpretations keep us moving through a world of objects with gravity. Our perceptual interpretations pick out what we have evolved to take as important objects to discriminate in an environment of proximate visible light. Sometimes we think about what we see, a kind of intellectual interpretation, but more often we see what we need to in order to keep on our track of thinking. Our interpretations are organized according to our purposes and needs. But purposes and needs take place within an inherited and appropriated culture with its values and semiotic distinctions, and they rest within the interpretive habits of our bodies. Imagine the density of the bizillion interpretations going on when we drive a familiar winding road, thinking about theology of world religions and not reflecting on what we are observing, but still seeing the twists in the road, judging the other drivers' intents, kinesthetically feeling when to brake or accelerate, and suddenly turning attention to the driving only when we get downtown and have to find a parking place. Think of the interpretive values and purposes that put us in the car in the first place, heading downtown, and thinking about theology. Our engagements with all dimensions of reality are shaped by symbols actually used in context to interpret them.

Interpretations refer symbols to objects in a variety of ways, often many ways together. The philosopher Charles Sanders Peirce distinguished three important ways: conventional, iconic, and indexical.[9] Conventional reference is determined by the conventions of one's culture's semiotic system, as, for instance, when language tells us what is referred to. Any interpretation expressed in words refers conventionally (and may also refer in other ways). Religion is a family of subsets of a semiotic system, and religious symbols are interdefined with semantic and syntactical structures determining how one symbol can refer to another. In "iconic" reference, reality is taken to be *like* the symbol, an icon of it. Peirce's example was the cross in church that is iconic of the cross on which Jesus was crucified. The notion of iconic reference is more general than isomorphism, however, because any description supposes that its object is like what it describes. Scientific theories, for instance, say that reality is like their mathematical equations. To the extent that metaphors describe, they assert a likeness between the expression and its object. Finally, "indexical" reference *points* (like an index finger); it establishes a causal connection between the object and the interpreter so that the interpreter engages the object. Contrary to the theories that say that mind only mirrors its objects, Peirce's theory (and mine) says that the signs in mind connect us with reality so that we interact with it in discriminating ways, hopefully being corrected when wrong.

Indexical reference establishes the causal connection between interpretation and its object. Therefore, if interpretation always requires engagement, then most interpretations must be indexical, at least in part. It is particularly important to notice the indexical reference of religious symbols because many of them aim to transform the interpreter so that something religiously important can become accessible to her. People often are religiously blind, skating on the surface of ultimate matters. Deep religious symbols, learned in scriptures, liturgies, religious speech, and specific practices, are aimed to transform the soul over time so that the soul becomes able to grasp what is really important religiously.

So what makes a religious interpretation true? First, a true religious interpretation genuinely engages its object; and second, it carries what is important or valuable in the religious object over into the interpreter, in the respect in which the symbol refers to the object.[10] The criteria are pragmatic because they focus on whether the interpretation works; does it transmit what is important about the object? They are contextual because a symbol that works for one person or one culture and hence is true there may well fail in another context and hence be false there. The criteria for telling whether an interpretation is true should always be expressed as hypotheses. That is, hypotheses of the first sort say that "the interpretation actually engages its object in such and such a way, and here are the arguments." Hypotheses of the second sort say that "the message the interpreter actually got is the important one to get for such and such reasons, and here are the arguments." A culture's conventional signs are worthy to the extent that they pick up on and do not distort what is really important or valuable in reality. But of course reality shows us that no language is fully adequate to what is important, hence the necessity of inquiry and poetry.

Many people complain that traditional religious symbols today are used without real engagement, only as habitual thought patterns. The language of substitutionary atonement, for instance, runs throughout many liturgies, but it is not meaningful to most Enlightenment people because they believe that responsibility is always moral responsibility and cannot be transferred. Or perhaps the symbols are engaging for some people but not for others, as when persons abused by their fathers cannot engage God with the symbol *Father*, even though they know intellectually what the symbol is supposed to mean.

Suppose that the symbol does engage, however. Does it do so truly? What I mean by this is, does it convey what is valuable or important in the religious object? Does the symbol *Father* tell the interpreter what is important about God? The symbol is false within that interpretation if it indicates something else. In order to tell whether the right meaning is conveyed, we need some kind of other corroboration, which is why interpretations are set within reinforcing and corrective interpretive frameworks. In religious matters, it is often difficult to discern what is really conveyed and whether it is true, because a symbol that means one thing for one person can mean something entirely different for another. What the symbol actually means depends on the interdefinition of symbols in the semiotic system, as well as the context of the actual interpretation, the surrounding cultural values and human purposes, the mode of reference involved, and the respect in which the symbol is taken to refer to the object in that specific interpretation.

So, only concretely contextualized interpretations are true or false. Some contexts are very nearly universal, such as those within which mathematical judgments are made. Others aim to be universal, such as scientific contexts. Religious contexts, by contrast, are highly specific and particular. Why? First, the meaning systems of their symbols are historically particular. Jews and Christians can dispute about whether Jesus was the Messiah because they share the evolution of that office in Israelite religion, and interpret it differently in terms of the affairs of Second Temple Judaism. The symbol of the Messiah would neither engage nor be true or false for Buddhists or Confucians, unless they adopted the history of Israel as Paul's Gentile Christians did. Second, the modes of reference in religion depend greatly on indexicality, and the causal connections established by indexical reference are particular: either they are made or they are not. Third, religious groups have their own historical and social contexts, with variations in social location, generational characteristics, and a host of other variables. Some religious claims might be unique in context to an individual. People in the same religious community might interpret the same religious dimension with the same symbol, and yet, because of their existential differences, that symbol might be true for some individuals and false for others.

For these reasons, the theological assessment of religious truth applies to real interpretations and is always contextual. This is not relativism in the sense that anyone's opinion is as good as any other's. But it does mean that a Hindu with no background in messianic Judaism would not receive the reality about Jesus as the Christ through the usual Christian words. Perhaps Jesus could be likened to Krishna as one who comes down from God, but even the symbols of Krishna do not convey the same things as the symbols of Jesus. This theory of symbols supposes that reality is what it is, but that the interpretation of it depends on what the various symbol systems can convey and on the contexts within which actual interpretations are made. Only in homogeneous cultural situations where everyone shares the same symbols and the same contexts of life can we assume that interpretive propositions are universally true for everyone in those situations. And even then, it may well be a problematic assumption. The feminist movement has shown that the so-called "universal" theology of European Christianity did not convey to women the same things that it did to men.

The context for any interpretation involves at least three elements I have mentioned: the symbol systems, the modes of reference, and the actual social and personal location of the interpreter with layers of values and purposes. To judge whether an interpretation is true, it is necessary to identify all of these to see whether what is important in the object of the interpretation is carried over into the interpreter. It is never possible to find an absolute standpoint. The best standpoint we can find is one that has taken into account all the counterarguments so far. One part of theology is the assessment of truth in religious interpretations, and so it is a theological obligation to identify these and most likely other elements to see whether the interpretations are engaging and true. Theology in this sense requires the work of anthropology, sociology, psychology, neurophysiology, and history, as well as theology in the old-fashioned sense.

In this light, the theology of world religions is suddenly transformed from the formal abstractions of exclusivism, inclusivism, and pluralism. No need exists at all to suppose that religions are bounded entities. Rather, the task is to look into particular contextualized interpretations to see just what symbol systems are in play. They might be central to a textbook religion, but they surely will not be the whole of the symbols that show up in the textbook. Moreover, they are likely to arise from contextualized biases within the textbook religion, as Protestants take different slants on Christian symbolism than do the Orthodox and Roman Catholics, not to speak of the Nestorians, Monophysites, or African Independent Churches. The theology of a Protestant living next door to a Buddhist or Jew is likely to be different in the shadings of its symbols from the theology of a Protestant who knows only Protestants. Theological assessment of truth should be sensitive to the actual symbol systems involved, as well as to differences in social context and personal existential situation. Because religion is crucial in today's affairs, theological assessment of religious truth is an issue of commanding importance, a crucial task for public intellectuals.

This robust conception of theology as in part the assessment of the truth of religious interpretations implies that one should treat the truth of one's own religious tradition contextually as well. We have to abandon the nonsense of saying that, for instance, Christianity is wholly true. Instead, we should ask what kind of Christianity makes a valid truth claim in the specific contexts under consideration. In contexts where Roman Catholicism of a certain particular sort is true, Methodism might not be true, and vice versa. Consider the claim that many Catholics would make, that "Mary remained a virgin all her life." In order to evaluate this claim, we need to start by deciding what kind of reference the speaker intends. If the claim is meant to refer iconically, we should ask whether there is evidence that she did remain a virgin. That evidence would likely involve interpreting church traditions about Mary. If it is meant to refer indexically, so that it bears spiritual meaning, it might well convey the notion of divine purity to Catholic interpreters. In contrast, Protestant interpreters, who have no special symbolic engagement with Mary, would not find that Mary's putative virginity would mean anything of spiritual importance, whether it were descriptively true or false. Or perhaps a generous person would see that in contexts where a particular Roman Catholic interpretation is true, a Wesleyan interpretation might be equally true. The point is that the assessment of truth is an empirical inquiry which determines whether what is important or valuable in the religious object is carried over into the interpreter in the respect in which the symbols interpret the object, relative to all the contextual variables.

We are accustomed to think that the truth of a particular religion should be judged by theologians attached to that religion. Practically speaking, those are the people most likely to have an interest to learn enough of the subtleties of the contextualized interpretations to do so. Yet a theologian from another tradition might make equally good judgments in the matter. In fact, given our propensity to self-deception, wisdom suggests that each tradition should hire theologians from other traditions to raise questions of the actual symbol systems at hand, the modes of reference involved, and the contextual factors of social location, cultural values, and purposes. Or better yet, perhaps we should think of theologians as persons adept at assessing religious truth across a wide variety of contexts.

I see no way to avoid reductionism if we think of theology of world religions as the study of what one religion—say, Christianity—

ought to think about other religions. On the other hand, we *can* think of theology of world religions as simply theology, and argue that one of its central tasks is the assessment of religious truth in the various contexts in which such truth claims are made. One marker to identify contexts is to trace their traditional roots through the history of core texts and motifs. Another marker to identify contexts is the comparison of religious symbols across different systems. To determine what is true and what false, however, a theology of symbolic engagement needs to assess what symbols allow for engaged interpretation in each context, and whether they in fact deliver what they promise.

NOTES

1. Immanuel Kant, *Critique of Pure Reason* (trans. Kemp Smith), B13. See also B16.
2. See the "Second Analogy" in the *Critique of Pure Reason*, B232–56.
3. The plagues Moses brought to Egypt are recounted in Exodus 7–12.
4. We should not think that theology has always been merely reductionistic. In the Hellenistic and Late Antique periods of Western society a rich interchange of religions took place in which people recognized differences as well as similarities among religious options. The medieval European discussion among Jews, Muslims, and Christians had something of that openness to difference as well, even as each side believed the others were mistaken or limited. Debates between pro-Vedic and anti-Vedic groups, such as Buddhists and Jains, in ancient and medieval India were marked by serious recognition and consideration of radically different views that were not reduced to what could be fitted into one's own encompassing view. The rise of Neo-Confucianism in Song Dynasty China occasioned open debate with much mutual understanding, and rejection with reasons, among Confucians, Buddhists, and Daoists. Nevertheless, the rule has been theological reduction to one degree or another.
5. This idea is defended at some length in my *Boston Confucianism* (Albany: State University of New York Press, 2000), chap. 6.
6. The conception of comparison sketched here as an ongoing collaborative inquiry lay behind the Cross-Cultural Comparative Religious Ideas Project at Boston University, the results of which are published in volumes I edited: *The Human Condition, Ultimate Realities,* and *Religious Truth,* 3 vols. (Albany: State University of New York Press, 2001). These volumes contain not only comparative essays written in collaboration by historians of Hinduism, Buddhism, Chinese religions, Judaism, Christianity, and Islam, but also accounts of how the comparative categories were developed over four years of work.

7. On the importance of ultimacy in defining religion, see Neville, *Ultimate Realities*.

8. This theory of interpretation is a development of seminal ideas in the various writings of Charles S. Peirce. These writings are detailed in my *Truth of Broken Symbols* (Albany: State University of New York Press, 1996) but are mainly found in volume 2 of *The Collected Writings of Charles Sanders Peirce*, ed. Charles Hartshorne and Paul Weiss (Cambridge, Mass.: Harvard University Press, 1932).

9. The theory of religious symbols developed here from Peirce is discussed at great length in my *Truth of Broken Symbols*. The theory is illustrated in my *Symbols of Jesus: A Christology of Symbolic Engagement* (Cambridge: Cambridge University Press, 2001). Readers who want to penetrate beyond the terse technical language of the text here can consult those books.

10. The hypothesis that truth is the carryover of value from the object to the interpreters in the respect in which the symbols or signs refer to objects has been developed at exhausting length in my *Recovery of the Measure* (Albany: State University of New York Press, 1989), esp. chaps. 1–4.

PART III

Crossing Borders

When Hindus Become Christian: Religious Conversion and Spiritual Ambiguity
JOHN B. CARMAN

COSTLY CONVERSION: YOHAN OF MALLUPALLE

How do Indian converts to Christianity regard their previous religious heritage? Let me begin by telling you about the first new convert to Christianity I met after going to India in 1959 straight from graduate school at Yale. His new name given at his baptism happened to be the same as my own: *Yohan*. He was a member of the small Madiga community of Mallupalle. The Madigas are one of the two largest "outcaste" communities in the South Indian state of Andhra Pradesh, formerly called "Untouchables" because their touch—sometimes even their shadow—could pollute Brahmins and other high-caste Hindus. Here in the village everyone knew that they were formerly serfs, compelled to do the most menial and unclean tasks for the higher castes.

The Mallupalle community of about eighty people lived in a hamlet a mile from the main village. Because of that distance they did not share the sacrificial duties and the compulsory menial service required of other Madiga families living just outside the main village. They were unusual in another respect: they were farmers who owned their own lands, rather than tenants or day laborers.

Some years before I met Yohan, a Christian catechist living near Mallupalle had been temporarily dismissed from his paid position and therefore had to find another way to earn a living. He persuaded a number of men working on a road gang, one of whom was Yohan, to pay him four rupees a month each to teach them how to read. Although none of them were Christians, he used the Bible as the textbook. Yohan became sufficiently interested in the Gospel story that he occasionally attended Christian worship in nearby villages. A few years later, in April 1957, he, his wife, son, and daughter-in-law were baptized, thus becoming the first and only Christian family in Mallupalle.

When I met Yohan two years later, he had recently refused to contribute funds for the festival for the village goddess, precipitating a crisis in Mallupalle. His brothers punished him by denying his family fire from their hearths and water from the communal well. Despite this ostracism from his own relatives and verbal abuse and physical threats from powerful men in the main village nearby, Yohan stood firm, supported by his immediate family. Then his brothers accused him of invoking magical powers when he prayed to the "God possessing all power"[1] and said they would force him to leave the village. At this, Yohan walked to the nearest Christian congregation a few miles away to appeal for help. A meeting was arranged at which both sides presented their views in the presence of a number of Christians. Yohan's brothers argued that they had been very patient in allowing him to worship a foreign god as his "chosen deity" and to participate in his new sect's peculiar worship. Surely, they said, he knew that support of the village goddesses was a collective obligation of everyone in the village, and his failure to contribute might anger the goddess Poshamma and thus bring disaster to the Madiga community or even to the whole village. Moreover, they added, they were only asking him to do something that most Christians in the three neighboring villages regularly did: contribute to the festivals involving the whole village. But Yohan continued to insist that he and his family could not share in the worship of any other deity than Lord Jesus. At that point a compromise was suggested by the Christian mediators: if Yohan would contribute to the goddess's shrine, would the other eight Madiga families join Yohan the next day to build a prayer hall for Lord Jesus?

> This unexpected application of the principle of group solidarity threw the Mallupalle delegation into some confusion. They announced that they would have to talk the matter over further among themselves and would come back to the [meeting] after lunch. When they returned, Yohan's relatives and persecutors made a surprising announcement: "Either Yohan must become like the rest of us and worship the village goddesses, or we must become like him and worship Jesus Christ. Since we cannot per-

suade him to fulfill his obligations to Poshamma, we shall all have to become Christians!"[2]

What seemed to the Christians present a miraculous decision was followed by a formal request for baptism by all nine families.

That was not the end of the story, however. The next six months brought severe rain, and the catechist who was supposed to instruct the families and prepare them for baptism became ill. Meanwhile, in an effort to dissuade them from converting, the Hindu leaders in the main village threatened to burn down their houses. Furthermore, they pointed out that if the villagers were to become Christian, they would cease to be *Harijans* and would therefore not receive any of the special *Harijan* benefits,[3] such as the larger well they wanted to build. The most effective deterrent, however, was the powerful threat that, if they became Christians, the government lands they had cultivated for twenty years would certainly not be registered in their name. Indeed, the lands would be taken away and given to others. Not knowing that this would have been illegal, the Mallupalle residents asked the Christian catechist not to visit them any more.

For two years the community remained undecided, and Yohan was subject to continuing threats and one beating that sent him to the hospital. Finally the families learned of their legal rights, and the lands they had been cultivating were registered in their names. At this point, about half of the community chose to be baptized; the others were no longer hostile to Yohan, but decided to "wait and see." The majority of baptized Christians in the community still participated in Hindu festivals. Only Yohan and his little family continued their "exclusivist" stance.

CONVERTS PRACTICING TWO RELIGIONS

Yohan's story reveals a variety of converts' attitudes toward their previous religious heritage. Yohan represents what Protestant missionaries have considered the ideal: both an outward and an inward turning around. External conversion requires rejecting the idolatry and caste prejudice of the original religion and joining the Church, while internal conversion requires being convinced of one's sinful state and of the deliverance from sin offered by God in Christ. Through his own reading of the Bible without formal Christian instruction, Yohan experienced a complete turnaround in his inmost being, both intellectually and emotionally (Greek: *metanoia*). He made a conscious individual decision to replace the village religion that had shaped his life to this point with a new, Christ-centered identity that left no room for the fulfillment of social obligations requiring him to participate in non-Christian religious activities. Even ostracism and persecution could not sway him from his newfound identity.

The various responses of the villagers to Yohan's conversion and, subsequently, to their own reflects a different conception of "conversion." This appears to outsiders as an ambivalence influenced by their Hindu background, which is initially seen in their willingness to allow Yohan to expand the Hindu pantheon to incorporate this new foreign god called Jesus. Their acceptance of Jesus as a deity reflects an attitude rooted in the theological concept of the *ishtadevata*, "chosen deity," whereby an individual comes to find his or her own personal meaning in a relationship with one particular deity. This relationship does not preclude the obligations one has to other deities, however, especially those who watch over the village. It is possible to dedicate oneself to one deity while at the same time participating in communal festivals dedicated to other deities whose sphere of influence is concerned with the community's well-being. Yohan's refusal to participate in the village festivals simply made no sense in the context of this world view. In these initial conversations, therefore, we see a response to the presence of Jesus in Yohan's life that is rooted in Hindu theology.

Later, when the other villagers accepted Christ, they did so using a more traditional Hindu framework. Moreover, their initial willingness to follow Yohan expressed a communal solidarity which individualistic Western missionaries encountered in many parts of the world. Because Protestant missionaries were accustomed to the norm of individual decisions and personal conversion experiences, decisions by whole families or larger caste groups to become Christian presented a theological problem. How was one to know for certain that true conversion had taken place?[4] Indeed, the fact that the villagers reversed their group decision to become Christians in the face of threats from the residents of the main village would seem to support this skepticism. Yet, religious identity in India is usually a shared tradition of families and much larger caste and sectarian communities. From this Indian standpoint, Yohan had elevated his individual decisions over the well-being of the community. The villagers' decision to become Christians, therefore, was motivated in large part by a desire to restore the group's solidarity. By being baptized as a group, they thought that they could reincorporate Yohan and his family into the community.

As time passed, however, that solidarity failed and, in the end, Mallupalle became split into two religious groups. The registration of the land in the name of each family may have provided an alternative to their religious affiliation. They were freed to reassess their religious stance with the larger village. Those who chose to become Christians had to relate the new to the old; not all of their religious life was easily rejected. Many developed what might be called a "dual religious citizenship": they gave their allegiance to Christ while at the same time participating fully in the Hindu traditions such as the goddess festivals that Yohan had refused to support.

The double identity of many Christians was already present in the neighboring villages. P. Y. Luke and I have described this as follows in our study of village Christianity in India:

> Most Christians have a Hindu or a Muslim name as well as a Christian name. Some tie a cross round their necks, and on the same thread put a Hindu charm or talisman. Once when the author (P. Y. Luke) was invited into a home to pray with a woman in acute pain, he found the sacred ashes of Kamudu (kept from the bonfire at Holi) smeared over her body in order to ward off the evil spirits. Christians give thank-offerings to Christ, and also pay considerable sums to the wandering religious mendicants of their own caste. They meet regularly to worship Christ, but also on occasion sacrifice a chicken to Poshamma, the goddess of smallpox. They respect their presbyter and sometimes bring him through the village to the evangelist's house in great procession, yet they consult a Brahmin about auspicious days and hours and ask him to draw up horoscopes for various purposes. They keep a picture of Jesus Christ on the wall of their houses, but in a niche in the same wall they have a little image of their household goddess, Balamma or Ellamma. They want the blessings of "Lord Jesus" without incurring the displeasure of any of the village goddesses. Each year many of them celebrate twelve or thirteen Hindu festivals and one Muslim festival (*Muharram*) as well as the two Christian festivals of Christmas and Easter.[5]

Missionaries, especially Protestants, expected Indian converts to meet their standards of inward or spiritual conversion. They often expressed their disappointment that the new Christian converts maintained their caste identities or participated in Hindu rituals. In India, however, joining or leaving sectarian communities sharing devotion to a particular deity or religious teacher has been much easier than caste membership. New converts have had to make decisions for themselves, entering a long debate among Indian Christians about what it means to be Christian in a predominantly Hindu society.

HINDU-CHRISTIAN INTERACTION IN POPULAR CATHOLICISM

Roman Catholic missions adapted more easily than Protestant missions to the caste structure of Indian society and were less concerned with the initial decision for baptism than with the ongoing process of spiritual nurture through the Christian sacraments. Thus they were much more willing to adopt and adapt existing religious forms to express Christian worship. This expression of Christianity through Hindu religious or social forms can been seen in a variety of "popular" forms of Indian Catholic practices. There are two important examples of this in Tamil Nadu: the festivals of the goddess Velankanni Arokkiyam Mata and of the martyr Saint John de Britto.

For the ten days between August 29 and September 8, close to a million people, both Hindus and Christians, come to the little village of Velankanni on the southern coast of Tamil Nadu in order to participate in the festival of Velankanni Arokkiyam Mata, "Velankanni the Healing Mother" (hereafter called Velankanni).[6] Initially this appears to be a typical South Indian festival.[7] It has all of the elements typically associated with these festivals: hoisting of a flag, daily processions of the deities, and the steady stream of people taking *darshan* of Velankanni, who is dressed in a sari and garlanded with gifts from the pilgrims.[8]

Some elements of this festival, however, reveal its Christian orientation. Most important is how people interpret Velankanni herself. Those who know the stories of Velankanni will be aware that she is a form of the Virgin Mary. In the main temple image of Velankanni she bears the Christ child in her arms. Yet, as Paul Younger discovered in his conversation with pilgrims, many do not see the child during their few moments taking *darshan*.⁹ This creates a certain ambiguity that allows both Christians and Hindus to see Velankanni through the lens they bring with them. For some she is Jesus' mother, for others a Hindu *mata* goddess whose powers are far more extensive (because she comes from over the sea) and more permanent than those of the local, fickle village goddesses.¹⁰ This identification is reinforced by the familiarity of the festival elements.

Even here, however, there are Christian reinterpretations of these rituals. Most visible are the ongoing masses that take place in the main church building (which is separate from the shrine), the Way of the Cross pathway, and the tableaus depicting the Mysteries of the Rosary on the way to the temple reservoir (said to be the location where Velankanni first revealed herself to some local boys). The processions are led by a priest, a crucifix, and candles. Prayers are said before the processions begin and songs are sung throughout. There are also elaborate ceremonies each day when the flag is raised, which breaks from the typical Hindu festival, where this occurs only on the first and last day of a festival. These ceremonies at Velankanni are occasions for prayer and petitions "lifted on high" to God. Even here, however, there are elements that remind one of other specifically Hindu contexts, for people speak of what they experience during these ceremonies in language that hints at experiences of possession.¹¹

This festival is an excellent example of the way that popular Christianity can take a Hindu worship form and introduce Christian elements, thereby reinterpreting the festival in Christian terms. Yet this leads to a high degree of ambiguity. Festivals like that of Velankanni allow Indian Christians to remain Indian through the structure of the ritual while expressing their Christianity through the details.¹² Hindu pilgrims, on the other hand, interpret Velankanni through the theological lenses of the Hindu tradition, at the same time acknowledging that she does not quite fit into that paradigm. Both the Christian devotees and Velankanni have hybrid identities.

A similar ambiguity in the interpretation of the object of veneration can be seen in the figure of Saint John de Britto, whose shrine is in Oriyur, a village in southern Tamil Nadu. De Britto was a Portuguese Jesuit missionary who was martyred in 1696 at the instigation of the local king, Setupathi of Ramnad.¹³ Tens of thousands of pilgrims from throughout Tamil Nadu come to this shrine to venerate de Britto, the largest number during the festival occurring from August 29 through

September 8.[14] This festival too is modeled on the South Indian Hindu festival, beginning with the hoisting of a flag and frequent processions. What is unique about de Britto's festival, however, is the emphasis placed upon fertility, especially as seen in the continual circumambulation of his shrine by pilgrims carrying coconut saplings (a folk symbol of fertility in Tamil Nadu). Even more striking is the practice of animal sacrifice, which the priests participate in only with great reluctance, and only to sprinkle the animals with holy water.[15]

This connection of de Britto with fertility is rooted in his martyrdom. During his stay in the Ramnad kingdom, he converted large numbers of people to Christianity. The converts came from the lower caste groups, which meant that de Britto was threatening not only the religious but also the social and political fabric of Tamil society. As a result, he came to be viewed as extremely powerful. The degree to which this power was respected and feared by the people is marked by the way he was martyred: he was beheaded, and his limbs were nailed down so as to prevent the dispersal of his power though them.[16]

It is often very difficult to tell whether people at the shrine view de Britto as a Hindu deity or a Christian saint. Indeed, the ritual form could be said to be more Hindu than Christian, the typical Christian forms of worship (masses and sacraments) being largely ignored by the Christians (although, ironically, most Hindus attend the masses). One priest commented in 1990, "We [clergy] preach about faith, the cross, and the kingdom of God, but for them [rural Catholics] religion is pilgrimage, festivals, and rituals. Official Catholic rituals like the Mass and sacraments have only secondary importance."[17]

These two festivals and many smaller Catholic festivals illustrate more than one of the models already mentioned. For Catholics there appears to be something that we only rarely see among village Protestants: a synthesis of Catholic and popular Hindu rituals. Although participants identify themselves as Christian, they utilize elements from the Hindu tradition to interpret the personage they are worshipping or venerating. The resulting theology is deeply informed by the Hindu worldview, an interpretation that is reinforced by the ritual forms.

However familiar the ritual forms, Hindus are aware that these festivals are expressions of a different and indeed a foreign religious community, whose rituals, including the masses, they should attend with respect if they are to benefit from their power. The Hindus encountering Lord Jesus among village Protestant congregations are comparable in their attitudes to other Hindus participating in festivals to Christian saints in a Catholic milieu. In most cases I would not call them converts; they have been "touched" but not "turned." Even so, every pilgrim's experience is slightly different, and some of these Hindu pilgrims might say not only that their lives have been touched by the presence of Lord Jesus or of Christian saints, but that they have also been turned in a new direction, even though remaining in Hindu society.

The views of most past converts to Christianity were never recorded and rarely survive in the memory of their own families. Still less are the attitudes of participants in Hindu or Christian festivals accessible to outside observers. Not surprisingly, therefore, studies of conversion have focused on the relatively few educated Indians, mostly of high-caste Hindu background, who have written about their experiences and articulated their convictions in prose or poetry. In this essay I have deferred considering the evidence of such educated converts until now. They are not the whole story, but they are an important part of it. Indeed, we find in their writings specific examples of the ambivalence or ambiguity already noted.

INDIVIDUAL EXAMPLES OF COMBINING
ACCEPTANCE AND REJECTION

The three high-caste Hindus described here who became Christian converts both rejected and retained their particular Hindu heritage, each in his or her own characteristic way. I cannot mention the first, Pandita Ramabai, without also saying a word about the two men who most influenced her. One was the scholar and publicist Rammohan Roy, who founded a new Hindu Unitarian movement under the influence of Islam, Protestant Christianity, and Western rationalism.[18] The second was Nilakantha (later Nehemiah) Goreh, one of the few Indians to write both against Christianity before his conversion and in support of his new religion after he became a Christian.[19] Equally noteworthy are his multiple changes of religious alliances: from the worship of Śiva to the worship of Vishnu, to Rammohan Roy's Unitarian reform, and finally to orthodox Anglicanism.

The neatly "orthodox" conclusion of Goreh's spiritual quest did not, however, apply in the case of the multiple "conversions" of his younger friend Pandita Ramabai, who was recognized as an orthodox

Brahmin scholar before she was drawn to the Unitarian theism of the Brahmo Samaj. Goreh was instrumental in her decision to become a Christian, as she commented in a letter to a friend:

> It was Father Goreh's letter that proved that the faith which I professed (I mean the Brahmo faith) was not taught by our Veda as I had thought, but it was the Christian faith which was brought before me by my friends disguised under the name of Brahmo religion. Well, I thought if Christ is the source of this sublime faith, why should I not confess Him openly to be my Lord and my Divine Teacher?[20]

Unlike her Indian Christian mentor, Ramabai's own statement of faith leans in the direction of Unitarianism. She would only accept Christ as the messenger of salvation, not as one identical with God, and the Christian doctrine of the Trinity seemed too close to the polytheistic Hindu doctrine of "God having Three Personal Forms" (the *Trimurti*), which she emphatically rejected. While her Anglican missionary sponsors were horrified at her heretical views, they conceded that her uncompromising monotheism might make her a more effective teacher in India, where Hindus so readily understand God in terms of polytheism or pantheism.[21] In fact, Ramabai shared much of Rammohan Roy's critique of traditional Hindu polytheism and of the Vaishnava doctrine of divine descent (*avatara*). Ramabai made a much more decisive break with her Hindu past than did Roy, however, and therefore criticized the existing translation of the Bible for using many Hindu theological terms.[22] When we add to this her vigorous involvement in efforts to improve the lot of Hindu women and her sharp criticism of both Hindu and British patriarchy,[23] we have a glimpse of a very independent-minded theologian.

The Roman Catholic theologian Brahmabandhav Upadhyay[24] exemplifies a different kind of ambivalence toward the Hindu tradition and his Christian "establishment." He distinguished between being a Hindu culturally and following a Catholic Christian spiritual practice. He considered himself a "Hindu-Christian" at a time when the Western missionary leadership, both Roman Catholic and Protestant, rejected the possibility of such a hyphenated religious existence. For him, Indian asceticism and Śankara's philosophy both provided appropriate means for expressing the truth of Christianity—indeed, for expressing Christian truth *better* than the religion of Western missionaries and colonial authorities.²⁵ He shared with Pandita Ramabai a pride in their Brahmanical tradition and a questioning of foreign Christianity. While she saw an emphasis in the Christian Gospel sharply different from traditional Hindu doctrine and social morality, however, Brahmabandhav saw Christian and Hindu truth merging in both his theology and his new form of asceticism. By the time of his death, his relations with Roman Catholic officials had become exceedingly strained, and his Hindu friends claimed that he had once again become a Hindu.

A final example is Krishna Pillai, from South India. Unlike the North Indian converts discussed above, Krishna Pillai never wrote in English. He did, however, write many books in Tamil and composed a number of hymns still sung by Tamil Protestants. Dennis Hudson has shown an intriguing parallel between the convert's former Tengalai Srivaishnava ritual status as Vishnu's slave and his understanding of his status as a Christian saved solely by Christ's atoning sacrifice.²⁶ Krishna Pillai himself, however, never seems to have recognized this parallel. He wrote later about his conversion and included the first verse he composed after becoming convinced to become a Christian. Hudson translates it as follows:

> O Sea of Grace, O Sun that dispels the world of Darkness, O God who has released precious life for this your slave. On this occasion when you make a devotee of me, a low wicked fellow not knowing the meaning of Truth, I offer my heart to only you, for the form of Dharma.²⁷

Hudson comments that this verse "in no way indicates the name of the Lord in whom he has taken refuge, and the final epithet *Dharma-murti* ("The Image of Dharma") calls to mind the figure of Rama, who embodied dharma on earth and to whom he had been devoted as a Hindu."²⁸ However Vaishnava his language, Krishna Pillai nevertheless considered himself chosen by Christ to be his devotee from that time on.

Krishna Pillai later wrote a number of polemical tracts against Hindu and specifically Vaishnava beliefs. The language of one was so extreme that the Christian missionaries responsible for its publication urged him to revise his statements to give less offense to Hindus. Krishna Pillai's poetry, however, continued to use typical Hindu terms. His major work, "The Pilgrimage to Salvation" (*Raksanyayatrikam*), was a Tamil version of John Bunyan's *Pilgrim Progress* that took the Tamil version of the *Ramayana* as its literary model. Thus the same convert who referred to the image-incarnation of Lord Vishnu in the central Srirangam temple as a "demon" retained his respect for that most human of Vishnu's incarnations, Lord Rama.

We should note briefly another important dimension to Krishna Pillai's life as a Christian. He and his brother continued the "pure" vegetarianism of his high-caste Hindu past, and Muthiah Pillai defended the right of Vellala Christians to retain their distinctive religious forms, specifically those setting them apart from low-caste Christians. From the standpoint of some English missionaries, the caste pride of Vellalas was un-Christian, but for the two brothers their own distinctive Tamil Christianity, "sitting together, separately," was a mark of their Christian integrity.[29]

Throughout, these three intellectuals questioned the need to abandon their religious heritage completely as they became Christians. Each found value in elements from that religious heritage; each argued that some elements, whether theological, ritualistic, or social, are compatible with the Christian message. However, they did not agree on what elements to keep, or on how their new Christian commitments differed from their earlier views. In other words, they were ambivalent over how to express their new identities in ways that did not deny their cultural identities as Indians. None of them believed that one must adopt Western cultural forms to become truly Christian. How to embody Christianity in Indian forms remains controversial.

THE CHALLENGE OF DALIT THEOLOGY

Many Christians want to affirm their solidarity with Hindus in a national culture that includes a distinctively Indian way of being religious. In this contemporary Indian Christian approach, articulated especially by some Roman Catholic theologians, "conversion" of any kind, whether of individuals, groups, or the nation as a whole, can suggest repentance and spiritual deepening, but certainly not a rejection of what is regarded as a common Indian spiritual heritage. Whereas evangelical Protestants continue to regard all Hindu religion as a demonic culture that must be rejected by true Christians, other Protestants desire to identify themselves with a much larger group outside the small Christian minority. However, the identification is not with

India's Hindu majority but with the substantial Dalit minority (at least one hundred million).

Dalit intellectuals, both non-Christian and Christian, claim that Dalits have never really been Hindus: they were ranked below the lowest Hindu castes and considered so polluted that in South India they could not live in the village proper; they were also excluded from worshipping at Hindu temples served by Brahmin priests. Dalit theologians frequently regard conversion as a group process involving corporate decisions by Dalit communities to move away from their traditional religion and toward a new religion, articulated by Christian missionaries. Their own tradition is interwoven with other strands of popular religion, all of which are informed by the Brahmanic world vision and place Dalits wholly outside the system, as Untouchables. In the converts' minds, conversion to Christianity might enable them to benefit from the missionaries' power to alleviate injustices (strengthened by their connection with the colonial government), and it also holds the potential for empowerment through education and "moving up" to more dignified forms of employment (often in the towns and cities).[30]

From the perspective of those speaking for Dalits, conversion to Christianity is a way of escaping the cosmically ordained oppression that is embodied in the caste system.[31] While missionaries have joined Dalits in a concerted attack upon the caste system, Dalits have learned that becoming Christians does not automatically lead to equality, freedom, and dignity, since Hindus continue to treat them as outcastes. Furthermore, the Christian community itself has come to be shaped along caste lines. Nevertheless, Dalits continue to envision a new social order, still unrealized.

The contemporary Roman Catholic and Protestant positions in India are each indebted to the experience of converts, but they identify opposite elements as important in the conversion process. The Catholic affirmation of Brahmanic spirituality as the core of generic "Indianness" (*Hindutva*) emphasizes one of the elements of the religious past and projects it into an anticipated future of interreligious harmony. Protestant Dalit theology, on the other hand, rejects everything Brahmanical, both in Indian society and in the theology and practice of Indian Christians. It seems difficult for Dalit theologians to agree on aspects of the Dalit religious heritage that are or could be revalorized in their new Christian existence. The memory of the past sufferings and indignities lends force to the theme of escape from caste oppression, but the religious resources of the village—those behind the unbending resolve and the quiet dignity of a Yohan of Mallupale—remain to be explored, if the promise of liberation is to become a reality within the village.

THE TRANSFORMING DREAM: FROM KRISHNA TO KRISTU

Indian converts to Christianity express diverse attitudes toward their previous religious heritage, as do those who have written about this subject. Some Hindu leaders regard "conversion" as an imperialist-induced betrayal of the Indian spiritual heritage. My interest in this subject was focused by a research assignment that seemed a distraction at the time. I had come back to India, which I had left fifteen years earlier, as a Christian missionary engaged in a doctoral research project. My theological interests in Christian views of Hindus had led to a study of one of the most important Hindu thinkers, Ramanuja. My research assignment to assist the Rev. P. Y. Luke in a study of village Christian congregations seemed to take me in a very different direction. Indeed, I thought I was postponing my study of Hinduism in order to address the situation of village Christians: What did it mean for them to live as a small Christian minority in the midst of traditional Hindu society? It turned out that our study had much more to do with Hinduism than I had expected, since the lives of these Christians were still intertwined with the established religious practices and beliefs of all the villagers. Our study also had more to do than I realized with the original theological questions that I never quite reached in my doctoral dissertation on Ramanuja: How should Christians view "other religions," particularly Hindu religious traditions? Only recently have I returned to this question directly, and it is still more recently that I have realized the importance of Christian converts' experiences in framing and trying to answer this question.

The strangest story I encountered was one I might not have believed if I had not heard it firsthand.

A young Sudra named Venkatesvara had a dream in which he thought he saw Krishna, who commanded him to accept the next marriage proposal received in the mail. A few days later such a letter did arrive, but it was from a Christian who wanted to find a husband of the same caste for his daughter, provided the young man would first become a Christian. The boy finally agreed, although this offer was less attractive financially than others he had previously received, because he came to believe that the figure he had seen in his dream was not Krishna but Jesus Christ. He was instructed in the Christian faith for several weeks by his prospective father-in-law, a landowning farmer who had himself become a Christian several years previously as the result of a miraculous healing.

This farmer had been a staunch Hindu who never listened to Christian preaching and had once beaten a Christian evangelist who had come to his village to preach. At one time he developed a chronic abdominal pain which he vainly tried to cure with various medicines. He also went to the hospital for treatment but secured no relief. One night in his dreams he had a vision of Jesus Christ, who told him that by a certain date he would be well. To his surprise, on exactly that date he felt perfectly all right. After this experience he became interested in the Christian Church and was subsequently baptized. Later he began to effect healing through prayer in the name of Jesus. According to his own report, his young son once became ill and actually died, but after he had "prayed with tears" at his bedside for two hours, his son came back to life. He is said to have healed many people in his locality through prayer.

After this instruction from his father-in-law, Venkatesvara was baptized with the name of Christopher Dayanand and soon afterwards married. Then he decided that he wanted to learn more about Christian faith, and enrolled in a one-year course at Medak. Before the end of the year he decided to offer himself for Christian ministry and take a three-year course in a theological college. Soon after coming to Medak, Christopher entered into regular conversations about Christianity with a group of young men of landowning caste in a village near Medak, where the Sudras had never previously shown any interest in the Gospel already accepted by the outcastes of that village. This is an actual occurrence, but it may also be a symbol of great significance: the attribution to the Lord Jesus of the power and the presence which have previously been ascribed to Lord Krishna or the other "Lords" of the village mind.[32]

This story and the others previously recounted suggest that the impact of the Christian Gospel on the South Indian village mind has sometimes been very different from the reception by educated Hindus in Indian cities. It appears that in those villages where the "Word of God" is least read and Christian social institutions are most fragile, the Word of God who became human in Jesus has escaped from the Bible and speaks directly to people—not only to Christians but also to Hindus. It is understandable that not only secular Westerners but also pious Christians in India are skeptical about Christ's appearances to those who have not spent years preparing for such a high point of religious experience, who do not faithfully pray to Jesus in their congregations or at home, who may not even recognize that it is Jesus Christ whom they have encountered. Certainly it is true that these reports come from those who do not find it unprecedented to encounter a deity in a dream. What made the appearance of Krishna in Venkatesvara's dream noteworthy was the command conveyed—"accept the next marriage proposal"—and the unexpected consequence of his obedience to that divine command. We in the West are more familiar with another kind of Hindu thought in which dreams are an evident metaphor for unreality—the world is a dream (*maya*). It is therefore worth remembering that for many Hindu traditions, quite notably in the theology of Ramanuja, dreams are real and the divine communication they convey must be taken seriously. Venkatesvara was a village Hindu of Vaishnava background. He was given the name of the great temple image-incarnation of Lord Vishnu in the hills above Tirupati—Venkatesvara. His subsequent drastic change of mind and social status—conversion in both the inner and outer sense—involved a good deal of conventional *catechesis*, unusual mainly because it was begun by a layman, his future father-in-law. There is nothing "supernatural" about the rest of Christopher Dayanand's story, but that story would not have started without the puzzling dream. Christopher came to believe that Jesus had appeared to him in the guise of Krishna.

In the experience of Christian encounter with "other gods," there have been two evident alternatives. One is to treat other deities as demons, real powers that are dangerous rivals to Christ for the possession of the soul. The second is to treat "other gods" as figments of human imagination. Whether or not they are given outward material form, they are "idols." However, I suspect that Christopher Dayanand accepted neither of these alternatives but was influenced by two other models. One was the theistic Hindu interpretation of "other gods" as real beings with great power who are ultimately subordinate to the Supreme Lord, of whom they are in fact devoted servants, even though their human devotees mistakenly give them supreme allegiance. From what Christopher told us of his own new theology, however, a fourth model can be discerned, for Vishnu did not remain a separate deity, but simply merged with the Second Person of the Trinity. Vishnu active in our world, however, is much more concrete and manifold. Krishna may be a genuine avatar for a previous age, but Jesus is the avatar for the present age, and, quite possibly, Krishna is to be regarded as the servant of Jesus Christ.

Venkatesvara was a young man from the washerman's caste who thought he was having a dream encounter with Lord Krishna, the patron deity of his family. It was only *after* he was persuaded to become a Christian—as a condition for marriage to the daughter of a new Christian convert—that he decided that the god who appeared in his dream was not Lord Krishna but Lord Jesus. In this case it was his father-in-law who had experienced Jesus' miraculous healing. Christopher Dayanand's "miracle," if we may call it that, was the entire process through which he decided not only to be baptized, joining the religion of the outcastes, but also to enroll in a theological seminary. His own Christian revision of the Puranic story of the world's creation, told to us *before* he started his Christian theological education, impressed me then as a remarkably genuine "Indian Christian theology."

Is the phenomenon of Lord Jesus appearing in dreams, rescuing people from illness and death, and giving strange commands a reflection of village Hindu beliefs that may be more familiar to the middle and higher Hindu castes than they are to the lowest castes? Certainly, Lord Jesus the Healer appears in a divine-human form familiar to Hindus who are acquainted with the avatars of Vishnu and the sudden appearances of Śiva, but this avatar is not enshrined in a temple from which outcastes are excluded. His shrine is in the middle of the outcaste corner of the village, across the road or even across a field from the rest of the village. Lord Jesus is worshipped there, but his power extends beyond the humble hall where services are held and the still humbler huts of his worshippers. Sometimes he enters into the dreams and into the bodies of Hindus with his healing power. Those who are attracted to him are welcome to worship him, but while they may pray in private, the public worship of Lord Jesus takes place in what Brahmins consider polluted ground, which higher-caste Hindus seek to avoid: the outcaste section of the village.

I began with Yohan and I end with Christopher Dayanand. These two converts represent millions whom I never met, many of whom were illiterate and most of whom never wrote down what they thought about the religious tradition they left—at least in part—when they became Christians. Once in a while some new document is discovered and published that gives us one more voice, but most of the voices we can only imagine, or else confess that we simply do not know what they thought. Even if we had been able to talk with them across the barrier of language, they might have been puzzled with our questions, and we might have been confused by their replies. In some cases we might learn more by observing their daily lives and their participation in festivals. In any case, we would gain a different impression from these converts than from the articulate, self-confident, but often one-sided pronouncements of Western Christian theologians.

In retrospect, I am grateful for the major delay in my doctoral research caused by the study of village Christians. I still believe that it is important to study major Hindu thinkers. I suggest, however, that we can also learn much from Christians who have pondered the challenges and the costs of Christian discipleship without the luxury of academic detachment or the freedom to avoid personal decisions. We can learn from stubborn exclusiveness and from imaginative synthesis, and also from failure of nerve or utter confusion. We shall understand these Christians better if we see them in their particular Indian contexts. Perhaps we shall discover something of what those converts saw in a command of the Gospel, a dream of Lord Jesus, or a miraculous healing.

NOTES

I thank my research and administrative assistant, Tamara S. J. Lanaghan, for the assistance she provided in preparing this essay.

1. The phrase he used is *Sarva śakti-gala Deva*. The word *śakti*, which has the generic sense of "power," has a number of specific and more emo-

tionally charged meanings for village Hindus. It can be used as the name for the great feminine Divine Power, consort of Śiva, or for local Powers (the village goddesses). It also can be used to refer to the specific mysterious power or powers invoked in performing black magic. Yohan's brothers feared that, in using this phrase, he was worshipping a mysterious Christian Śakti in the interests of black magic (P. Y. Luke and John B. Carman, *Village Christians and Hindu Culture: Study of a Rural Church in Andhra Pradesh South India*, World Studies of Churches in Mission [London: Lutterworth Press, 1968], p. 159).

2. Ibid., p. 160.

3. In an effort to reform Hindu attitudes, Mahatma Gandhi called the Untouchables *Harijans*, "children of Hari [God]," a name still used by the government, in efforts to improve their economic lot and educational status. The current pan-Indian name that some of their leaders give themselves is *Dalit*, "crushed" or "oppressed."

4. In the first American Baptist mission station in Andhra Pradesh, for example, it was initially expected that prospective converts would leave their homes and come to live near the missionary so that they could be daily tutored and observed in developing a Christian style of life, breaking completely with their previous Hindu practices. That practice was challenged by a recent convert named Periah, who insisted that the prospective converts could not leave their village to receive baptism. The young missionary John Clough went against established practice and acceded to this request. Within months, inquiries began to trickle in from Periah's relatives and neighbors in his Madiga outcaste community, and within a few years the "trickle" became a "flood" (Alvin T. Fishman, *For This Purpose: A Case Study of the Telugu Baptist Church in Its Relation with the South Indian Mission of the American Baptist Foreign Mission Societies in India* [Guntur: Andhra Christian College, 1958], p. 8). Many sought baptism during a famine, but Clough refused to baptize anyone until the famine was over; he wanted no "rice Christians." On the appointed day for baptism, when thousands came to the bank of the Gundlakamma River, he and his assistants spent all day interrogating the applicants to assure themselves of the sincerity of their conversion (Kenneth Scott Latourette, *The Great Century in North Africa and Asia A.D. 1800–A.D. 1914*, History of the Expansion of Christianity 7 [New York and London: Harper and Brothers Pubs., 1944], pp. 166–67).

5. Luke and Carman, *Village Christians and Hindu Culture*, p. 165.

6. Paul Younger, "Healing Mother Velankanni: Hindu Patterns of Worship at a Christian Shrine," chap. 9 in *Playing Host to Deity: Festival Religion in the South Indian Tradition* (Oxford and New York: Oxford University Press, 2002), p. 115.

7. Margaret Meibohm gives descriptions of this festival in her "Past Selves and Present Others: The Ritual Construction of Identity at a Catholic

Festival in India," in *Popular Christianity in India: Riting between the Lines*, ed. Selva J. Raj and Corinne G. Dempsey (Albany: State University of New York Press, 2002), pp. 63–66. Cf. Younger, "Healing Mother Velankanni."

    8. "Taking *darshan*" refers to the central ritual act in Hinduism that involves the reciprocal "seeing" between deity and devotee. Cf. Diana L. Eck, *Darśan: Seeing the Divine Image in India*, 2nd ed. rev. (New York: Columbia University Press, 1996), passim.

    9. Younger, "Healing Mother Velankanni," p. 112.

    10. Ibid., pp. 113–14.

    11. Meibohm, "Past Selves and Present Others," pp. 68–69.

    12. Ibid., p. 69.

    13. For a summary of the story of this martyrdom, see Selva J. Raj, "Transgressing Boundaries, Transcending Turner: The Pilgrimage Tradition at the Shrine of St. John de Britto," in *Popular Christianity in India*, ed. Raj and Dempsey, p. 86.

    14. Ibid., p. 87.

    15. Ibid., pp. 90, 97.

    16. Ibid., p. 86.

    17. Ibid., p. 103.

    18. Bruce Carlisle Robertson, *Raja Rammohan Roy: The Father of Modern India* (New Delhi: Oxford University Press, 1995).

    19. Richard Fox Young, *Resistant Hinduism: Sanskrit Sources on Anti-Christian Apologetics in Nineteenth-Century India*, Publications of the De Nobili Research Library 8 (Vienna: Indological Institute, University of Vienna; and Leiden: Brill, 1981).

    20. Gauri Viswanathan, *Outside the Fold: Conversion, Modernity, and Belief* (Princeton, N.J.: Princeton University Press, 1998), pp. 133–34, n. 31.

    21. S. M. Adhav, *Pandita Ramabai*, Confessing the Faith in India Series 13 (Bangalore: Christian Institute for the Study of Religion and Society; and Madras: Christian Literature Society, 1979), pp. 166ff.

    22. Ibid., p. 196.

    23. Meera Kosambi, ed. and trans., *Pandita Ramabai through Her Own Words: Selected Works* (New Delhi and Oxford: Oxford University Press, 2000).

    24. Cf. two recent studies of Brahmabandhav Upadhyay's life and thought: Julius J. Lipner, *Brahmabandhab Upadhyay: The Life and Thought of a Revolutionary* (New Delhi and Oxford: Oxford University Press, 1999); and Timothy C. Tennent, *Building Christianity on Indian Foundations: The Legacy of Brahmabāndhav Upādhyāy* (Delhi: ISPCK, 2000).

    25. See especially Lipner, *Upadhyay*, pp. 130–56, and Tennent, *Building Christianity*, pp. 208–99.

26. D. Dennis Hudson, "Hindu and Christian Parallels in the Conversion of H. A. Krishna Pillai 1857–1859," *Journal of the American Academy of Religion* 40, no. 2 (June 1972): 199.
27. Ibid., p. 197.
28. Ibid., pp. 197–98.
29. D. Dennis Hudson, "'New Missionaries' and the Tanjore Congregation," chap. 9 in *Protestant Origins in India: Tamil Evangelical Christians, 1706–1835*, Studies in the History of Christian Missions (Grand Rapids, Mich.: William B. Eerdmans; and Richmond, Va.: Curzon Press, 2000), pp. 153–72.
30. This section is indebted to a preliminary draft of a forthcoming article by Sathianathan Clarke, "Conversion to Christianity in Tamilnadu," in *Religious Conversion in India: Modes, Motivations, Meanings*, ed. Rowena Robinson and Sathianathan Clarke (Delhi: Oxford University Press, forthcoming). Professor Clarke wrote his doctoral dissertation on Dalit religion while at Harvard. It is now published under the title *Dalits and Christianity: Subaltern Religion and Liberation Theology in India* (Delhi: Oxford University Press, 1998).
31. In the British Methodist Mission to the semi-independent princely state of Hyderabad, one of the missionaries, C. W. Posnett, attained almost legendary status in the memory of village Christians. He was a huge man who came from England in the early twentieth century and imposed his vision on the mission, building a school, a hospital, and a huge cathedral in Medak, a few miles from Mallupalle. He had the reputation of being able to intervene forcefully to protect those whom he called "our village Christians" against the worst injustices against them by Hindu landlords (Luke and Carman, *Village Christians and Hindu Culture*, p. 65).
32. Ibid., pp. 182–83.

Christian-ish and Jew-ish: Childhood on a Religious Shuttle
WERNER GUNDERSHEIMER

In the public schools I attended during the Second World War and its aftermath, every day began in precisely the same way. The class remained seated while the teacher (and then, beginning in third or fourth grade, a pupil) stood at the front of the room and read brief passages from the Old and the New Testaments. The class then rose and, with heads bowed, recited the Lord's Prayer. Facing the flag in one corner, hands over hearts, we gave the Pledge of Allegiance. These rites remained constant until 1954, when, courtesy of the Congress of the United States, the words "under God" turned up in the pledge. The obligatory ritual, as amended, continued. By then, my age cohort was well into high school. Thanks to U.S. history and "civics" courses, we knew all about the doctrine of separation of church and state. We had recited the pledge more than two thousand times. Of course we were also being carefully taught to despise what was then called "godless communism," but it was hard to reconcile traditional notions of liberty with a newly mandated religiosity, not to mention the savage assaults on civil liberties then emanating from the House Un-American Activities Committee. Many of us chose the route of passive resistance; perhaps we were unconsciously in training for the civil rights and antiwar movements of the next decade. We skipped the new words and, at the end of the day, went home to cheer that great Boston lawyer Joseph Welch as he shamed and skewered the paranoid alcoholic senator from Wisconsin.

By then I was already the grizzled veteran of an inner religious struggle which provides the subject of this brief memoir. In writing about my early experience of the ritual and spiritual Other, I am deeply mindful as a survivor of the Shoah (at least in the technical sense) of

Christian-ish and Jew-ish 155

the rare privilege of having lived to have that experience, and to tell this story. The millions of ordinary humans who, because they were born into the same religious community as I, met their horrific fate while I and a few others lived to write memoirs—those dead souls offer mute witness to the real story, the one to which mine is in reality a trivial footnote. Yet, slight though it surely is, this narrative offers an affirmation of what seems to me most precious in the American tradition—pluralism, a certain generosity of spirit, and the freedom to choose.

I come from two long lines of German Jews. My mother's people, especially on her father's side, pursued their quiet lives in small towns in the Rhineland Palatinate, several generations removed from Orthodoxy. A measure of their assimilation is the fact that my maternal grandfather bore the name of the Norse hero Siegfried. Though not himself a hero, Siegfried Siegel was German enough to have served in the army in World War I. But he was also Jewish enough to have been shipped off to Theresienstadt in the deportations of September 1942, and then on to Auschwitz in May of 1944. My maternal grandmother's family was more urban, more cosmopolitan, and if anything even more assimilated. My grandmother, Anna Bamberger Siegel, had six brothers, five of whom managed branches of Bamberger & Hertz, the family's prosperous chain of men's clothing stores. There was actually some intermarriage among distant relatives on that side. Several of my mother's cousins, like the film director Max Ophuls (né Oppenheim), had attained a modest celebrity. Not so Grandmother Anna, who, despite a degenerative disease of the nervous system, was deported with Siegfried, and died during the infamous typhus outbreak at Theresienstadt in 1942.

My father, who was born in Würzburg, in Franconia, came from a far more observant family. The Gundersheimer side kept the Sabbath, obeyed the dietary laws, attended synagogue regularly, and had far less extensive contacts with the dominant Christian culture of pre-Nazi Germany. Samuel Gundersheimer, my paternal grandfather, was (like Siegfried Siegel) a wholesale wine merchant. Though a brilliant young man in his school days, he dropped out of school at sixteen to support his family when his father died. He always maintained a deep respect for the learning he was never able to continue. My father therefore became the first member of his family to go to university. He studied with eminent art historians, first in Würzburg, and then in Berlin, Munich, and Leipzig, where, at twenty-three, he received his

Ph.D. in 1926. Having specialized in German Baroque mural painting, on which he soon published an authoritative study, he served as a museum curator in Frankfurt until the Nuremberg Laws led to his immediate dismissal. After that, while hoping for, and indeed expecting, a reversal of the Nazi insurgency, he supported himself by free-lance writing and by teaching courses. He taught alongside people like Martin Buber, Nahum Glatzer, and Ernst Kantorowicz in the Jüdisches Lehrhaus, the celebrated adult school founded in Frankfurt by Franz Rosenzweig, as well as in its secular equivalent, the Frankfurter Bund für Volksbildung. In 1935, he became director of the newly established Jewish Museum, a project sponsored by the Frankfurt branch of the Rothschilds. Although my parents had briefly considered emigrating as early as 1935, my father decided he could not bear to leave his parents behind. But no country wanted older people of no particular distinction. His father died in the autumn of 1938, the victim of a botched operation. Several months later, his mother left to join her sister in Jerusalem, and so for the first time—from my father's viewpoint—we were free to go. I use the first-person plural here because I appeared in 1937, one of a very small cohort of Jewish children born in Germany in those years who survived the war and the Shoah.

The Germans took a different view of our emigration, and for two reasons. In the first place, the events of Kristallnacht—November 9, 1938—had very direct effects on my father. His museum, like all facilities identified with or owned by Jews, had been sacked—its cases smashed, ritual objects strewn about helter-skelter, ancient textiles ripped and trampled. There had been the usual looters, but since the place was a museum and not a temple it was not set ablaze. The next morning, the authorities, having recognized that what was left of the museum might hold value for them, sent for my father. Instead of being shipped off with thousands of other Jewish men to the concentration camp at Dachau, outside Munich, he was assigned to clean up the mess at the museum, relabeling the objects so as to clarify their importance for their new owners—the German *Volk*. It took him almost nine months to complete this assignment, working under armed guard in the otherwise deserted galleries.

The second, and equally serious, impediment to our departure was that no one could leave unless they could show that there was some place that would take them in. During the years of the German Jewish diaspora, various countries—the United States in particular—had raised the bar to Jewish immigration, so as to keep numbers down. For over a year, my father had braved the indignities of the application process at the now notorious U.S. consulate in Stuttgart, with its enormous lines, petty gatekeepers and other officials on the take, and brusque dismissals. No luck.

One day in the summer of 1939, when things seemed hopeless, a letter arrived from a village schoolteacher in the town of Witham, near Cambridge, England. She had learned of us through a relief agency, and was writing to announce that the ladies of her parish were prepared to sponsor a refugee family providing there were no school-age children who would strain the slender resources available. We met that test, the British Consulate in Frankfurt had been apprised of this, and the necessary visas for short-term residency in England would be processed immediately. We should emigrate as soon as possible, and we would be provided with a place to stay and other necessities, while we arranged for eventual transit to another country.

On August 10, 1939, we left the land where our ancestors had lived for a thousand years, more or less. A two-year old, I was far too young to understand that I would forever owe my life, if not precisely to the Church of England, at least to the kindness of strangers who worshipped at Saint Nicholas' Church, Witham, Essex. Their act of Christian intercession, and many similar ones which followed it, became part of the fabric of my childhood, and therefore of a life which, far from being rootless, has drawn its nourishment from diverse soils. The resulting hybrid is German-ish, English-ish, and solidly, if complicatedly, American; Anglican-ish, Quaker-ish, Congregational-ish, and both Sephardic and Askenazic Jew-ish; and also unrepentantly agnostic-ish. I am an extremely lucky hybrid. Raised in a climate of man-made catastrophes, great financial worries, and few easy choices, I was for the most part thoughtfully and lovingly nurtured. One of the more interesting peculiarities of that nurturing was that it exposed me at a very early and impressionable age to varieties of religious experience that might have made William James's head spin.

In May of 1940 we succeeded in coming to the United States, where my memories begin. We arrived on the *Brittanic,* one of the last passenger vessels to make the transatlantic crossing, accompanied by a few trunks of clothing and linens and $30 in cash (a parting gift from Baron de Rothschild, who had also provided a monthly stipend of £10 toward our support while in England). Our first home was a room in a squalid boardinghouse on the Upper West Side. From there, my father began to pound the pavements between the various refugee relief agencies. HIAS—the Hebrew Immigration Aid Society—was the logical first place to turn. But HIAS lacked either the resources or the will to help my father find a way to jump-start his suspended career as an art historian. Instead, they proposed to send us to Skokie, Illinois, where a new German-Jewish workers' suburb was developing around the growing factories. If he agreed to move there, he could be assured of work on an assembly line. He politely declined.

At what seemed like a hopeless moment, the Religious Society of Friends came through for us. From the office of the Emergency Committee in Aid of Displaced Foreign Scholars, an organization devoted to helping refugees find permanent academic appointments, my father learned of an eight-week summer seminar which the Quakers planned to hold for up to forty recently arrived refugee scholars. They and their families would assemble on the campus of Brewster Academy in Wolfeboro, New Hampshire. There the men would receive instruction in English and learn about the United States and its academic institutions. In the course of the summer, the Quakers would try to place them in academic jobs.

Wolfeboro claimed the distinction of being "The Oldest Summer Resort in America." Its local paper, *The Granite State News* (still the newspaper of record for those parts) reported almost weekly on the seminar, chronicling its lectures, excursions, chamber music concerts, and guest appearances by such notables as "the world's most famous Quaker, Dr. Rufus M. Jones." Significantly, one would never conclude, from these lengthy and detailed reports, that any of the participants—let alone, say, 90 percent—were Jewish. That is an eloquent and deliberate silence, one that surely reflects the generally unwelcoming stance that many New England summer resorts took toward certain minorities in those days.

The Brewster seminar was well documented in other places as well. The *New York Times Magazine* ran an article on it, with a group photograph, and participants received a nice little photo album as a keepsake. From these sources, the program can be reconstructed accurately. Meeting for worship took place each Sunday at 10:00 a.m., and the whole community—the forty scholars with their families, thirteen resident teachers, other staff, volunteers, and guests—gathered for silent contemplation. I actually remember those meetings—and the admonitions to sit still, not fidget, and be quiet. Quaker meeting turned out to be excellent training for me, for I was about to set forth on a long march of divine worship in church and synagogue services, as well as Friends' Meetings elsewhere.

As the days grew shorter at the Brewster Academy seminar, it became clear to my parents and to the Friends who were helping them that their prospects were extremely limited. Most of the leading German art historians had come to the United States years earlier, and the few choice jobs that had existed or been invented for them were all filled. Meanwhile, college and university enrollments and budgets were shrinking, as the nation mobilized for war. In what has become normal U.S. practice, the arts and humanities were affected first, and hit hardest. But someone at Wolfeboro knew a dean at the University of Pittsburgh, whose wife needed a housekeeper. Therefore, it was my mother who actually held the entry-level position—room, board, and $5 a week, in return for full-time cooking and cleaning—with my father tagging along to continue his English studies and to offer an occasional lecture (unpaid) at the university. The problem was that the dean and his wife absolutely refused to accept a child in their servants' quarters, and nothing else was available that held out even a minimal prospect of entry into academic work. A staff person at the seminar knew a Quaker lady in a nearby town, who, as it turned out, would be willing to take in a refugee child for an indefinite period. This left my parents a day or so to grapple with the agonizing decision of whether to break up the little family that had managed to stay together through traumatic times. They decided to meet these prospective foster parents, liked them, and agreed on an arrangement. And so it happened that in early September, 1940, my parents set out for Pittsburgh, leaving me with the Reverend Francis S. Tucker, minister of the Henniker Congregational Church, his Quaker wife Annah, and their daughters—Helen, Betty, and Anne. I was to spend the next year with them, and they were to receive $4 of my mother's weekly wages for my maintenance.

I have vivid memories of life in Henniker and Ossipee, where the Tuckers had a lakeside cabin. In those places, I can locate specific markers for the beginnings of religious consciousness. At once participant and observer, I became enmeshed in a family in which daily religious practice was perhaps the central defining trait. It is logical to see me, the refugee, as the stranger in this setting. But I was not bringing the stranger's religion to the Tuckers. The strangeness, and probably nearly all of the fascination and fear, resided in my experience of the Tuckers and their religion. I have written about life in general in Henniker as I remember it, but without emphasis on the issue of what Mary Louise Pratt has called "contact zones," the confrontational borders where travelers encounter their differences and similarities with native populations. For me, Henniker was the contact zone with U.S. culture, and with traditional rural New England Protestantism in particular. And I believe that nothing in my brief past, and certainly none of the ritual occasions I had witnessed, had prepared me in any way for life in a clergyman's household, let alone one that was, in addition, essentially a community of women.

It is evident from the letters that "Aunt Annah" wrote to my mother almost every Sunday afternoon during that year that the Tuckers easily and immediately came to see me as one of the family. Yet, while she noticed instances where I responded strongly to some specifically religious aspect of the environment, much of this must have remained private, or else it escaped her watchful eye, or it may have been simply too commonplace to be worth mentioning. For example, in what was surely the most casual and routine way, we all held hands during Uncle Frank's brief grace before meals. This simple ritual came to feel so normal to me that I was puzzled to find that—aside from brief words of thanksgiving for bread and wine [wine!]—the Hebrew grace came after the meal, took place in my parents' household only on the Sabbath eve, went on for quite some time, and did not involve any physical contact among the participants.

But Aunt Annah couldn't help noticing my wayward, or even resistant, behavior at the annual Christmas Pageant, when I decided to improvise my little part instead of doing what I had practiced to perfection. Even earlier, in her letter dated December 8, 1940, she reported that I seemed worried that Santa Claus would be covered with smoke when he came down the chimney and that she had observed me on hands and knees trying to look up the chimney. She adds: "I must tell you of what happened tonight. We were singing songs [clearly meaning hymns] at the piano and [Werner] was choosing them. When I said 'one more'—he said 'I want three, six.' I didn't know what he meant whether three or six more songs or what. When I asked him he said 'This is My Father's World,' which is Hymn 36 in the hymnbook which is used in our older Sunday School where he sometimes visits! Imagine his remembering a number like that!" With the benefit of hindsight, it seems likely that the name of that hymn might have been what made it important to me. I had lost touch completely with my father's world; perhaps that anthem would help to keep it present in some magical way.

Life in Henniker was not easy, but there was great beauty in it. And indeed, much of that beauty—as seen through the wide eyes of a three-year-old foreigner—lay in the comforting rituals of Christian family life. Of course Jews tell bedtime stories, sing songs, and hold kids on their laps. But the fact was that I didn't actually know any Jews as such. Even the Jews at Brewster Academy had adopted the silent practice of the Friends, thus eliminating such vestiges of foreignness as their thick middle-European accents. Saying grace, holding hands, singing hymns, praying, going to church, hearing the Word, trimming the tree, finding the stocking, dyeing the eggs—that was ostensibly the stranger's religion, but it soon came to feel like my own. I loved it because it was pretty and accessible, and because I loved the people who lived it so fully. By the time my parents came to take me to yet another home, still to be found, in September of 1941, that religion—that practice—had found its way inside me. Though the Tuckers scrupulously reminded me that I was Jewish, I had no idea what that meant. No longer a stranger, but now a sojourner in their midst, I had happily and comfortably morphed into a four-year-old New England Congregationalist.

But not for long. By cobbling together small grants from three different agencies, Temple University had managed to create a one-year instructorship in History of Art at its Tyler School of Fine Arts for my father. We were to move to Philadelphia toward the end of the summer of 1941. It was arranged that my parents would come to stay for a week with me and the Tuckers at their summer quarters on Ossipee Lake, after which we would take the train south. The arrangements at Ossipee were far from ideal. The Tucker cabin was fully occupied, and afforded little or no privacy. There was no room for my parents, who therefore stayed in an ice-fishing cabin that had been hauled onto a bare patch in the woods about fifty yards from the main cabin. A path connected the two buildings, and also gave access to a common privy. Aside from the obvious discomforts of the ice-fishing shack, there was no room in it for me, so I stayed in my usual place with the Tuckers. Therefore, the physical arrangements served to reinforce my perception that I was part of the Tucker family, whereas my parents were merely visitors. During their stay, they too became part of the religious rhythms of the Tucker family, a circumstance that surely complicated my confusion when those rhythms disappeared, superseded by a vastly different set of observances.

In the few photographs preserved from this period, my parents appear preoccupied and unhappy. If, as they later recalled, this was a time of joyous reunion, the visual evidence seems to belie the memory. It must have been difficult as well as reassuring for my parents to discover that I had grown a lot, spoke very good, unaccented American English, and was fully adjusted to my new life. In addition to all the other changes and challenges they were facing, they now had to accommodate to the added demands of a familiar, yet somehow changed, child. For me, though, and also for the Tuckers, my impending departure was at least as painful as the original separation may have been for my mother and me. A few days after they saw us off from the little depot at Center Ossipee, Annah wrote: "It has seemed so quiet and queer without Werner. Nap times and after supper we still whisper and think he must be around somewhere." A few days later, having returned to Henniker from Ossipee, she wrote: "It seems so natural to be sitting here in my room writing to you, but what doesn't seem natural is to be wondering what Werner is doing instead of telling you. I had thought that the worst of missing him would be over when we came back here but I have missed him much more here. It just doesn't seem right not to have him either upstairs or down, outdoors or in. We had a picnic tonight with the Chase family and they all spoke of it not seeming right not to have Werner."

It was certainly no picnic for me, figuratively as well as literally. Suddenly the Gundersheimers were strangers again, not only to each other, but also in a big city, staying in a room at a Society of Friends building on Arch Street, while my parents looked for a place to live. Cobblestone streets, stifling mid-Atlantic heat, and urban din and traffic replaced the verdant New Hampshire countryside. The silence of Quaker meetings, which I had taken in stride at Wolfeboro, now seemed strangely oppressive in contrast with Uncle Frank's church services. All my new friends and family had disappeared, replaced by a pair of strict, harried aliens who didn't talk right and weren't much fun to be with. After the richly textured days with the five Tuckers and their large and affectionate circle of friends, relatives, and parishioners, I had no one to play with, and little to do. I desperately missed all the Tuckers: Aunt

Annah, with her humor, her endless competencies, and her relaxed, accepting ways; the eldest daughter, Helen, my special friend and first sister; Betty, the prettiest, with her soulful cello playing; Anne, headstrong and contrary, ready to stir things up; and Uncle Frank, a wonderful male role model, studious, generous-spirited, strong, and physically active. I even missed Taffy, their annoying little cocker spaniel. There, on the streets of Philadelphia, I had my second set of lessons about loss, loneliness, and pain, more serious and enduring than the first ones. In that respect, perhaps, I was catching up with my parents.

There was no way to reconcile this affective alienation with the cognitive awareness that I was now expected to feel completely happy. Didn't I have my mother and father back? Wasn't the long nightmare over? Well, hardly. The toughest parts were yet to come. We moved into a dank, depressing apartment that—it soon emerged—was infested with fleas. This was hardly one of the plagues of Egypt, but I was covered with bites and welts that made New Hampshire mosquito bites feel like caresses. The fleas were eventually eliminated, but immediately in their wake came an even more peculiar encounter—my first Jewish holidays. For starters, the ritual of the Sabbath seemed totally alien to me. Here, in coming home to Judaism, I really did encounter the stranger's religion. It made no sense to me that the prayers were rattled off in yet another foreign language in what seemed like great haste—it wasn't even German, which my parents now used in conversation with each other on the assumption that I wouldn't understand it. It also made no sense that one said those words with a hat on, or that there were all sorts of peculiar rules governing what we might or might not eat or drink. I disliked the melodies, didn't understand any of the words, and found the rules preposterous. None of this was scary, and it certainly wasn't fascinating; it just seemed unaffecting, and a bit dull.

But if these domestic observances were strange, the services at our synagogue appeared absolutely bizarre. This need not have been the case. There were, of course, many Reform Jewish temples where a little Congregationalist like me would have felt very much at home. In their services, most of the prayers and hymns were in English. The rabbi wore a robe pretty much like Uncle Frank's, and no other paraphernalia. There was responsive reading. A choir and an organ delivered melodious, familiar-sounding tunes. Families sat together. The whole thing was over in an hour and a half at the most. Because these temples were by and large German-Jewish, an outgrowth of the assimilationist ideas of the Haskalah, the Jewish enlightenment of the nineteenth century, my parents would have found them quite congenial too (and, much later, they did).

However, my father made a different and, as it turned out, somewhat unfortunate choice. A chance acquaintance had suggested that Congregation Mikveh Israel tended to attract an intellectual and religiously serious group and that its dues were significantly lower than those of most of the other synagogues. Mikveh Israel, however, was a Sephardic synagogue, physically and liturgically far different from the Askenazic rite in which both of my parents had been raised. What's more, it was Orthodox. Therefore I saw what seemed to me very much the stranger's religion, and it did feel strange. The men wore big hats, the kind they used out on the street. The women sat up on balconies, segregated but in full view, watching the men swaying back and forth wrapped in their big white scarves, even though it wasn't cold. The men didn't seem to be praying, or thinking much about what they were saying; they just read and chanted aloud or moved their lips silently, all in that language that nobody I knew used in everyday life. And there was a lot of talking, with people wandering in and out. None of it made much sense to me, even when my father tried to explain it. Why would anyone do things this way if they could sing the Doxology, or listen to the neat Bible stories read aloud in plain English in the Henniker Sunday School?

As time went on, I began to understand why Judaism seemed to matter to my father as much as it obviously did. I heard the stories of what my immediate family had been through, and eventually we all learned about the sufferings and the fate of other relatives. In that context, it seemed right to accept his decision that I should have a thorough Jewish education. Consequently I spent innumerable Sunday mornings and weekday afternoons acquiring the rudiments of written and spoken Hebrew; ancient, medieval, and modern Jewish history; and, of course, the Torah and the festivals. None of this study was freely chosen, and much of it I cordially disliked—not because of anything intrinsic to the subject, but because it was often badly taught, and because it was forced down my throat. But given the terrible stresses my parents lived with during those years and the sacrifices they were making for my sake, it would have been shameful to express such feelings to them. Self-censorship had taken hold early for me, and my internal delete key got heavy use. Instead of practicing candor at home,

I acted out in Hebrew School, and blithely brought home mediocre grades and wearily negative comments concerning my classroom attitude and behavior. Judaism was a non-negotiable topic. Unlike me, as I learned a bit of Jewish history, my father seemed unwilling to consider the possibility that the tragic history of our people might cast some doubt on the validity of God's promises. He said the words of the ancient prayers and promises, and appeared to believe them. I said the words because I had to. For the most part, I didn't believe them, and I found little comfort or beauty in them. Yet, it was not so bad to have become religiously, as well as linguistically, bilingual at an early age; for one thing, it established an enduring platform for a relativistic or even skeptical outlook. What did move me, deeply, was the creation of the State of Israel, in 1948. The idea that Jews could have their own homeland, defend themselves against persecution, and build a modern secular society seemed wonderful. I resolved to learn all I could about that fledgling democracy, and filled scrapbooks with newspaper clippings and photographs of the sturdy pioneers, who with their tanned faces and work clothes reminded me of the people I had known in New Hampshire.

If I had never seen the Tuckers again after leaving Henniker, my adjustment to the religion of my ancestors might have been more complete and less ambivalent. But through the war years, I was invited to return to New Hampshire nearly every summer. For a few precious weeks, there would be the same sights and smells as before; there would be a family—my Tucker family—with children, and lots of friends, and a dog. Marshmallows would be roasted, berries picked, frogs caught and released, lake perch caught and fried up for breakfast, songs sung on the beach, in the cabin, and in church. When the religious shuttle (which was actually the Boston & Maine and the Pennsylvania Railroads) finally took me south, it was to reenter that other world, the one without Christmas, the one in which "36" no longer signified "This is My Father's World."

Fast-forward now to April 1950, and my Bar Mitzvah. At Mikveh Israel, this was no perfunctory exercise, but rather a kind of spiritual immersion in Jewish learning. I was assigned a tutor, a gentle young clinical psychology student named Irving Kidorf. He was a fine Hebraist and, more importantly, he coached me with great patience as I learned the complex Sephardic chants needed for the introductory prayers, and the readings from the Torah and the prophets. After many months of rigorous instruction, I was ready to perform all the parts. I had been fitted with a natty, double-breasted blue gabardine suit, given a haircut and a quite grown-up rayon talit. I had written a graceful little speech thanking various adults, especially my parents, whom I was determined not to embarrass before what I knew to be a highly critical, and rather gossipy, audience.

It all went according to plan, but the best thing about it, the source of the most enduring memory, was that the Tuckers were there. They drove from Frank's new parish in Franklin, New Hampshire, north of Concord, and they had to leave the modest reception at our house early and drive for fifteen hours, so that he would be back in time to preach the next morning. That very day, Annah wrote to all of us, saying "This will not be a long note but will let you know we reached home safely—made very good time, getting here at 6 AM. Frank had time for a nap and I lost consciousness almost immediately and didn't wake up until noon! He drove until we were on the Merritt Parkway nearly to Connecticut and I drove the rest (on the strength of benzedrine to keep me awake!) But it was worth it . . . we loved every moment of the time." On an embossed white Bar Mitzvah card, perhaps the only one she ever bought, Annah had written me a very moving note, on behalf of "your second family—the Tuckers."

Shortly after those events, and driven by the example of the authentic Orthodoxy of Irv Kidorf and perhaps also by the incipient hormonal imbalances of adolescence, my life took a profoundly devotional turn. Donning skullcap, prayer shawl, and with the traditional phylacteries bound to arm and forehead, I performed all the daily Hebrew prayers with punctilious zeal. The stranger's religion had become my own, and with a vengeance. To my parents' great credit, they did nothing either to encourage or to discourage this entirely unexpected behavior, which they seemed to regard with a mixture of respect and resignation. Then suddenly one day, five or six months later, I let it go. It was as though by immersing myself in ritual practice I had given myself a vaccination against extreme religious piety, a small dose of the live virus, which has provided lifelong protection against the disease itself. But whence came this unbidden religiosity? Did it derive from fear or fascination; from Jewish guilt or a Calvinist sense of unworthiness in the eyes of God; from a Hebraized version of Lutheran *sole-fide*-ism or a delayed reaction to the heady experience of reading God's words from the very Scrolls of the Law? Or was it just a momentary need for certainty at a time of the mysterious, ill-understood, and totally unexplained changes imposed by maturing glands?

These are not answerable questions. What I do know, though, is that my own spiritual seeking, such as it is, ultimately became completely nondenominational. While institutional religions and many of their followers have a demonstrated capacity to scare me, religions as belief systems and sources of wisdom continue to exert a certain fascination. But my tendency is to cull what seem to me to be the good parts, and set the rest aside. In this, my role model is the Renaissance philosopher Giovanni Pico della Mirandola (1463–94), who in a work called the *Conclusiones* published nine hundred propositions he considered true. He had taken these from all the religious systems he could find—Greek, Roman, Jewish, Christian, Hermetic, Chaldean, Zoroastrian, and more. He was horrified by what turns out to be the recurrently fashionable notion that a single religion might hold a monopoly on the truth, and I agree with him. If I could pick my seatmate on the religious shuttle, it would be someone like Pico.

Like the Reformation in England, my religions were imposed from above. Unlike a scientific experiment, this odd sort of childhood experience cannot, and probably should not, be replicated. I sometimes think that I belong to a communion of which I am the only member. But, like Montaigne and the last Shaker lady, I prefer to accept what I cannot change. It's fine being an odd sort of hybrid; especially since, mule-like, I cannot replicate the trait. Having moved back and forth in early life, I see little to admire or applaud in any form of doctrinal orthodoxy. As a historian, moreover, I am deeply cognizant of the atrocities committed in God's name over the centuries, and the dangers religious zeal continues to pose to millions of innocent people around the world. Fanaticism or dogmatism of any sort revolts me. I can't understand Jews for Jesus any more than I could relate to Christians for Moses, if there were so curious an entity. And while acknowledging everyone's absolute right to choose and change, I find most conversions, except perhaps those made to accommodate a life partner, puzzling. I cannot imagine that the world will offer a peaceful, humane environment unless and until people become willing, once and for all, to put aside their beliefs in the exclusivity of their religious opinions. To me, one of these belief systems seems just as good or bad as the next. In my case, the default option turns out to be Judaism, so "Jew-ish" is what I write on official forms.

Perhaps these are the most lasting, albeit tentative, conclusions from my early rides on the religious shuttle. But the word *shuttle* has another, much earlier meaning: "an instrument used in weaving for passing the thread of the weft to and fro from one edge of the cloth to the other between the thread of the warp" (OED). That kind of shuttle served to fashion the richly textured, tightly woven textiles that have endured through the ages. While some became altar cloths and tapestries celebrating Christian revelation, others adorned the scrolls of the Law, or sheltered the Ark of the Covenant. For me, it seems, the warp of Christianity and the weft of Judaism have woven a coat of many colors, conferring greater warmth and conveying a bit more beauty than your basic gabardine.

The Convert—Stranger in Our Midst: Crossing Borders in Two Worlds
PRAVRAJIKA VRAJAPRANA

An alternate title for this essay could have been, "That's funny, you don't *look* Hindu." This remark, which has been directed to me over the years, reminds me that my WASP appearance is an explicit contrast to my religious identity. The remark further reminds me that though today's societies are increasingly diverse—racially, culturally, and religiously—people nevertheless continue to associate race and culture with a specific religious identity. Finally, it is precisely this rigid association which helps create the "stranger"—one who has crossed existing borders to enter into new territory.

What are these borders, how are they crossed, and why? What is the experience of "strangers" in their inherited traditions, as well as in their adopted traditions? Although my discussion will be largely from a Hindu viewpoint—specifically that of a Caucasian American convert to Hinduism—much of it will be applicable to conversions across religious borders that span different cultures.

Most Westerners find my religion—I am a Vedanta nun—strange indeed. Vedanta means "end of the Vedas,"[1] and the Vedas are Hinduism's sacred texts. To identify myself with Vedanta is to identify myself with Hinduism, and Hinduism is foreign to most Americans. So also is monasticism, which flies in the face of mainstream contemporary U.S. values. On the other hand, my U.S. heritage makes me a stranger to many Hindus as well. How did I arrive in the stranger's borderland?

I first crossed the border into Hinduism via windshield wipers. As a young antiwar activist in 1967, I quite accidentally stumbled upon the Vedanta temple in Santa Barbara. Our antiwar organization was advertising a peace march by leafleting cars in church parking lots. Having briskly finished the Catholic Church, my co-worker suggested that we go to the Vedanta temple. "What's *that*?" I asked. "Oh, it's a really beautiful place with a big parking lot." Great. Anything for more windshield wipers.

Leaflets dispersed, my co-worker suggested we go inside the temple to hear the Sunday lecture. I wasn't enthused but I acquiesced, listening to the heavily accented words of a thin swami with an austere appearance. Not knowing better, I assumed he fasted. Not *my* kind of religion, I thought. There was something in the serene atmosphere of the temple which attracted me, but a swami who seemed altogether too skinny was not greatly appealing.

After the lecture the speaker was thanked by Swami Prabhavananda, the head of the Vedanta Society of Southern California—a smaller, mercifully rounder swami. I cannot say why shaking his hand after the lecture touched me so profoundly. If one has never encountered real holiness before, how is one supposed to react to it? I certainly was not looking for holiness (since I was personally responsible for saving the world); the very idea was appalling. But somehow this small, luminous, elderly man made holiness not only palpable but inexplicably sweet. He radiated purity. I had always thought that "holy" meant cloying piety and churchiness; instead I encountered a radiant swami who instantly redefined "holiness" for me with his warmth and infectious love for God.

That chance encounter reoriented my life. Naturally and effortlessly, I found myself moving into Hinduism. It was not a shock to my system. Though I was raised a quasi-Protestant, my parents had taught me many ideas found in Hinduism. While other children heard about heaven, I heard about reincarnation. It was only after that personal encounter, however, that I decided to study Vedanta seriously. I vividly remember the first time I read "Brahman and Atman are one."[2] I put the book down. The exaltation was indescribable. The stories of Rama and Krishna, Śiva and Ganesha, Durga and Kali, filled me with delight. Most importantly, the words of Hinduism's towering nineteenth-century figures—Ramakrishna, Sarada Devi, and Swami Vivekananda—rang true for me. That was when I fell in love with the Hindu tradition.

Unbeknownst to myself, I was slipping across borders. The process was so smooth and natural that I would not have characterized myself as a "convert." I was no Saul-on-the-road-to-Damascus. It was not until much later that I discovered that "conversion is," as Lewis Rambo describes it, "a process, not a specific event."[3]

CONVERSIONS

There was no defining moment when I became "Hindu." As Rambo observed, "For some [conversion] is abrupt and radical, for others, it is gradual and very subtle in its effects on a person's life."[4] My own conversion was gradual enough to be nearly imperceptible. A few ideas planted by my parents were given impetus with my Vedanta Society encounter and then slowly gestated within me. Externally, I led a prosaic life—college, graduate school, career—but it was ultimately unsatisfying. The fulfillment I hoped to find in career and relationships was not the fulfillment I craved.

Why would a reasonably sane person become a nun? When monasticism ends up being the best way for her to get what she needs out of life. That was what happened in my case. I had had whatever I thought I wanted, and—sweet as it was—it was simply not enough. A friend of mine who became a Trappist left a promising career at Columbia. "What do you do when God taps you on the shoulder?" he explained. Eventually one succumbs to the insistent push. In 1977 I joined the Ramakrishna Order and eleven years later took my *sannyasa* vows—final vows of renunciation. I have never looked back. Though it is not an "easy" life in the ordinary sense of the term, it provides deep satisfaction and great happiness.

Still, I never thought of myself as a "convert" until the term was thrust upon me in India, where I —finally and unexpectedly—felt very much at home. Traveling with two other Western Vedanta nuns in the holy city of Varanasi, we were staying in the guesthouse of the Ramakrishna Order. The swami in charge of our monastery was attempting to gain us entry into the Viswanath temple, as it is said that unless you have *darshan*[5] of Lord Viswanath ("Lord of the Universe"), you haven't been to Varanasi. But even though we were nuns of the Ramakrishna Order—one of the most respected Hindu monastic orders in India—we were not allowed to enter. After a week of fruitless appeals, our swami gave it one final try. Their conversation went as follows:

"Are they converts?" the head priest inquired.

"Of *course* they are converts!" replied our swami.

"Well, if they converted to Hinduism, they could convert *back*," the priest retorted. "They could even become Muslim!"

So much for the Lord of the Universe. Dedicating our lives to the ideal of Hindu dharma was not enough.[6] In the eyes of Viswanath's head priest, those who were not born Hindu could not become "real" Hindus.[7] I discovered that, as a convert, I was inherently suspect—and that my self-definition of religious identity could cross someone else's inviolable border. I became viscerally aware of the fact that I was a stranger within my own religious tradition.

Those inviolable borders were not only in India. I was recently introduced to a fellow Westerner as a Hindu nun. With barely concealed derision he said, "Don't you need more arms?" Apparently my religious orientation was an affront to *his* sensibilities as well. Again I became aware that I was a stranger and this time it was within my own country and culture.

From these experiences a few epiphanies have emerged, and I have continued to think about my encounters a great deal. When I was in Varanasi some years ago, I had never really thought about myself as a "convert" and I didn't particularly like being told that I was one. The label seemed pejorative, as if my religious commitment were some cheap veneer, peeling off with use, age, or convenience. The label can—and often does—make me a stranger within my own national borders as well as in the very country where my religious identification is shared.

Clearly I inhabit two worlds that remain separated by borders of different kinds. Converts stray beyond the borders of their inherited cultural, ethnic, or religious community to embrace the religion of the stranger. They often find, however, that they have become double strangers—strangers both within their adopted religious community and strangers within their inherited religious community.

CONVERSION VS. THE RELIGIOUS DEFAULT

What is the spiritual homeland whose borders I cross in the United States? Despite our much-vaunted religious pluralism, this country remains resolutely Protestant in its outlook. Only in recent memory have Catholicism and Judaism been generally accepted, and it is no secret that anti-Semitism surfaces with disturbing regularity. Before the events of September 11, it appeared that Muslims might be allowed to tiptoe into the People-of-the-Book Club and be accepted as part of the religious mainstream. But September 11 changed all that. While there remains a segment of U.S. society which regards Islam as a worthy second cousin because of its Abrahamic roots, a larger segment of society increasingly stereotypes Muslims as fanatics and proto-terrorists.

With or without pluralism, the United States possesses a powerful religious default: secularized Protestantism. It is unconsciously accepted as the country's normative religious status, and it provides a lens through which the United States views itself and others. For most Americans this lens defines the stranger, either inside or outside the country's borders.

This default is so ingrained in our national consciousness that its assumptions are taken for granted—that is, until someone converts to Islam or Judaism or Hinduism or even becomes a Seventh-Day Adventist or a Mormon. In each of those cases, the question of religion and religious identity has been taken seriously enough to merit bucking the system to cross borders. Further, both religious and secular borders have been crossed. To take religion seriously enough to convert is to eschew secular values.

Despite the many problems inherent in becoming a convert, there are converts in every religion and in every part of the world. The motives for such movement have been suspect historically, since leaving the religion of one's community is inherently transgressive. Even if one's parents and ancestors for fourteen generations were religiously nonobservant, abandoning one's ancestral religion is censured. When we cross religious borders we cross societal borders as well.

Some brief examples: Edith Stein's conversion to Catholicism remains a bitterly divisive subject. Hindus in India who convert to Christianity, Islam, or Buddhism are generally suspected of having economic or political motives. Muhammad Ali's conversion to Islam was thoroughly condemned; and, more recently, John Walker Lindh's conversion to Islam was seen as the result of poor parenting and Marin County hot tubs. ISKCON (International Society for Krishna Consciousness) members in Russia have faced harrowing brutality.

To convert is to leave tradition aside to follow one's individual star. As individualism is *the* defining U.S. characteristic, conversion is much easier in this country than in many others. In North America one faces at most social ostracism and ridicule, not the overt repression that is found in many nations across the globe. The counterpoint to this is the presumption that if conversion is easy, then it is facile.

Some conversions are presumed more facile than others. Choices within Christian congregations are rarely second-guessed in this country, and conversions to Christianity from other faith traditions are seen as understandable changes of heart. While conversions from Christianity to Judaism are questioned and often criticized, they are at least taken seriously. But when other religious borders are crossed, different presumptions are made. If one becomes a Muslim, one is a rebel. If one becomes a Buddhist, one is trendy. To become a WASH—a White Anglo-Saxon Hindu[8]—is to open oneself up to disbelief or ridicule. To cross this border is deemed facile if not downright silly.

If this seems overstated, let me provide a brief but telling example. Last summer I was contacted by a BBC reporter in London who said that he wished to interview Vedanta Society monastics. He later visited the Vedanta Society in Los Angeles and interviewed several Western monastics. When I heard the brief broadcast, I was outraged. The reporter had in mind a parody, a fact he never mentioned. He seemed particularly amused by Westerners following Hindu traditions and dismissed our existence as "a summer camp for adults." I found the reporter's questions tasteless and rude, but what disturbed me most was the later dubbing of his laughter and sarcastic remarks over both the monastics' responses and our *arati* (vesper) hymns. I shot off an e-mail to NPR, a portion of which said:

> I am shocked that NPR would choose to air a story so breathtakingly contemptuous of Hindu religious and monastic traditions. . . .
>
> The listener hears the words of our evening prayer—a prayer we consider deeply meaningful and sacred—with [the reporter's] snarky comment about those who "mumble certain things." When the congregation sings our evening liturgy, [the reporter] chirps: "They're able to sing it longer than you're able to listen to it." This brief, nasty segment mocks Hindu religious names, mocks the monastic community and mocks the spiritual values that practicing Hindus cherish.

The Convert—Stranger in Our Midst 175

While you manage to be sensitive to the sentiments of other religious minorities in this country, you've decided that we don't merit the same respect and dignity.[9]

Why is crossing *this* border, the border from a Western religious background to Hinduism, so easily trivialized? Perhaps because Hindu religion has been inextricably linked to the alluring exoticism and eroticism of Indian culture as the popular mind in the West understands it. The immediate question, however, is whether Hindu religion is ineluctably chained to Indian culture or whether Hindu religious practice can be universal.

CULTURAL BORDERS, RELIGIOUS BORDERS

There are Hindus who have argued that "Hinduism is the culture of Indians in India" and thus restrict Hindu membership to Hindus from the Indian subcontinent and their descendants.[10] Obviously I would argue to the contrary since, if nothing else, I have to explain myself and others like me. Swami Vivekananda—the founder of the Ramakrishna Order to which I belong—had a dream of creating a vibrant Hindu monastic foundation in the West with Western monastics.[11] The process is already well on its way. Vivekananda outraged many in India by doing what was then considered preposterous: giving *sannyasa* to Westerners. This pioneering act had far-reaching consequences not unforeseen by Vivekananda: As Hindu monks and nuns, Westerners became eligible to enter the doors and belong to the most ancient tradition of monasticism in religious history.

Vivekananda cheerfully outraged both Indians and Westerners. Many Indians were outraged that he crossed the ocean, defying caste restrictions and mixing freely with Westerners. Westerners were outraged that he staunchly defended Hinduism and freely, and occasionally fiercely, criticized the West. Vivekananda inhabited truly liminal territory when he brought Hinduism to the world stage at Chicago's World Parliament of Religions in 1893. Yet from that marginal place Vivekananda put Hinduism on the world's religious map, pulling Hinduism across national, ethnic, and religious borders, creating outrage but also the possibility of a Western Hindu dharma.

The global Hinduism that we see today is very much Vivekananda's offspring. As Gavin Flood noted, "Vivekananda might be seen as the first effective proponent of Hinduism as a world religion."[12] It was Vivekananda who pulled together Hinduism's varying strands to create a unifying vision of Hindu dharma.

This brings us to a significant issue. Vivekananda was an ardent, even defiant, champion of Hinduism, so why did he form "Vedanta Societies" and not "Hindu Societies" in the West? Certainly Vivekananda was not diffident about proclaiming Hinduism's greatness. But as critical as Vivekananda was about the West's foibles, he was equally so of India's. He railed against untouchability, the fetish for ritual purity, and a thousand other ills which made Hinduism seem exclusionary rather than inclusionary. Vivekananda wanted Hinduism to be a global religion delinked from Indian culture, and that form of Hindu dharma without Indian cultural accretions he called "Vedanta."

This puts us on slippery turf. Which part of Hindu dharma is "cultural accretion" and which part constitutes religion? The issue is vexed because Hinduism itself is notoriously difficult to define. It has no founder, no centrally affirmed creed, no dogma, no unifying praxis. It is quite possible to find sects of Hindus who, for all practical purposes, have hardly anything in common with one another.[13]

Given that, how can one define who fits into the category of Hindu? What borders do Hindus place around themselves? Below are some typical examples:

1. I am a Hindu because I was born in India and I am neither Muslim, nor Christian, nor Sikh, nor Jain, nor Parsi, nor an Adivasi.[14]
2. I am a Hindu because I was born to Hindu parents and my ancestors have always been Hindu.
3. I am a Hindu because I do puja to Śiva or Ganesa or Krishna or Durga or the local goddess near our home.
4. I am a Hindu because I accept the Vedas as true.
5. I am a Hindu because I follow the Hindu dharma.
6. I am a Hindu because the ideas of the individual, the world, and the Supreme Reality expressed in Hinduism correspond with my own.
7. I am a Hindu because the Hindu way of life fulfills my deepest aspirations and goals as a human being.

These self-definitions show that a person can be ethnically or culturally Hindu without being religiously Hindu at all. But the last four definitions reinforce my argument that the reverse of the equation is equally valid: One can be religiously Hindu without being culturally or ethnically Hindu. The borders can be porous in both directions. As Douglas Renfrew-Brooks has written:

> One can nowadays be "religiously Hindu" from any number of cultural or ethnic backgrounds, much to the chagrin of those who might prefer it otherwise. To put it another way, *Hinduism* names a religion, whereas the term *Hindu* may be used religiously, ethnically, culturally, politically, or in other ways.[15]

By delinking the spiritual essence within Hinduism from Indian culture we cross another border, for Hinduism can be a global rather than a nationalistic religion only by shedding some of its "Indianness."[16] While some Hindus have realized this, many others have not. Clearly much work remains to be done in this direction.

CROSSING BORDERS TO A WESTERN HINDU DHARMA

In an increasingly mobile world where borders are crossed with the click of a mouse, the most important —and the most intractable— border is psychological rather than geographical. Religions have traditionally been identified with geographical locations, but the determining factor today is not the individual's location but her mind, and where that mind feels religiously attuned.

Further, North America is currently witnessing an increasing number of second- and third-generation American Hindus who are ethnically and religiously Hindu but culturally North American. They crossed cultural borders simply by being born in the West. For these Hindus, a Hinduism delinked from Indian culture is a daily reality. Just as there is a viable and thriving Western Buddhist dharma, so there is a viable Western Hindu dharma that, I believe, will one day be thriving. Does a Western Hindu dharma mean a compromised Hinduism? I don't think so—at least no more so than a Westernized Buddhism means a compromised Buddhism. Just as Buddhism has adapted to new cultures by assimilating the character of each country it inhabited, so has Hinduism. When Buddhism crossed the physical borders of India to inhabit other lands, it also crossed religious and cultural borders. The Buddhisms found in Tibet, Japan, China, Thailand, Vietnam, and Korea vary considerably. In each country, Buddhism has adapted to the host country and culture and created a distinct hybrid attuned to the population's needs and values.

Similarly, in the West today, we can see a version of Hinduism which is still an evolving, richly innovative entity. One has only to visit some of the Hindu temples in North America or see the performance of Hindu rituals—by both American-born Hindu practitioners and immigrant Hindus from India—to witness a distinctive combination of imported customs as well as local needs.

The Hinduism of my experience embraces variety and strongly affirms human dignity and potential. It has molded my life as it has molded the lives of one-sixth of the world's population. Thus, I am profoundly disturbed by the diminished stereotype of Hinduism that is so often presented to the West by the media and, on occasion, by the academy. It affects me directly, in both the worlds I straddle, making me more of a stranger in my own land—and also in my adopted religion, since my Western heritage is often associated with disrespect toward Hinduism.

The vast majority of North Americans are not aware that they are often presented a parody of Hinduism. The media reflect the stereotypes the popular culture already believes to be true. Since the time India was colonized, Hinduism has been the irrational, mysterious, and occasionally dangerous religion of the stranger.

Example after colonial example demonstrated just how irrational, silly, superstitious, and weak-minded Hindu religious practice was. People madly threw themselves under the juggernaut, worshipped cows and elephant-headed gods, monkey-gods, and, purportedly, even phalluses. Indeed, the more incomprehensible and bizarre Hinduism appeared, the more rational and imbued with *gravitas* the Western religious model became. The less respect Hinduism was given, the more respect the Western model acquired, if only by default. Ronald Inden's *Imagining India* asks: "What is the essence that Hinduism . . . lacks?" "A 'world-ordering rationality'" is his reply.[17] Small wonder, then, that crossing the border into Hinduism has been consistently slighted and trivialized, and that converting to Hinduism transforms me into a stranger.

Why is Hinduism regarded as so strange? One of the foremost reasons is the Protestant taboo against graven images and the West's rejection of "idolatry." The West, with its deeply ingrained belief in "progress," has long viewed "polytheism" as a childish way station en route to the mature monotheism of the West. The Hindu worship of deities seems akin to the play of children who refuse to abandon their dolls and grow up. Hinduism has gods with lowercase *g*'s, which contrasts unfavorably with the adult religions whose God merits a capital *G*.[18] Anyone, therefore, who would willingly cross borders to become a Hindu is viewed as puerile. Such a conversion can not be taken seriously.

THE STRANGER AND THE REBIRTH OF THE COLONIAL MODEL

Despite all the talk of religious pluralism and multiculturalism, the legacy of colonialism remains a powerful force in the way the West views Hinduism. This is a significant reason why Hinduism remains a religious stranger. As Edward Said observed:

> One aspect of the electronic, postmodern world is that there has been a reinforcement of the stereotypes by which the Orient is viewed. Television, the films, and all the media's resources have forced information into more and more standardized molds. So far as the Orient is concerned, standardization and cultural stereotyping have intensified the hold of nineteenth-century academic and imaginative demonology of "the mysterious Orient."[19]

Through cultural stereotyping, the media serve as a great cookie cutter, both defining and enforcing the imprint of strangeness upon the stranger. This reinforces the borders which define "the Other" in contrast to "us." The larger culture accepts and internalizes the stereotype and then proceeds to define the stranger's religion *to* the stranger. In the convert's borderland, it is a bizarre view indeed when one's inherited culture projects a caricatured view of one's adopted religion. *I* know the projected image is akin to that of a funhouse mirror. Alas, most of my countrymen and countrywomen do not.

What are we to make of a *Time* cover story on yoga that defines yoga as "exercise cum meditation," an article which mentions a "yoga butt" but never once discusses yoga as something deeply sacred to Hindus, something that has nothing to do with stretching and flexing?[20] This is but one small example of how the West appropriates a few aspects of Hinduism's sacred traditions, trivializes the rest, and then throws them back flattened, devalued, and desacralized. It is nothing less than colonialism redux.

What are we to make of scholars who apply psychoanalytic theory to Hinduism even though the validity of applying its methods to Western religious figures is questioned and even though much psychoanalytic theory is passé even in psychoanalytic circles? As Alan Roland, psychoanalyst and author of *Cultural Pluralism and Psychoanalysis*, has noted: "Psychoanalysis has played a surprisingly major role in South Asia studies, much more so than in other area studies, not to mention other intellectual disciplines."[21]

In a number of cases, the Western psychoanalytic model has served to pathologize that which Hindus find sacred. As the late psychoanalyst Renuka Sharma wrote in her review discussion of *Kali's Child: The Mystical and the Erotic in the Life of Ramakrishna*: "The imperialistic use of some outdated dogmas of psychoanalysis perpetuates a kind of psycho-orientalism"; both she and other Indian feminists, such as Gayatri Spivak, characterize this as "a well-known colonial ruse."[22]

One key example is Hinduism's great bête noir, "phallus" worship. Hindus do not worship phalluses. Hindus worship the *linga*, the emblem of Śiva. When a Hindu worships a *linga*, she or he is not worshiping a phallus; she or he is worshipping divinity. Even if we grant the *linga* a phallic origin in bygone millennia, the symbol has referred to Śiva as the ultimate Reality for centuries.

The West's original understandings of Hinduism came from Christian missionaries whose Ten-Commandment worldview defined Hindu deities as "graven images." To worship them was to commit the serious sin of idolatry. "The heathen in his blindness bows down to wood and stone," the Christian hymn rang out. The missionaries could not fathom that Hindus never viewed their images as wood and stone. Idolatry, as Theodore Roszak observed, is in the eye of the beholder. While Christianity's perception of truth was defined by text and historical events (particularly the advent of Jesus), Hinduism's truth was to be found in image and story, which Hindus understood to be no less significant than text and history.[23]

Images can be aniconic as well as iconic, the latter being directly representational (an icon representing Jesus, for example) while the former bears no representational likeness. Diana Eck clarifies: "The plain cross . . . is aniconic, as is the *linga* of Śiva or the natural stone *salagrama* of Vishnu."[24] About the *linga,* Eck writes:

> It is true that some of the myths of the *linga*'s origin are myths of castration. . . . However, the *linga* as it is worshiped in India today is more accurately seen as an aniconic image . . . its origins [found] in a magnificent hierophany of a fiery column of light, rather than in a primal act of castration. Those who worship Śiva in the *linga* form are consistently appalled to hear it understood as phallic, and again we suspect the interpretation of the "eye of the beholder."[25]

Coming from such a vastly different worldview, it is not difficult to understand why Christian missionaries immediately reduced the *linga* to a phallus. What puzzles Hindu practitioners, however, is how even supposedly neutral academics have continued to reinforce the old stereotype.[26] We need to remember that the primary meaning of the word *linga* itself is "symbol" or "sign" or "defining characteristic"; *linga* as "phallus" is only an extension of that meaning.[27] What is the *linga*—the defining characteristic—of a male? The phallus. What is the *linga* of a female? The *yoni.* The *linga* of a sannyasin? The ocher robe. The Śiva *linga* is the sacred symbol of Śiva; it is not his phallus.[28]

A STRANGER IN THE ADOPTED TRADITION

At the time of my Varanasi experience I did not understand the Hindus' profound sense that they had been hurt and betrayed by those who had come to India as tourists, scholars, journalists, or missionaries. Now, after many more years in the stranger's borderland, I can clearly see the cause-and-effect relationship between the grievances of the colonized and the outraged reaction to the colonizers. For those colonized, the tourists, scholars, journalists, and missionaries who mock or misunderstand what Hindus find sacred are not far removed from the earlier invaders. Whereas the previous weapons of colonization were boots, bottles, and Bibles, the modern colonizers brought Western wealth and arrogance and, above all, the entitled sense that *their* view of the world was the only valid view and certainly the only view that mattered.

What happens when one's religion is trivialized? The borders which protect—and insulate—that religion are reinforced and hardened. That means that those of us who live inside the convert's liminal territory are denied access into temples because our appearance reminds the arbiters of access of their bitter colonial experience.

Fear that the truth might offend should not prevent us from pursuing truth wherever it may lead. One would hope that all human beings, regardless of religious affiliation, would see the search for truth as indispensable to their religious life. But methodology and cultural and historical context are equally important.

Now, why should Hindus expect their religion not to be deconstructed as Christianity has been? Christians also have serious reservations about the academic treatment of Christian texts. That is true. But let us remember that there are many more practicing Christians teaching Christianity than there are practicing Hindus who teach Hinduism. Let us also remember that "Religious Studies" is a Western enterprise. When any religious tradition is examined, it is necessarily through a lens that was created *by* the West *for* the West with Western values and Western understandings of religion. Finally, we need to remember that the origins of Indology were colonial, with significant political and religious agendas, and that some of that baggage remains to this day.

The study of Hinduism should be rigorous, fearless, and bold. Let Hinduism be subject to the same standards as other religious traditions. But the writings and interpretations of those who deconstruct Hinduism must be subject to equally rigorous criticism and deconstruction. The scholars' critics must not be presumed to be credulous believers (fearing the truth lest their faith be shaken) when they are disputing what they find distorted or fallacious.

Mine is a plea for the validity and importance of border crossings. Borders can be crossed, and *should* be crossed, but always with respect and as much understanding as one can muster. In our multicultural and religiously diverse world, we all need to cross borders in order to understand and connect meaningfully with other people and their traditions. Moreover, such knowledge allows us to understand and connect with ourselves in a healthier way.

Most border crossings will necessarily be of short duration, but even a brief excursion will be a broadening experience if we are willing to learn. In a few cases, the crossing of a border will bring about permanent change, creating a genuine inner transformation. Such an irreversible crossing creates the "stranger," who is then provided a scenic view of both sides of the border without being locked into either of them. It is a lovely perch from which one can learn a great deal.

The most important baggage for all border crossings—whether brief or permanent—is a profound respect for those outside our own borders. With that respect we bring the stranger's experience of the sacred into our own lives—as much as our minds will allow and our hearts can expand. The more we are able to do this, the fewer strangers there will be.

NOTES

1. The Sanskrit word *anta* can also mean "essence." Thus *Vedanta* can also be translated as "essence of the Vedas."
2. Brahman is the Reality behind the universe; Atman is the Reality behind the individual.
3. Lewis R. Rambo, *Understanding Religious Conversion* (New Haven, Conn.: Yale University Press, 1993), p. 7.
4. Ibid., p. 6.
5. Sanskrit *darshan* (lit. "seeing") is a term used to express "seeing" a deity installed in a Hindu temple and, occasionally, meeting a holy person.
6. *Dharma* literally means "what holds together" and therefore is the basis of moral and social order. Dharma thus includes all of these various shades of meaning: "way of life," "justice," "righteousness," "duty," and "truth."
7. It may well have been that at the time of our visit, political forces at play in Varanasi made our attempted temple visit unsuccessful. In previous years, other Western monastics in our Order were allowed to have *darshan* of Viswanath without any difficulty. Nevertheless, there are any number of Hindu temples (for example, the Jagannath temple in Puri, the Pashupatinath temple in Kathmandu, and a number of temples in southern India) which still would have forbidden our entry; our entry would still be forbidden today.
8. This term is used by Douglas Renfrew-Brooks, "Taking Sides and Opening Doors," *Journal of the American Academy of Religion* 68, no. 4 (December 2000): 823–24.
9. Pravrajika Vrajaprana, e-mail to National Public Radio, 31 July 2002, regarding Chase Peters's report, "Monastery Training Ground," on National Public Radio's *Marketplace*, 29 July 2002.
10. For example, Ed Viswanathan, *Am I a Hindu? The Hinduism Primer* (San Francisco: Halo Books, 1992), p. ix.

11. See, for example, *Complete Works of Swami Vivekananda*, 10th ed. (Mayavati: Advaita Ashrama, 1973), 5:105, 5:106; 7:93. See also Marie Louise Burke, *Swami Vivekananda in the West: New Discoveries: The World Teacher*, 1:128–30.

12. Gavin Flood, *An Introduction to Hinduism* (Cambridge: Cambridge University Press, 1996), 258.

13. Vivekananda addressed this issue and drew attention to what he called the "common bases of Hinduism"; see *Complete Works of Swami Vivekananda*, 3:122–32, 3:372–78, 3:455–60.

14. I was amused to discover that in the British census of the 1920s and 1930s, Hindus were defined as "Hindus" if they were nothing else. "Hindus were what was left after others—Muslims, Untouchables, Christians, Sikhs, and so forth—had set themselves apart," writes John Stratton Hawley in "Naming Hinduism," *The Wilson Quarterly* 15, no. 3 (Summer 1991): 23.

15. Renfrew-Brooks, "Taking Sides and Opening Doors," pp. 822–23.

16. The issue is particularly relevant today, in the West as well as in India. As Flood observed, "In Hinduism we see two contemporary cultural forces which are characteristic of modern communities: on the one hand a movement toward globalization and identity formation which locates Hinduism as a transnational world religion alongside Christianity, Buddhism or Islam; on the other, a fragmentation which identifies Hinduism with a narrowly conceived national identity" (Flood, *Introduction to Hinduism*, p. 4).

17. Ronald Inden, *Imagining India* (Oxford: Blackwell Publishers, 1990), p. 86.

18. The Sanskrit word *deva* literally means "the shining one." Once *deva* was mistranslated as "god," it became easy to contrast the "many gods" as opposed to the "one [true] God." Thus in the popular mind, Hinduism became polytheistic in contradistinction to the monotheistic Semitic religions.

19. Edward W. Said, *Orientalism* (New York: Vintage Books, 1979), p. 26.

20. Richard Corliss, "The Power of Yoga," *Time*, 23 April 2001, pp. 51–62.

21. Alan Roland, "The Uses (and Misuses) of Psychoanalysis in South Asian Studies: Mysticism and Child Development," paper delivered at the South Asia Conference, University of Wisconsin, Madison, 11 October 2002; reproduced on the *Sulekha* website http://www.sulekha.com/column.asp?cid=270005.

22. Renuka Sharma, "'The Foot in the Lap or Kripal's Discontent': A Review of *The Mystical and the Erotic in the Life and Teachings of Ramakrishna* by Jeffrey John Kripal," *Sophia International Journal for Philosophy of Religion, Metaphysical Theology and Ethics* 42, no. 2 (December 2001): 78. Later in the same article (p. 80), Dr. Sharma adds: "Oh Calcutta! There [the author] discovers 'phallus erectus-lingam worship' under the guise of a tormented sage proclaiming his love of the terrifying goddess Kali. . . . Here

we leap straight into the bedcrust with a whole tradition of colonial psychoanalysis which neatly defines 'the Indian personality'—as being homophobic, mother-hating, full of vagina-envy, anally-possessed, and deeply feminized, obsessive compulsive males. . . . So much for the postmodern transference upon subaltern masculinity."

23. For an enlightening discussion of this topic, see S. N. Balaganghadhara, *"The Heathen in His Blindness": Asia, the West and the Dynamic of Religion* (Leiden: E. J. Brill, 1994), pp. 398–413.

24. Diana L. Eck, *Darśan: Seeing the Divine in India*, 2nd rev. ed. (Chambersburg, Pa.: Anima Books, 1985), p. 32.

25. Ibid., pp. 35–36.

26. See, for example, Wendy Doniger O'Flaherty, *Siva, the Erotic Ascetic* (New York: Oxford University Press, 1981), pp. 4, 84, 324; Wendy Doniger O'Flaherty, trans., *Hindu Myths: A Sourcebook Translated from Sanskrit* (Harmondsworth, England: Penguin Books, 1975), p. 137; Paul B. Courtright, *Ganesa: Lord of Obstacles, Lord of Beginnings* (New York: Oxford University Press, 1985), p. 121; Jeffrey J. Kripal, *Kali's Child: The Mystical and the Erotic in the Life and Teachings of Ramakrishna*, 2nd ed. (Chicago: University of Chicago Press, 1998), pp. 29, 161, 231.

27. See, for example, Monier Monier-Williams, *A Sanskrit-English Dictionary* (Delhi: Motilal Bandarsidass, 1899), pp. 901–2. See also John Grimes, *A Concise Dictionary of Indian Philosophy* (Albany: State University of New York Press, 1996), pp. 175–76.

28. Interestingly, the linga of Vishnu is a smooth, oval-shaped stone called *shalagrama*.

Author Index

Adams, Hannah, 21
Aristotle, 101–2

Bethge, Eberhard, 38–39, 52
Bonhoeffer, Dietrich, 38, 51
Bunyan, John B., 143

Carman, John B., 7–8, 133–50

Daggett, Mabel Potter, 25
Daly, Mary, 31
Davis, David Brion, 28–30
De Gruchy, John W., 2–3, 38–52
Delano, Amaso, 21, 28
Deutsch, Eliot, 5–6, 99–111
Devi, Sarada, 170
Dillard, Annie, 79
Doniger, Wendy, 4–5, 79–96
Douglass, Frederick, 26

Eck, Diana, 19, 180–81
Emerson, Ralph Waldo, 19, 21–23

Flood, Gavin, 175–76
Franchot, Jenny, 30
Freud, Sigmund, 80, 90, 92, 94

Goldman, Robert P., 92–95
Goreh, Nilakantha, 141–42
Gundersheimer, Werner, 8–9, 154–68

Herberg, Will, 31
Hick, John, 100–101, 107, 109–10, 117

Hudson, Dennis, 143

Inden, Ronald, 178
Isaacs, Harold, 31

Jabir, 117
James, William, 13, 157

Kant, Immanuel, 100, 114–16
Kuschel, Karl-Josef, 41

Lännström, Anna, 1–10
Levinas, Emmanuel, 79
Lévi-Strauss, Claude, 85
Luke, P. Y., 137, 146–48

Mandela, Nelson, 44
Marx, Karl, 80, 92
McClintock, Martha, 91
Monk, Maria, 129
Müller, Max, 25
Myers, Frederic, 91

Nasr, Sayyed Hossein, 117
Neville, Robert Cummings, 6–7, 113–29
Newman, John Henry, 116

Otto, Rudolf, 100, 106

Parekh, Bhikhu, 3–4, 54–74
Pico della Mirandola, Giovanni, 167
Pierce, Charles Sanders, 124–29
Pillai, Krishna, 143–44

Pillion, Numa Jay, 92
Plato, 87–90
Pratt, Mary Louise, 160
Priestley, Joseph, 21
Prothero, Stephen, 2, 13–32

Ramabai, Pandita, 141–43
Ramakrishna, 14, 117, 170–71, 180
Ramanuja, 146, 148
Rambo, Lewis, 171
Reed, Elizabeth A., 25
Renfrew-Brooks, Douglas, 177
Roland, Alan, 180
Roszak, Theodore, 180
Roy, Rammohan, 141–42

Said, Edward, 179
Samaj, Brahmo, 142
Saud, Ibn, 51
Sedick, Sheik Achmat, 49–50
Seuss, Dr. (Theodore Geisel), 91
Shakespeare, William, 23, 81, 82

Sharma, Renuka, 180
Smith, Huston, 117
Smith, Wilfred Cantwell, 20,
    80, 109
Soueif, Ahdaf, 47
Southey, Robert, 21
Spivak, Gayatri, 180

Thoreau, Henry David, 2, 22–23
Toulmin, Stephen, 104
Tracy, David, 82–83
Twain, Mark, 20

Upadhyay, Brahmabandhav, 142

Vrajaprana, Pravrajika, 9–10,
    169–83

Whitman, Walt, 20
Williams, Rowan, 41

Younger, Paul, 138

Subject Index

Abrahamic faiths, 2–3, 27, 38–52, 56, 173
AIDS, 19, 44, 47, 50, 94
al-Qaeda, 54, 57
apartheid, 39, 41–43, 45, 50, 51

Baha'is, 17, 116
Bernard, Pierre ("Oom the Omnipotent"), 17–18, 20, 25, 27, 30
Bhagavad Gita, 19, 23, 26, 109, 120
Bin Laden, Osama, 3–4, 54–74
Brahman, 7, 101, 170
Buber, Martin, 69, 156
Buddhism, 19–20, 23, 26, 80, 83, 109–10, 118, 120–21, 122, 177
  Buddhists, 19–20, 26, 80, 82–83, 126, 127, 174
  scriptures of, 25, 120
  Zen Buddhism, 82, 84
Bull, Sara, 13–17, 18, 20, 25, 27, 30, 32
Bush, George W., 70, 71

caste, 7–8, 9, 16, 82, 85, 133, 141, 144, 145, 150
China, 79, 118, 120, 177
Chinese, in U.S., 24–27
Christ, 69, 135–138, 143–144.
  See also Jesus

Christianity, 2, 7, 8, 22, 28, 32, 38–52, 109–10, 117, 118, 121, 127, 133–50, 168, 182
  African Independent Churches, 127
  Anglicanism, 8–9, 41, 141, 142, 157
  Calvinist, 166
  Christians, 3, 15, 38–52, 56, 59, 62, 69, 83, 118, 126, 133–50, 176, 182
  Congregationalism, 9, 157, 159, 161, 163
  Dutch Reformed Church, 44
  Lutheran, 166
  Methodism, 128
  Monophysites, 127
  Nestorian, 120, 127
  Orthodox, 117
  Protestantism, 9, 10, 24, 30–31, 141, 145, 160, 173, 178
  Protestants, 2, 27, 29, 38, 44, 81, 83, 117, 127, 135–36, 138, 140, 143, 144
  Quakerism, 9, 157, 158, 159, 161, 162
  Roman Catholicism, 2, 26, 28–31, 40, 117, 128, 138–41, 142, 145, 173
  Roman Catholics, 8, 19, 27, 28–30, 44, 82–83, 127, 143, 144
Clinton, Bill, 57

Subject Index

compassion, 46, 110
Confucianism, 118, 121, 126
Confucius, 121
conversion, 7–8, 9–10, 133–50, 169–83

Dao, 7, 122
Daoism, 118, 120–21
De Britto, St. John, 138, 139–40
death penalty, 3, 49–50
dialogue, 2, 3–4, 5, 7, 13, 39, 42–43, 52, 73–74, 119, 121

ecumenism, 41, 50
Egypt, 48, 121, 163
Europe, 55–57, 59, 61, 81
evil, 3, 59, 63–64, 68, 73, 87
exclusivism, 6, 116–17, 135

Farmer, Sarah, 15, 17, 18, 20, 25
feminism, 51–52, 80, 106, 127
France, 56, 68
freedom, 57, 102, 105, 155
friendship, 38, 52

Gandhi, Mohandas, 3–4, 54–55, 57, 59–74, 79
gay rights, 3, 50
gender equality, 3, 47, 50–51
Germany, 8, 38, 155–59, 163
God, 3, 6, 7, 15, 16, 22, 24, 46–52, 55, 61–62, 83, 101, 107, 110, 125, 126, 134–35, 139–140, 142–43, 148, 154, 165–76, 170, 171, 179
  justice of, 3, 4, 44, 46, 48
Great Britain, 56, 66, 68, 157

Hinduism, 2, 7–8, 9, 13–32, 59, 80, 83, 88–96, 109–10, 118, 120, 169–83
  Hindu Unitarianism, 141–42
  Hindus, 7, 8–9, 13–14, 16, 20–22, 24–26, 28–29, 44, 65, 80, 82–83, 87, 133–50, 169–83
  Tantric Hinduism, 17–18

Holocaust, 38–39, 40, 45. *See also* Shoah
homosexuality, 67, 92
human rights, 50–51

I Ching (Yijing), 121
Iliad, 84
inclusivism, 6, 116, 117–18, 119
India, 59, 63, 66, 68, 79, 82, 84, 87, 133–50, 171, 175–77
Indians, 23–25, 65, 175–77
Indonesia, 40, 48
injustice, 8, 48
Iraq, 58, 68, 70, 72
Ireland, Northern, 1, 43, 83
Islam, 19, 32, 39–52, 55–57, 59–61, 67, 69, 70, 72, 109–10, 117, 118, 121, 173
  Muslim festival, 137
  Muslim societies, 56–57, 60, 63, 65, 70, 72
  Muslims, 3, 4, 24, 39–52, 55, 58–60, 65–66, 69, 74, 172, 173, 174, 176
  Nation of Islam, 19
Israel, 1, 56–57, 63, 64–65, 68, 126, 165

Jainism, 120, 176
Japan, 118, 177
Japanese, in U.S., 24–27
Jesus, 28, 38–39, 69, 121, 124, 126, 134, 136–37, 139–41, 147–50, 157, 180. *See also* Christ
Judaism, 8, 31, 38–52, 109–10, 117, 118, 121, 126, 160, 161, 163, 165, 167, 168, 173
  Ashkenazic, 9, 157, 164
  Jews, 3, 8, 19, 38–52, 56–57, 59, 62, 69, 82, 83, 126, 127, 155–58, 161, 165, 167
  Orthodox, 164, 166
  Reform, 163, 165
  Sephardic, 9, 157, 164
justice, 3, 40–41, 60, 67, 74

Subject Index 191

Kamasutra, 4, 85–87
karma, 4–5, 85, 87–96
Khan, Abdul Gaffar, 65–69
King, Martin Luther, Jr., 71
Korea, 118, 178
Krishna, 120, 126, 146–49, 170, 176

Mary (the Virgin), 28, 40, 128, 138
Mencius, 121
Middle East, 2, 39, 57
missionaries, 8, 21, 26, 116, 135–36, 138, 142, 144, 145–46, 180–81
Moses, 21, 167
Muhammad, 69, 110

Native Americans, 27, 31
Neo-Confucianism, 121, 122
nondualism, 100–101, 109
nonviolence, 3, 54, 65, 71
Norway, 13, 15

"Oom the Omnipotent." *See* Bernard, Pierre

Pakistan, 40, 57, 65
Palestine, 1, 57
Palestinians, 39, 56–57, 62–63, 64–65, 68
Paul, St., 121, 126
peace, 32, 38–39, 48, 57, 63, 67, 70, 110
perennial philosophy, 117–18
pluralism, 5–6, 44, 47, 49, 82, 99–111, 116, 118–19, 155, 179
Poshamma, 134, 137
psychoanalysis, 180

racism, 51–52, 80–81
Rama, 143–44, 170
Ramakrishna Order, 171, 175
Ramayana, 84, 143

rationality, 102–5, 107–8, 115, 141, 178
reductionism, 6, 114–18
reincarnation, 87–96
relativism, 99–100
Rouner, Leroy, 113–14
Russia, 94, 173

secular society, 27, 44, 45, 47–52, 57, 67, 173
sexism, 52, 80
Shoah, 154–56. *See also* Holocaust
Siva, 141, 149, 170, 176, 180–81
South Africa, 2–3, 38–39, 41–52, 62
Soviet Union, 57, 69
Spain, 40, 42, 57
Spiritualism, 16, 17
symbols, 122–29

terrorism, 3–4, 54, 57–59, 63, 68, 72–73, 173
Theosophy, 16, 23
Tibet, 120, 177
truth, 7, 41, 102–11, 116–19, 125–29
Truth and Reconciliation Commission, 3, 44–46

United States, 2, 8–9, 13–32, 55, 56–58, 59–62, 66–72, 79, 83, 93, 154–59, 169, 171, 174

Vedanta, 169, 171
Vedanta Society, 10, 13, 15, 26, 28, 170–71, 174, 176
Vedas, 118, 120, 121
Vietnam, 118, 177
violence, 4, 52, 54, 57–58, 59, 64–65, 68, 71–73
Vishnu, 141, 143–44, 148–49

Viswanath, 171–72
Vivekananda, Swami, 10, 13–15, 17, 170, 175–76

West, 3, 4, 5, 10, 39, 54, 59–60, 67, 80, 87, 117, 148, 169, 171–72, 174–81

yoga, 14–16, 32, 120, 179
   bhakti yoga, 15, 23
   hatha yoga, 31
   jnana yoga, 23

Zoroastrianism, 121, 167

www.ingramcontent.com/pod-product-compliance
Lightning Source LLC
Chambersburg PA
CBHW051924160426
43198CB00012B/2025